A Book-by-Book Guide to Septuagint Vocabulary

A Book-by-Book Guide to Septuagint Vocabulary

Gregory R. Lanier

William A. Ross

HENDRICKSON ACADEMIC

A Book-by-Book Guide to Septuagint Vocabulary

Hendrickson Publishers Marketing, LLC
P. O. Box 3473
Peabody, Massachusetts 01961-3473
www.hendrickson.com

ISBN 978-1-68307-196-9

Printed in the United States of America

First Printing — December 2019

Library of Congress Control Number: 2019946437

CONTENTS

INTRODUCTION

Interest in the Greek Old Testament, commonly called the Septuagint, has been on the rise in recent decades. Those who study the Hebrew Bible, early Judaism and Christianity, Hellenistic Greek, and the New Testament are increasingly recognizing the central importance the Septuagint plays within each of these fields. In step with these developments has been the publication of two Septuagint-focused lexicons, a handful of important introductory books, numerous monographs, and a "reader's edition" (see bibliography below). However, apart from a simple vocabulary guide in German[1] and a few Greek-Latin glossaries now centuries out of date, there have been no publications that aim to help students and scholars acquire competency in Septuagint-specific vocabulary. Yet, flashcards and other vocabulary aids abound for the Hebrew Bible and Greek New Testament. This volume aims to fill the void for the Greek Old Testament.

While the Greek Old Testament (including the Apocrypha/Deuterocanon) at first feels familiar to anyone who has studied Hellenistic Greek or the Greek New Testament, the diversity in literary style and expansive range of vocabulary across the corpus present major challenges to anyone seeking to acquire a broad but detailed familiarity. Our aim is not to replace full lexicons. Rather, we aim to provide a convenient way for students to obtain proficiency with both general and book-specific Septuagint vocabulary for their personal, scholarly, or ministry purposes.

Organization and Contents of the Book

As with the other *Book-by-Book* vocabulary guides published by Hendrickson, the core of this book consists of the twenty-eight chapters devoted to vocabulary for specific books or groups of related books (e.g., the twelve Minor Prophets, the Jeremiah corpus, and the Daniel corpus are treated in one chapter each).[2] Within these chapters, vocabulary words are arranged according to frequency, from highest

1. Friedrich Rehkopf, *Septuaginta-Vokabular* (Göttingen: Vandenhoeck & Ruprecht, 1989).

2. We have departed from the ordering of the books in Rahlfs-Hanhart, which itself is often contentious among Septuagint scholars. Instead, the chapters are arranged according to categories we hope are useful to readers. Though the "Wisdom" label is debated at present, we retain it due to its common use in biblical studies.

to lowest, as found *in that given book/section of the Septuagint*. This allows the user to focus on the most important words (by frequency of appearance) in a given portion of the Septuagint.

These sorted lists in turn have been segmented into word lists consisting of fifteen words each (arranged alphabetically), which we judged to be the most manageable size for study and review. The header of each list provides the range of frequency covered by that list within the given book/section of the Septuagint: for instance, the first fifteen-word list in Genesis gives the range "81 to 25×."

Importantly, we have also provided the following three general lists, which we strongly recommend that all users consult before using the book's core twenty-eight chapters:

(1) *Greek New Testament Refresher* [pp. 9–18]

Most individuals who study the Septuagint also have at least some experience with the Greek New Testament and its vocabulary. Moreover, a substantial number of words are, of course, shared between the two corpora. It would have been tedious for the user—and would have substantially lengthened this volume—had we included all such shared words in the twenty-eight core chapters. Therefore, we have provided a "refresher" list consisting of approximately 300 words that appear ≥50× in the Greek New Testament *and* that appear one or more times in the Septuagint. Note that none of these words appear in the remaining chapters of this book.

(2) *High-Frequency Septuagint Vocabulary* [pp. 19–22]

In addition to the words shared with the Greek New Testament that were mentioned immediately above in (1), there are approximately 120 words that occur with very high frequency in the Septuagint (>100×) but with only moderate frequency in the Greek New Testament (30×–49×) and that, hence, are not covered in the list described in (1) above. These words cumulatively appear over 32,000× in the Septuagint and are found in most, if not all, of the books. Thus, we have consolidated them into a single list that is the best place for any Septuagint student to begin vocabulary acquisition. Note that, as with the list described in (1), none of these words appear in the remaining chapters of this book.

(3) *Common Septuagint Proper Nouns* [pp. 23–24]

Names of people and places occur over 23,000× in the Septuagint, and some, like Ισραηλ, occur in practically every book. Thus, rather than clutter the core chapters of our book with repetitive proper nouns, we have consolidated the most frequent 80 into a single list. The remainder are excluded altogether, as they are readily intelligible in nearly all cases (either as transliterations or as something that can be "sounded out").

Design of the Individual Lists

Our goal is to enable users to obtain proficiency in the vocabulary of the Septuagint in a way that is both efficient (hence the emphasis on frequency) and targeted (hence the focus on books or groups of books). We did not, however, want to include all of the approximately 11,000 words in the vocabulary stock of the Septuagint (excluding proper nouns). Thus, for each chapter of the book we had to develop a cutoff point that made sense for that chapter. Our guiding question in designing each chapter was this: What words would the user need to know to "get up the curve" and reach reading competency for this particular Septuagint book?

In answering this question, we could not simply pick the same number of words (and thus the same quantity of fifteen-word lists) for each chapter. The books vary in length, and as any reader knows, the degree of variety of vocabulary also varies. Some writings use an immense range of vocabulary, while others have a more confined range (e.g., compare Hebrews to John in the Greek New Testament). In other words, obtaining a certain level of reading competency for one book may require mastering far more words than would be required for obtaining the same level of competency for another book. As it turns out, 1–2 Chronicles has the simplest vocabulary, while 2 Maccabees has the most varied. A brief comparison of the two helps illustrate the dynamics involved in "getting up the curve" for each:

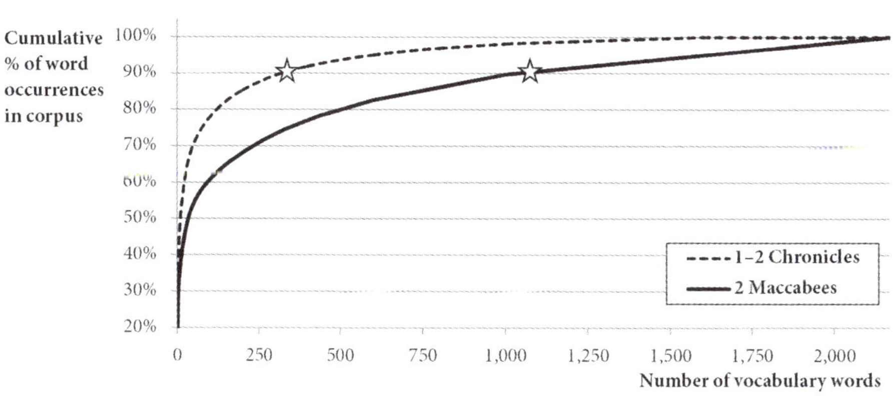

Though 1–2 Chronicles is over three times the length of 2 Maccabees, the reader is required to memorize *over three times* the number of individual vocabulary words for 2 Maccabees in order to reach the same 90 percent level of cumulative word occurrences as for 1–2 Chronicles (as shown with the stars on the graph). Put differently, to enable the user to attain the same level of overall reading competency for each of these books/sections of the Septuagint, the vocabulary set for 2 Maccabees needs to be triple the size of that for 1–2 Chronicles, even though the simple word counts of each book are precisely the reverse.

We have taken all these considerations into account when establishing frequency thresholds individually for each book or group of books. Each chapter will—when used in conjunction with the consolidated lists for the entire Septuagint discussed above—enable the user to get to over 90 percent reading competency for each book. This means that some chapters in this vocabulary guide are longer than one might expect based simply on the length of the book they treat, but this is the result of that book's vocabulary complexity relative to the other books in the Septuagint.

Our textual base is the edition of Rahlfs-Hanhart, including the so-called "double texts" for Judges, the Daniel corpus, Tobit, and portions of Joshua.[3] To determine word frequencies, we have used computer software as well as the standard lexicons that provide frequency counts. However, given that various editors or software developers do not always agree on morphology, lexical form, and so on, it is not uncommon for various sources to disagree on precise frequency counts for specific words. It is possible, then, that the reader may find that the frequency of a given word as presented in this volume differs from that found in, say, his or her preferred Bible software package. Perfect consistency across sources in this regard is impossible to achieve. We trust, however, that the overall experience of using this resource will not be impacted by such minor variations.

Guide to Using the Vocabulary Lists

Each list consists of fifteen vocabulary words that are sorted alphabetically. However, any word that is found frequently in the Greek New Testament—but that is not already provided in lists (1) and (2) mentioned above—is moved to the end of the list and italicized, allowing users to more easily skip words they may already be familiar with.

All entries consist of the lexical form of the word followed by at least one (though usually more than one) English gloss, which we have developed by consulting

3. Alfred Rahlfs and Robert Hanhart, *Septuaginta: Editio Altera* (Stuttgart: Deutsche Bibelgesellschaft, 2006).

a variety of lexicons. These glosses are only generalized English translation equivalents and not full definitions or descriptions of a word's entire semantic range. We have attempted to be as precise and comprehensive as possible, but the reader is encouraged to consult the main lexicons for fuller treatment of each word. Though in general we have aimed for consistency in the glosses we provide for a given word that appears in multiple chapters of this book, we have also tailored the glosses at points to reflect the meaning a word has in a given book/section of the Septuagint if this differs from what the word means elsewhere.

Verbs are provided in the first-person singular, but our glosses take the form of "to ______" rather than "I ______," which we found to be a more elegant presentation.

Nouns are accompanied by genitive endings and the article corresponding to the noun's grammatical gender. Adjectives are accompanied by feminine and neuter endings.

Other supplemental information is provided using the following conventions:

;	partitions the gloss list according to distinct functions or uses
( )	provides contextual variations in meaning, or disambiguates the sense of the gloss provided
[ ]	encloses noteworthy Greek phrases in which a given vocabulary word commonly appears, such as "[ἀνὰ μέσον] among, between"
+gen, *+dat*, or *+acc*	specifies the contextual meaning of a word (e.g., preposition) when followed by another word in the specified case
adv	adverb
conj	conjunction
fem	feminine
Heb	Hebrew
inf	infinitive
interj	interjection
mid or *pas*	specifies a particular meaning of a verb in these voices, if relevant
perf or *plpf*	perfect or pluperfect (respectively)

prep	preposition
sg or *pl*	singular or plural (respectively)
+subj	indicates that the word in question is followed by a verb in the subjunctive mood
subst	specifies a common substantival use of an adjective
trans or *intrans*	transitive or intransitive (respectively)
translit	transliteration
×	number of times

Select Bibliography

Septuagint Lexicons

Lust, Johann, Erik Eynikel, and Katrin Hauspie, eds. *Greek-English Lexicon of the Septuagint*. 3rd ed. Stuttgart: Deutsche Bibelgesellschaft, 2015.

Muraoka, Takamitsu, ed. *A Greek-English Lexicon of the Septuagint*. Leuven: Peeters, 2009.

Other Lexicons

Danker, Frederick W., Walter Bauer, William F. Arndt, and F. Wilbur Gingrich. *Greek-English Lexicon of the New Testament and Other Early Christian Literature*. 3rd ed. Chicago: University of Chicago Press, 2000.

Danker, Frederick W., and Kathryn Krug. *The Concise Greek-English Lexicon of the New Testament*. Chicago: University of Chicago Press, 2009.

Gingrich, F. Wilbur. *Shorter Lexicon of the Greek New Testament*. Revised by Frederick W. Danker. Chicago: University of Chicago Press, 1979.

Liddell, Henry George, Robert Scott, and Henry Stuart Jones. *A Greek-English Lexicon with a Revised Supplement*. 9th ed. Oxford: Oxford University Press, 1996.

Moulton, James H., and George Milligan. *The Vocabulary of the Greek Testament Illustrated from the Papyri and Other Non-Literary Sources*. London: Hodder & Stoughton, 1929.

Introductions to the Septuagint

Aitken, James K., ed. *T&T Clark Companion to the Septuagint*. London: Bloomsbury T&T Clark, 2015.

Dines, Jennifer. *The Septuagint*. London: T&T Clark, 2004.

Fernández Marcos, Natalio. *The Septuagint in Context: Introduction to the Greek Version of the Bible*. Leiden: Brill, 2000.

Jobes, Karen H., and Moisés Silva. *Invitation to the Septuagint*. 2nd ed. Grand Rapids: Baker Academic, 2015.

Kreuzer, Siegfried, ed. *Introduction to the Septuagint*. Translated by David A. Brenner and Peter Altmann. Waco: Baylor University Press, 2019.

Septuagint Reading Resources

Jobes, Karen H., ed. *Discovering the Septuagint: A Guided Reader*. Grand Rapids: Kregel Academic, 2016.

Lanier, Gregory R., and William A. Ross. *Septuaginta: A Reader's Edition*. 2 vols. Peabody, MA: Hendrickson, 2018.

McLean, Bradley H. *Hellenistic and Biblical Greek: A Graduated Reader*. Cambridge: Cambridge University Press, 2014.

Acknowledgments

We would like to thank the editorial team at Hendrickson for the opportunity to undertake this project as a complement to our work on *Septuaginta: A Reader's Edition*. It has been a joy to partner once more with Jonathan Kline, Phil Frank, and Tirzah Frank on a complex project focused on primary sources, for their attention to detail is unsurpassed. We also thank our wives for encouraging us in the work, despite its unusual nature. This guide is dedicated to our students, for whom we hope it will be yet one more stepping stone toward a lifelong appreciation of Greek and, in particular, the Greek Old Testament.

GRL and WAR
Summer MMXIX

GREEK NEW TESTAMENT REFRESHER

▷ List 1	88,461 to 4,907 × in LXX
αὐτός, -ή, -όν	he, she, it
δέ	and, now, then
ἐγώ	I; [*pl* ἡμεῖς] we
εἰμί	to be, become, exist
εἰς	(+*acc*) into, toward, until, with regard to
ἐν	(+*dat*) in, on, among, with, when, at
ἐπί	(+*gen*) upon, near, in the time of; (+*dat*) on, owing to, during; (+*acc*) over, toward, against
καί	and, also, then, so, even
κύριος, -ου, ὁ	master, sir, lord, (Lord)
ὁ, ἡ, τό	the, this (one), that (one)
ὅς, ἥ, ὅ	who, that, which
οὐ, οὐκ, οὐχ	no, not
πᾶς, πᾶσα, πᾶν, (*gen* παντός, πάσης, παντός)	each, every, all
σύ	you; [*pl* ὑμίν] you (all)
υἱός, -οῦ, ὁ	son, descendant, community member

▷ List 2	4,419 to 2,145 × in LXX
ἀπό	(+*gen*) from, out of, after, because of
βασιλεύς, -έως, ὁ	king, ruler
γῆ, -ῆς, ἡ	earth, ground, region
γίνομαι	to be, become, come about, happen
ἐκ, ἐξ	(+*gen*) out of, from, due to, after
ἡμέρα, -ας, ἡ	day, period (of time)
θεός, -οῦ, ὁ	God, god, deity
κατά	(+*gen*) down (from), against, toward; (+*acc*) at, facing, according to, concerning
λέγω	to say, speak, tell
μετά	(+*gen*) with, by, among; (+*acc*) behind, following, after
μή	not, lest
ὅτι	that, so that, because, since
οὗτος, αὕτη, τοῦτο	this (one), (*pl*) these (ones)
ποιέω	to do, act, make, produce
πρός	(+*gen*) in the interest of; (+*dat*) at, near, in addition to; (+*acc*) to, toward, in order to, against, concerning

▷ List 3	2,130 to 1,357× in LXX
ἀνήρ, ἀνδρός, ὁ	man, person, husband
ἄνθρωπος, -ου, ὁ	man, husband, person, humanity
γάρ	for, since, as
διά	(+*gen*) through, after, by means of; (+*acc*) because of
δίδωμι	to give, grant, provide
ἐάν	if, perhaps, when(ever)
ἕως	until, as long as, up to, while
λαός, -οῦ, ὁ	people, nation, humankind
οἶκος, -ου, ὁ	house, possessions, kin, descendants
ὁράω	to see, notice, look; (*pas*) to appear
πατήρ, πατρός, ὁ	father, parent, ancestor
πόλις, -εως, ἡ	city, town
τίς, τίς, τί, (*gen* τίνος)	who?, which (one)?, what (sort)?
χείρ, χειρός, ἡ	hand, possession, power, control
ὡς	like, when, so that; (*interj*) how!; [ὥς *adv*] so, thus

▷ List 4	1,336 to 950× in LXX
ἀκούω	to hear, listen (to), obey, understand
γυνή, γυναικός, ἡ	woman, wife
ἔθνος, -ους, τό	people (group), nation, (*pl*) non-Israelites
εἷς, μία, ἕν, (*gen* ἑνός, μιᾶς, ἑνός)	one, a/an, someone
ἔρχομαι	to go, come (to), arrive (at)
ἤ	or, (rather) than, as
ἰδού	see!, look!, watch!
καρδία, -ας, ἡ	heart, (spiritual) center, (seat of) emotion
λαλέω	to speak, tell
λαμβάνω	to take, grasp, acquire, catch
λόγος, -ου, ὁ	word, matter, statement
ὄνομα, -ατος, τό	name, reputation
πορεύομαι	to go, come, proceed, walk
πρόσωπον, -ου, τό	face, front (side), surface, appearance
ψυχή, -ῆς, ἡ	soul, life, person

▷ List 5 — 926 to 747 × in LXX

ἅγιος, -α, -ον	holy, sacred, pure
ἀδελφός, -οῦ, ὁ	brother, fellow person
αἰών, -ῶνος, ὁ	age, eternity
γι(γ)νώσκω	to know, realize, understand
εἰ	if, perhaps, whether
ἐκεῖ	there, in that place
ἐκεῖνος, -η, -ον	that (person *or* thing)
ἵστημι	to set, situate, position; (*intr*) to stop, hold out, present oneself
μέγας, μεγάλη, μέγα	large, great
μέσος, -η, -ον	middle; (*prep +gen*) among, within, between
ὁδός, -οῦ, ἡ	way, road, journey, conduct
οὕτως	so, thus
παρά	(+*gen*) from; (+*dat*) beside, in the presence of; (+*acc*) alongside of, for the reason that, more than, contrary to
περί	(+*gen*) about, concerning, with regard to; (+*acc*) around, near, with
πολύς, πολλή, πολύ, (*gen* πολλοῦ, πολλῆς, πολλοῦ)	much, many

▷ List 6 — 743 to 633 × in LXX

ἀγαθός, -ή, -όν	good, upright, beneficial
ἄν	(*particle of contingency*)
ἀναβαίνω	to go up, rise up, ascend
ἀποστέλλω	to send (out), dispatch
δύο	two
ἑαυτοῦ, -ῆς, -οῦ	himself, herself, itself
εἰσέρχομαι	to enter, go in(to)
ἐξέρχομαι	to exit, depart, come out
ἐσθίω	to eat, consume
νῦν *or* νυνί	now, at present
ὄρος, -ους, τό	hill, mountain
οὐρανός, -οῦ, ὁ	sky, heaven(s)
ὀφθαλμός, -οῦ, ὁ	eye
ὕδωρ, ὕδατος, τό	water
φωνή, -ῆς, ἡ	sound, noise, voice

▹ List 7 — 621 to 543× in LXX

ἀλλά	but, rather, nevertheless
ἁμαρτία, -ας, ἡ	sin (offering)
ἀποθνῄσκω	to die
δύναμις, -εως, ἡ	power, ability, authority, army
ἐνώπιον	(+*gen*) in front of, in the presence of
ἔργον, -ου, τό	work, task, action, product
ἔτι	yet, still, even
εὑρίσκω	to find (out), discover, obtain
ζάω	to live, be alive
ἵνα	(+*subj*) that, in order that, so that
ὅσος, -η, -ον	as great as, as much as, as many as
οὐδέ	and not, nor, neither
ῥῆμα, -ατος, τό	expression, statement, matter, thing
τίθημι	to set, place, establish
τόπος, -ου, ὁ	place, region, position

▹ List 8 — 541 to 428× in LXX

ἀνίστημι	to raise (up), set up, restore
βασιλεία, -ας, ἡ	kingdom, dominion, reign
δίκαιος, -α, -ον	just, righteous
δόξα, -ης, ἡ	glory, majesty, reputation
ἔχω	to have, possess, hold
θάλασσα, -ης, ἡ	sea
καιρός, -οῦ, ὁ	time, period, opportunity
καλέω	to call, invite, summon
κεφαλή, -ῆς, ἡ	head, top, leader
νόμος, -ου, ὁ	law, regulation, rule
πῦρ, -ός, τό	fire
στόμα, -ατος, τό	mouth, opening, entrance
ὑπέρ	(+*gen*) for (the sake of), on behalf of, concerning; (+*acc*) beyond, more than, over
ὑπό	(+*gen*) by; (+*acc*) below, under, during
φοβέω	to fear, become frightened

▷ List 9 — 423 to 351 × in LXX

ἄγγελος, -ου, ὁ	angel, messenger
αἷμα, -ατος, τό	blood
ἀπόλλυμι	to destroy, conceal; (*mid*) to perish, vanish
δοῦλος, -η, -ον	enslaved; (*subst*) servant, slave
ἕκαστος, -η, -ον	each, every
ἑπτά	seven
θάνατος, -ου, ὁ	death
κακός, -ή, -όν	bad, evil, harmful
καταβαίνω	to go down, come down, descend
πίπτω	to fall, collapse, perish
πνεῦμα, -ατος, τό	wind, spirit, soul
πονηρός, -ά, -όν	evil, bad, harmful
συνάγω	to bring together, assemble, invite
σῴζω	to save, rescue; (*pas*) to escape
τρεῖς, -εῖς, -ία	three

▷ List 10 — 350 to 295 × in LXX

ἄρτος, -ου, ὁ	bread, food
γράφω	to write (down), record
δικαιοσύνη, -ης, ἡ	righteousness, uprightness, justice
δύναμαι	to be able, be capable
εἰρήνη, -ης, ἡ	peace, well-being
ζητέω	to seek, look for, inquire about
ζωή, -ῆς, ἡ	life, existence
λίθος, -ου, ὁ	stone
μήτηρ, μητρός, ἡ	mother
νύξ, νυκτός, ἡ	night
πούς, ποδός, ὁ	foot, step, track
προφήτης, -ου, ὁ	prophet
τέκνον, -ου, τό	child, son, offspring
τις	someone, something, anyone, anything, (a) certain one
τότε	then, next, at that point

▷ List 11	294 to 262 × in LXX
ἀγαπάω	to love, delight in, enjoy
ἄγω	to bring, lead, take
αἴρω	to lift, take up, remove
ἀποκρίνομαι	to answer, reply
ἕτερος, -α, -ον	other, another, different
καθώς	as, just as
κρίνω	to consider, judge, decide, condemn
οἶδα	to know (about), understand, be(come) aware
οἰκία, -ας, ἡ	house, household, family
ὅλος, -η, -ον	whole, entire, complete
ὅπως	(+*subj*) (in order) that
παραδίδωμι	to give up, hand over, deliver
πίνω	to drink
τε	and
φέρω	to carry, bear, endure

▷ List 12	259 to 223 × in LXX
ἀπέρχομαι	to go away, depart, leave
ἀποκτείνω	to kill, destroy
ἀρχή, -ῆς, ἡ	origin, beginning, ruler
γεννάω	to father, give birth to, produce
δεξιός, -ά, -όν	right (side)
ἐντολή, -ῆς, ἡ	commandment, order, precept
ἱμάτιον, -ου, τό	clothing, garment
καλός, -ή, -όν	good, beautiful, useful
μέν	yet, now, rather
οὖν	so, thus, consequently, therefore
προσκυνέω	to worship, bow before in reverence
πρῶτος, -η, -ον	first, earlier, former
σοφία, -ας, ἡ	wisdom, skill, shrewdness
σύν	(+*dat*) with, in addition to
συναγωγή, -ῆς, ἡ	congregation, assembly, gathering place

▹ List 13 — 223 to 173 × in LXX

ἀλήθεια, -ας, ἡ	truth, truthfulness
ἀνοίγω	to open
ἄρχω	(+*gen*) to rule, administer; (*mid*) to begin
κάθημαι	to sit, stay, reside
μόνος, -η, -ον	only, alone
ὅταν	when, whenever
ὅτε	when, while
οὐδείς, οὐδεμία, οὐδέν	no one, none, nothing
οὐχί	no, surely not
πείθω	to persuade; (*pas*) to obey; (*perf/plpf*) to trust, feel confidence
πρεσβύτερος, -α, -ον	older; (*subst*) elder, official
σάρξ, σαρκός, ἡ	flesh, meat, body, humanity
τρίτος, -η, -ον	third
φῶς, φωτός, τό	light
ὥστε	so that, in order that, for the purpose of

▹ List 14 — 169 to 133 × in LXX

αἰώνιος, -ος, -ον	eternal, without end
ἀφίημι	to forgive, release, permit, leave (behind)
βλέπω	to see, look at, watch
γλῶσσα, -ης, ἡ	tongue, language, bar (of metal)
δοξάζω	to extol, magnify, hold in honor
ἔσχατος, -η, -ον	last, final, remotest
θέλω	to be willing, want
θρόνος, -ου, ὁ	throne, seat (of power)
μηδέ	and not, nor, not even
παιδίον, -ου, τό	young child
παρακαλέω	to comfort, exhort, encourage, summon
σῶμα, -ατος, τό	body, slave, person
ὑπάρχω	to exist, be (present), belong to
χάρις, -ιτος, ἡ	grace, favor, kindness; (*prep* +*gen*) on account of
χρόνος, -ου, ὁ	time, duration, period

▷ List 15 — 133 to 107× in LXX

ἄλλος, -η, -ον	other, another
διδάσκω	to teach, instruct; (*pas*) to learn
ἐλπίς, -ίδος, ἡ	hope, expectation
ἔξω	outside; (*prep +gen*) out from, outside of
καρπός, -οῦ, ὁ	fruit, (offspring)
κράζω	to cry out, scream, call
λοιπός, -ή, -όν	remaining; (*subst*) rest, remainder
ὅστις, ἥτις, ὅ τι	whoever, whichever, whatever
οὔτε	and not, neither, nor
πληρόω	to fill (up), complete, bring to an end
προσέρχομαι	to go to, approach, arrive
προσεύχομαι	to pray
πῶς	how, in what way
σάββατον, -ου, τό	sabbath, week
σημεῖον, -ου, τό	sign, signal, identifying mark

▷ List 16 — 105 to 79× in LXX

αἰτέω	to ask (for), request
γραμματεύς, -έως, ὁ	scribe, secretary
δώδεκα	twelve
ἐγείρω	to raise up, rouse
ἐκβάλλω	to throw out, move out, sever a relationship with
ἐκκλησία, -ας, ἡ	assembly, gathering, (social) organization
ἐμός, -ή, -όν	my, mine
ἐξουσία, -ας, ἡ	authority, control, power
μένω	to remain, wait for
νεκρός, -ά, -όν	dead; (*subst*) dead person
πάλιν	again, once more
πιστεύω	to trust, believe in
τοιοῦτος, -αύτη, -οῦτο(ν)	of such a kind, like this
χαίρω	to rejoice, be glad
ὧδε	here

▷ **List 17**	**79 to 62× in LXX**
δέχομαι	to receive, accept
δοκέω	to think, suppose; (*intr*) to seem
ἐπερωτάω	to question, consult, ask
ἐρωτάω	to ask, consult, question
εὐθύς, -εῖα, -ύ	straight, direct, immediate
ἤδη	now, at this time, already
θεωρέω	to see, look at, watch
ἴδιος, -α, -ον	own, one's own
ἱερόν, -οῦ, τό	temple
κόσμος, -ου, ὁ	ordered world, ornamentation, accessories
μακάριος, -α, -ον	blessed, happy
μηδείς, μηδεμία, μηδέν (*or* μηθείς *etc.*)	no, nobody, nothing
πιστός, -ή, -όν	faithful, trustworthy
φημί	to say, assert
ὥρα, -ας, ἡ	hour

▷ **List 18**	**62 to 44× in LXX**
ἀλλήλων, -οις, -ους	of each other, of one another
ἄρα	so, then
ἀρχιερεύς, -έως, ὁ	high priest
βάλλω	to throw, put
γραφή, -ῆς, ἡ	writing, document, scripture
δεῖ	to be necessary
θέλημα, -ατος, τό	will, desire
μᾶλλον	rather, more
μέλλω	to be about to (do something)
ὄχλος, -ου, ὁ	crowd, army
παραβολή, -ῆς, ἡ	proverbial saying, illustration, taunt
πίστις, -εως, ἡ	faith, faithfulness, loyalty
σπείρω	to sow, scatter (seed)
χαρά, -ᾶς, ἡ	joy, cause for delight
χριστός, -ή, -όν	anointed

▷ List 19 — 42 to 13× in LXX

ἀγάπη, -ης, ἡ	love
ἀγαπητός, -ή, -όν	beloved
ἀκολουθέω	to follow, go after
ἀπολύω	to dismiss, release, acquit; (*mid*) to depart
δαιμόνιον, -ου, τό	demon
διό	therefore, for this reason
εὐαγγελίζω	to convey good news, announce
κηρύσσω	to proclaim, declare
μαρτυρέω	to witness, testify
ὅπου	where, whereas, wherever
πέμπω	to send
περιπατέω	to walk around, traverse, conduct oneself
πλοῖον, -ου, τό	boat, ship
τηρέω	to guard, keep, watch over
τυφλός, -ή, -όν	blind

▷ List 20 — 12× or fewer in LXX

ἀμήν	amen (*Heb* truly)
ἀσπάζομαι	to greet
βαπτίζω	to baptize, wash, dip
διδάσκαλος, -ου, ὁ	teacher
εἴτε	or, either/or, even if
ἐπαγγελία, -ας, ἡ	promise
εὐαγγέλιον, -ου, τό	good news
ὑπάγω	to go away, draw off

HIGH-FREQUENCY SEPTUAGINT VOCABULARY

▷ List 1 — 904 to 438× in LXX

ἀποστρέφω	to turn away, remove, reject
ἄρχων, -οντος, ὁ	ruler, commander, governor
ἐναντίον	(+*gen*) before, in the presence of
ἐπιστρέφω	to turn, return, bring back
ἔτος, -ους, τό	year
εὐλογέω	to bless, confer favor, praise
ἐχθρός, -ά, -όν	hostile; (*subst*) enemy
θυγάτηρ, -τρός, ἡ	daughter
ἱερεύς, -έως, ὁ	priest
κατοικέω	to reside, inhabit, settle
ὅδε, ἥδε, τόδε	this (one), here
οἰκοδομέω	to build, construct
παῖς, παιδός, ὁ	child, boy, servant
φυλάσσω	to guard, watch (over), defend
φυλή, -ῆς, ἡ	people group, tribe

▷ List 2 — 437 to 359× in LXX

ἀνά	(+*acc*) up; [ἀνὰ μέσον] among, between
ἀντί	(+*gen*) instead of, in place of
ἀργύριον, -ου, τό	silver, money
βασιλεύω	to be king, rule, install as king
ἐντέλλομαι	to command, order, instruct
ἔρημος, -ος/η, -ον	desolate; (*subst*) desert, wilderness
θυσία, -ας, ἡ	sacrifice, offering
θυσιαστήριον, -ου, τό	altar
ἰσχύς, -ύος, ἡ	power, strength, capability
ὀπίσω	behind; (*prep* +*gen*) after
πατάσσω	to hit, strike (down), afflict
πόλεμος, -ου, ὁ	war, battle, fight
πύλη, -ης, ἡ	gate, door, entrance
σκηνή, -ῆς, ἡ	tent, tabernacle, booth
σφόδρα	very much, extremely

▹ List 3 — 358 to 303× in LXX

ἀλλόφυλος, -ος, -ον	foreign, Philistine
δέκα	ten
δή	now, then, indeed, surely
διαθήκη, -ης, ἡ	covenant, treaty, testament
διότι	for, since, so
ἔλεος, -ου, τό	mercy, compassion, pity
θυμός, -οῦ, ὁ	anger, wrath, rage
μήν, μηνός, ὁ	month, moon
ξύλον, -ου, τό	wood, timber, tree
ὀργή, -ῆς, ἡ	anger, wrath, indignation
ὅριον, -ου, τό	border, region
παρεμβολή, -ῆς, ἡ	army, encampment, company
προστίθημι	to add to, increase; (+*inf*) to continue
σκεῦος, -ους, τό	object, item, stuff
χιλιάς, -άδος, ἡ	one thousand

▹ List 4 — 300 to 245× in LXX

ἀγρός, -οῦ, ὁ	field, land, countryside
ἁμαρτάνω	to sin, do wrong
ἀπαγγέλλω	to proclaim, declare, inform
ἐπιτίθημι	to lay on, place upon, impose
κρίσις, -εως, ἡ	(legal) case, sentence, judgment
οἶνος, -ου, ὁ	wine
πέντε	five
πλῆθος, -ους, τό	quantity, multitude, crowd
πλήν	rather, nevertheless, but; (+*gen*) except
πρό	(+*gen*) ahead of, before, prior to
πρόβατον, -ου, τό	sheep
σήμερον	today
σπέρμα, -ατος, τό	seed, children, descendants
τέσσαρες, -ες, -α	four
ὥσπερ	(just) as, like

▹ **List 5**	**240 to 178× in LXX**
ἁμαρτωλός, -ός, -όν	sinful; (*subst*) sinner
ἀποδίδωμι	to give back, repay; (*mid*) to sell
βιβλίον, -ου, τό	document, scroll, letter
γενεά, -ᾶς, ἡ	generation, family group, birthplace
δεύτερος, -α, -ον	second
δυνατός, -ή, -όν	strong, powerful, capable
ἐπικαλέω	to call, (give a) name; (*mid*) to call upon
ἥλιος, -ου, ὁ	sun, sunshine
θύρα, -ας, ἡ	door, entrance
καθίζω	to sit down, settle, reside
μισέω	to hate, detest, disdain
οὖς, ὠτός, τό	ear
παραγίνομαι	to arrive, be present, present oneself
σεαυτοῦ, -ῆς, -οῦ	yourself
φόβος, -ου, ὁ	fear, dread, reverence

▹ **List 6**	**176 to 149× in LXX**
ἀκάθαρτος, -ος, -ον	impure, unclean
διέρχομαι	to go through(out), pass (through)
ἐγγίζω	to bring near, come near, approach
ἐκεῖθεν	from there, from that point
ἐκπορεύομαι	to go out, emerge, leave
ἔμπροσθεν	(+*gen*) before, in front of, prior to
ἐπιγινώσκω	to recognize, realize, notice
ἑτοιμάζω	to prepare
θηρίον, -ου, τό	wild animal
κλαίω	to cry, weep, lament
κρατέω	to grasp, take control (of), gain strength
μικρός, -ά, -όν	small, little, insignificant
προσφέρω	to bring to, offer, present
σωτηρία, -ας, ἡ	salvation, deliverance
τέλος, -ους, τό	end, conclusion, goal

▹ List 7 — 148 to 120× in LXX

ἅπτομαι	(+*gen*) to touch, grasp, affect, reach
βούλομαι	to desire, be willing, consent to
δείκνυμι	to point out, show, make known
ἐκλέγω	to select, choose, elect
ἐλεέω	to have pity (on), show mercy (to)
ἐργάζομαι	to work, labor; (*trans*) to accomplish
θλῖψις, -εως, ἡ	distress, suffering, oppression
καθαρίζω	to purify, cleanse
λογίζομαι	to devise, regard as, consider, notice
μέρος, -ους, τό	part, piece, section
πλανάω	to lead astray, deceive; (*mid*) to wander (away)
ποῦ	where?, at which place?
πτωχός, -ή, -όν	poor, oppressed, needy
σκότος, -ους, τό	darkness
φυλακή, -ῆς, ἡ	watch, guard, prison

▹ List 8 — 119 to 100× in LXX

διώκω	to pursue, chase
ἐλπίζω	to hope (for), expect
ναός, -οῦ (*or* νεώς, -ώ), ὁ	temple
ὀλίγος, -η, -ον	little, small, few
οὐκέτι	no more, no longer, not again
προσευχή, -ῆς, ἡ	prayer

COMMON SEPTUAGINT PROPER NOUNS

▷ List 1	2,747 to 227× in LXX
Ααρων	Aaron
Αιγυπτος	Egypt
Βαβυλων	Babylon
Δαυιδ	David
Ιακωβ	Jacob
Ιερουσαλημ	Jerusalem
Ιησους	Joshua
Ιουδας	Judas; Judah; Jew
Ισραηλ	Israel
Ιωσηφ	Joseph
Λευιτης	Levite
Μωυσης	Moses
Σαλωμων	Solomon
Σαουλ	Saul
Φαραω	Pharaoh

▷ List 2	216 to 131× in LXX
Αβρααμ	Abraham
Αιγυπτιος	Egyptian
Αμμων	Ammon
Ασσυριος	Assyrian
Βενιαμιν	Benjamin
Εφραιμ	Ephraim
Ιορδανης	Jordan
Ιουδαια	Judea
Ιουδαιος	Judaean; Jewish, Jew
Ιωαβ	Joab
Ιωναθαν	Jonathan
Μωαβ	Moab
Σαμουηλ	Samuel
Σιων	Zion
Συρια	Syria, Aram

▹ List 3 — 131 to 92× in LXX

Αβεσσαλωμ	Absalom
Αβιμελεχ	Abimelech
Αμορραιος	Amorite
Αχααβ	Ahab
Γαλααδ	Gilead
Δανιηλ	Daniel
Ελισαιε	Elisha
Ησαυ	Esau
Ιερεμιας	Jeremiah
Ιεροβοαμ	Jeroboam
Ισαακ	Isaac
Μανασση	Manasseh
Ναβουχοδονοσορ	Nebuchadnezzar
Σαμαρεια	Samaria
Χαλδαιος	Chaldean

▹ List 4 — 92 to 72× in LXX

Βααλ	Baal
Βαιθηλ	Bethel
Γαδ	Gad
Δαν	Dan
Εζεκιας	Hezekiah
Ελεαζαρ	Eleazar
Ηλιου	Elijah
Ιωας	Joash
Ιωσαφατ	Jehosaphat
Λευι	Levi
Ρουβην	Reuben
Σιμων	Simon
Χανααν	Canaan
Χαναναιος	Canaanite
Χεβρων	Hebron

GENESIS

▹ List 1	81 to 25×
ἀδελφή, -ῆς, ἡ	sister, beloved woman
βοῦς, βοός, ὁ/ἡ	ox, cow
γένος, -ους, τό	kind, people group, family (lineage)
ἑκατόν	one hundred
ἡγεμών, -όνος, ὁ	leader
ἡνίκα	when
θάπτω	to bury
κιβωτός, -οῦ, ἡ	box, chest, ark
κοιμάω	(*mid*) to lie (down), sleep; [κ. +μετά] to have sexual intercourse
κτῆνος, -ους, τό	(domesticated) animal; (*pl*) herd, cattle
νέος, -α, -ον	new, young; (*subst*) child
παιδίσκη, -ης, ἡ	young woman, female servant
πληθύνω	to increase, multiply
τίκτω	to give birth to, bear, produce
φρέαρ, -ατος, τό	pit, well

▹ List 2	24 to 17×
αὐξάνω	to grow, increase, intensify
βρῶμα, -ατος, τό	food, provisions
ἐκλείπω	to abandon, neglect; (*intr*) to fail, run out, cease
ἐνύπνιον, -ου, τό	dream
ἑρπετόν, -οῦ, τό	reptile, creeping thing
καθά	as, just as
κάμηλος, -ου, ὁ/ἡ	camel
λιμός, -οῦ, ὁ	hunger, famine
μήποτε	lest, in order that . . . not
πεδίον, -ου, τό	plain, field, level area
πετεινός, -ή, -όν	winged; (*subst*) bird
ποτίζω	to give drink to, water
πρωί	in the morning; (*subst*) morning
συλλαμβάνω	to capture, catch; to become pregnant
τριάκοντα	thirty

▷ List 3 — 17 to 14×

ἀναγγέλλω	to report, announce, publicize
γένεσις, -εως, ἡ	beginning, birth, family origin
δουλεύω	to serve (as a slave)
ἕνεκα *or* ἕνεκεν/εἵνεκεν	(+*gen*) on account of, because of
ἐξάγω	to lead out, take out, bring out
εὐλογία, -ας, ἡ	praise, blessing
κτάομαι	to get, acquire
μάρσιππος, -ου, ὁ	bag
οἰκέω	to inhabit, live
ὄνος, -ου, ὁ	donkey
περιτέμνω	to circumcise
ποταμός, -οῦ, ὁ	river, stream
πρωτότοκος, -ος, -ον	firstborn
σπήλαιον, -ου, τό	cave
τεσσαράκοντα	forty

▷ List 4 — 14 to 12×

ἀναβλέπω	to look up
ἄρσην, -εν	male
δῶρον, -ου, τό	gift, offering
εἰσάγω	to bring in, lead in, introduce
ἐξαποστέλλω	to dispatch, dismiss, permit to leave
ἐπονομάζω	to (give a) name, call (a name)
καθαρός, -ά, -όν	pure, clean
κατακλυσμός, -οῦ, ὁ	flood, inundation
ὄμνυμι *or* ὀμνύω	to swear, take an oath
ὅρκος, -ου, ὁ	oath
παράδεισος, -ου, ὁ	orchard, enclosed garden
παροικέω	to dwell as a foreigner
πηγή, -ῆς, ἡ	spring, fountain
ποιμήν, -ένος, ὁ	shepherd
σῖτος, -ου, ὁ	grain

▷ **List 5**	**12 to 10×**
αἴξ, αἰγός, ὁ	goat
ἀνατολή, -ῆς, ἡ	sprouting, rising; morning; (*pl*) east
ἀποδιδράσκω	to run away, escape
γαστήρ, γαστρός, ἡ	belly, womb
εἴκοσι	twenty
ἐπάνω	over, more than; (+*gen*) above, higher than
ἑσπέρα, -ας, ἡ	evening
καταλείπω	to leave (behind), abandon; (*pas*) to remain
μηρός, -οῦ, ὁ	thigh, flank
μιμνῄσκομαι	to remember, recall
μισθός, -οῦ, ὁ	payment, wages, reward
ῥάβδος, -ου, ἡ	rod, staff, scepter
στήλη, -ης, ἡ	pillar, stele, monument
συντελέω	to finish, complete, accomplish
φιλέω	to love, kiss

▷ **List 6**	**10 to 9×**
ἀναστρέφω	to return, change course; (*mid*) to conduct oneself, live
γῆρας, -ως, τό	old age
διαχωρίζω	to separate, distinguish; to depart
ἑξήκοντα	sixty
ἥκω	to have come, reach, be present
θῆλυς, -εια, -υ	female
κατάγω	to bring down, reduce
κληρονομέω	to inherit, become heir to, give as inheritance
λεπτός, -ή, -όν	small, thin, fragile
ὀρύσσω	to dig (out)
πεντήκοντα	fifty
ποικίλος, -η, -ον	multicolored, various
στάχυς, -υος, ὁ	head of grain
συνάντησις, -εως, ἡ	meeting
ὕπνος, -ου, ὁ	sleep

▹ List 7 — 9 to 8×

ἅμα	at once, together
ἀπαίρω	to remove, take away
ἀρχιοινοχόος, -ου, ὁ	chief cupbearer
βουνός, -οῦ, ὁ	hill
βρῶσις, -εως, ἡ	food, consuming
διακόσιοι, -αι, -α	two hundred
εἶδος, -ους, τό	form, appearance
ἐπακούω	to hear, listen to, comply
εὐοδόω	to lead safely, ensure success, grant; (*pas*) to prosper
θήρα, -ας, ἡ	hunting; prey, game; snare
κτῆσις, -εως, ἡ	acquisition, property
στερέωμα, -ατος, τό	firmness, strength; firmament
ὑδρία, -ας, ἡ	pitcher, jug
ὑψόω	to lift up, raise high, exalt
χώρα, -ας, ἡ	country, land, region

▹ List 8 — 8 to 7×

διάλευκος, -ος, -ον	white-spotted
ἑβδομήκοντα	seventy
ἕβδομος, -η, -ον	seventh
κατεσθίω	to eat up, devour
κινέω	to move, disturb
κριός, -οῦ, ὁ	ram
λάκκος, -ου, ὁ	pit, cistern, cavity
οὐθείς, οὐθέν	no one, none, nothing
παιδάριον, -ου, τό	child, little boy, servant
σπεύδω	to hasten, hurry
τριακόσιοι, -αι, -α	three hundred
χιτών, -ῶνος, ὁ	tunic, shirt
ἀγοράζω	*to buy*
μνημεῖον, -ου, τό	*tomb, memorial, monument*
φαίνω	*to shine;* (mid) *to appear, seem*

▷ **List 9**	7×
ἀδικία, -ας, ἡ	unrighteousness, wrongdoing, injustice
ἀκροβυστία, -ας, ἡ	uncircumcision
ἀναλαμβάνω	to take up, carry, assume
ἀριστερός, -ά, -όν	left
ἀρχισιτοποιός, -οῦ, ὁ	chief baker
ἀφαιρέω	to separate, remove; (*mid*) to deprive, seize, take away
διάνοια, -ας, ἡ	mind, thought, understanding
διασπείρω	to scatter, spread around
διηγέομαι	to describe in detail, relate fully
διπλοῦς, -ῆ, -οῦν	double
εἰρηνικός, -ή, -όν	peaceful, peaceable
ἐκλεκτός, -ή, -όν	chosen, select, elite
ἐκτρίβω	to rub out, destroy
ἐμβάλλω	to throw in, put inside
ἐνισχύω	to strengthen, grow strong(er), prevail (over)

▷ **List 10**	7×
ἐννακόσιοι, -αι, -α	nine hundred
ἐννέα	nine
ἐπάγω	to bring (up)on
εὐαρεστέω	to please
εὐλογητός, -ή, -όν	praised, blessed
καθίστημι	to place, appoint, establish; (*mid*) to stand against
καταλύω	to lodge, bring down, destroy
κλέπτω	to steal, carry off
κόνδυ, -υος, τό	cup, drinking vessel
μάχαιρα, -ας, ἡ	sword, dagger
μερίς, -ίδος, ἡ	share, part, portion
οἰκογενής, -ής, -ές	(*subst*) member of a household, servant
ὁλοκάρπωσις, -εως, ἡ	whole burnt offering
ὄφις, -εως, ὁ	snake
παρθένος, -ου, ἡ	unmarried woman, virgin

▷ List 11 — 7 to 6×

αἰσχρός, -ά, -όν	ugly, revolting, shameful
ἄμμος, -ου, ἡ	sand
ἀπάγω	to lead away, divert
ἀπέναντι *or* ἀπεναντίον	(+*gen*) opposite, contrary to, against
πένθος, -ους, τό	grief, mourning
ποίμνιον, -ου, τό	flock
ῥαντός, -ή, -όν	spotted, speckled, sprinkled
σκληρός, -ά, -όν	difficult, harsh, rough
στολή, -ῆς, ἡ	robe, cloak
συγκρίνω	to interpret; (*pas*) to be compared
τόξον, -ου, τό	bow (to shoot arrows)
τράχηλος, -ου, ὁ	neck, throat
ὑπολείπω	to leave remaining; (*mid*) to remain
χόρτος, -ου, ὁ	grass, hay
ὡσεί	as (if), like, approximately

▷ List 12 — 6×

ἀποσκευή, -ῆς, ἡ	household member, belongings
ἀφίστημι	to keep away, remove; (*mid*) to depart, withdraw
γίγας, -αντος, ὁ	giant, mighty person
διαβαίνω	to go through, cross (over)
διατίθημι	to treat; (*mid*) to grant, arrange
ἔδεσμα, -ατος, τό	food, provisions
εἰσφέρω	to lead in, bring in
ἐκτείνω	to stretch out, reach out, extend
ἐνυπνιάζομαι	to dream
ἐπειδή	when, since
ἐπιβάλλω	to lay upon, throw upon
ἐπικατάρατος, -ος, -ον	cursed
ἐπιπίπτω	to fall upon, embrace, attack
ἑπτακόσιοι, -αι, -α	seven hundred
ἐμαυτοῦ, -ῆς, -οῦ	*myself*

▷ List 13 — 6×

ἔριφος, -ου, ὁ	young goat, kid
εὐθηνία, -ας, ἡ	prosperity, abundance
κατάσκοπος, -ου, ὁ	spy
κοιλία, -ας, ἡ	belly, stomach, womb
κρύπτω	to hide, conceal
λευκός, -ή, -όν	white
λύπη, -ης, ἡ	sorrow, pain
νεανίσκος, -ου, ὁ	young man
ὄρνεον, -ου, τό	bird
παρέρχομαι	to go past, pass by, move on
παύω	to stop, prevent; (*mid*) to cease, come to an end
περιστερά, -ᾶς, ἡ	dove, pigeon
πίμπλημι	to fill, satisfy
πλάτος, -ους, τό	breadth, width
πλήρης, -ης, -ες	full, complete

▷ List 14 — 6 to 5×

ἀμφότεροι, -αι, -α	both
ἀναφέρω	to bring up, offer, bear
ἀνεμόφθορος, -ος, -ον	wind-blasted
ἀριθμέω	to number, count
ἀρσενικός, -ή, -όν	male
σός, σή, σόν	your, yours
ταράσσω	to trouble, disturb
τελευτάω	to die
τετρακόσιοι, -αι, -α	four hundred
τρέχω	to run, advance
ὑδρεύω	to draw water, transport water
ὑπακούω	to obey, comply (with)
ὑποκάτω	(+*gen*) under, below
φεύγω	to flee, escape, vanish
χεῖλος, -ους, τό	lip, language, edge

▷ List 15 5×

ἀστήρ, -έρος, ὁ	star
ἀτεκνόω	to make childless, bereave
βοάω	to cry out, shout
βόσκω	to feed, graze
γελάω	to laugh (at)
γυμνός, -ή, -όν	naked
δεσμωτήριον, -ου, τό	prison
δεῦτε	come here!, come on!
δράγμα, -ατος, τό	bundle (of stalks), sheaf
εἰκών, -όνος, ἡ	image, (idol)
εἰσακούω	to hear, listen to, obey
εἰσπορεύομαι	to go in, enter
ἐνενήκοντα	ninety
ἐνευλογέομαι	to bless, praise, make happy
ἐνιαυτός, -οῦ, ὁ	year

▷ List 16 5×

ἕξ	six
ἐξανίστημι	to raise, bring about; (*intr*) to arise, emerge
ἐρευνάω	to search, investigate
εὖ	well, good
ἐχθές	yesterday
ἵππος, -ου, ὁ	horse
καταράομαι	to curse
καταφθείρω	to destroy
μανδραγόρας, -ου, ὁ	mandrake
νίπτω	to wash
νύμφη, -ης, ἡ	bride, daughter-in-law
οἰκέτης, -ου, ὁ	household servant
ὀκτώ	eight
ὅρασις, -εως, ἡ	seeing, appearance, (prophetic) vision
ὁρκίζω	to cause to swear, bind by oath

▷ **List 17**	**5×**
ὄψις, -εως, ἡ	appearance, face, perception
παλλακή, -ῆς, ἡ	concubine, mistress
παρατίθημι	to set before, present; (*mid*) to entrust
περίχωρος, -ος, -ον	nearby region, surrounding area
πῆχυς, -εως, ὁ	cubit, (length of the) forearm
πόρνη, -ης, ἡ	prostitute, harlot
πρίαμαι	to buy, purchase
πρότερος, -α, -ον	former, earlier, before
πρωτοτόκια, -ων, τά	rights of the firstborn
συμβαίνω	to happen, come about, befall
ὑγιαίνω	to be in good health, be well
φείδομαι	to spare, refrain, hold back
χράω	to use, employ; (*mid*) to treat (in a certain way)
χρυσίον, -ου, τό	gold
ποτήριον, -ου, τό	*cup*

▷ **List 18**	**5 to 4×**
ᾅδης, -ου, ὁ	Hades, the underworld
ἀδικέω	to do wrong, harm
ἄκρος, -α, -ον	(far) end, tip, top
ἀλλότριος, -α, -ον	foreign, strange, unfamiliar
ἀμνός, -οῦ, ὁ	lamb
ἀνατέλλω	to spring up, rise, appear
ἀποκαθίστημι	to restore, put back, pay
ἀρέσκω	to please, gain favor
ἀσεβής, -ής, -ές	ungodly, wicked, sacrilegious
δέομαι	to ask (for), pray (for)
δεῦρο	come!, go!
διαιρέω	to divide, split, dispense
διαστέλλω	to distinguish, separate, state precisely; (*mid*) to command
ἐκζητέω	to search for, seek out, demand
ὡραῖος, -α, -ον	beautiful, lovely

▷ List 19 4×

ἐκκλίνω	to bend, turn away; (*intr*) to avoid, deviate
ἐκχέω	to pour out, spill
ἐνδύω	to dress, clothe
ἐξαίρω	to raise up, remove, pack up camp and go
ἐξαλείφω	to wipe out, erase, obliterate
ἐπικρατέω	to rule over, prevail, hold power
ἐπιλανθάνω	(*mid*) to forget, overlook, ignore
θυμόω	to anger; (*pas*) to be(come) angry
καθαιρέω	to take down, overpower, destroy
καταδιώκω	to seek eagerly, chase down
καταλαμβάνω	to take hold of, overtake, capture
καταπαύω	to bring to an end, stop, cease
καταστρέφω	to turn over, overthrow, ruin
κατέχω	to prevent, restrain, gain control
κοιλάς, -άδος, ἡ	valley

▷ List 20 4×

λίψ, λιβός, ὁ	south, southwest wind
μήτρα, -ας, ἡ	womb
μιαίνω	to make unclean, defile, pollute
μόσχος, -ου, ὁ	calf, young bull
νεφέλη, -ης, ἡ	cloud
ξηρός, -ά, -όν	dry, withered, arid
ὀργίζω	to make angry; (*pas*) to be angry
ὀσμή, -ῆς, ἡ	fragrance, scent, smell
ὀστοῦν, -οῦ, τό	bone
ὀχύρωμα, -ατος, τό	stronghold, fortress
πενθέω	to grieve, mourn
περιτίθημι	to put on, put around
πλάσσω	to form, mold
παραλαμβάνω	*to receive, take along*
παρίστημι	*to place near, present;* (intr) *to stand near, be present to serve*

EXODUS

▷ List 1 — 66 to 28×

ἁγιάζω	to make holy, consecrate, sanctify
βάσις, -εως, ἡ	base, pedestal, foot
βύσσος, -ου, ἡ	linen
εἰσακούω	to hear, listen to, obey
ἐξάγω	to lead out, take out, bring out
ἐξαποστέλλω	to dispatch, dismiss, permit to leave
θεράπων, -οντος, ὁ	servant, aide
κλίτος, -ους, τό	side
κλώθω	to spin, twist
μαρτύριον, -ου, τό	proof, testimony, witness
πῆχυς, -εως, ὁ	cubit, (length of the) forearm
στῦλος, -ου, ὁ	pillar, column
συντάσσω	to command, prescribe, set in order
χρυσίον, -ου, τό	gold
χρυσοῦς, -ῆ, -οῦν / χρύσεος, -α, -ον	golden; (*subst*) golden coin

▷ List 2 — 28 to 22×

αὐλή, -ῆς, ἡ	court, courtyard
δακτύλιος, -ου, ὁ	ring
ἐκτείνω	to stretch out, reach out, extend
ἐπωμίς, -ίδος, ἡ	ephod, shoulder piece
καθαρός, -ά, -όν	pure, clean
κιβωτός, -οῦ, ἡ	box, chest, ark
κόκκινος, -η, -ον	scarlet, dark red
κτῆνος, -ους, τό	(domesticated) animal; (*pl*) herd, cattle
κύκλῳ	(*dat of* κύκλος) (all) around, surrounding
πορφύρα, ας, ἡ	(cloth of) purple (color)
ποταμός, -οῦ, ὁ	river, stream
πρωί	in the morning; (*subst*) morning
πρωτότοκος, -ος, -ον	firstborn
ὑάκινθος, -ου, ἡ	(cloth of) hyacinth (color)
χαλκοῦς, -ῆ, -οῦν	(made of) bronze

▹ List 3 — 22 to 18×

ἀμφότεροι, -αι, -α	both
αὐλαία, -ας, ἡ	curtain, tent flap
ἕβδομος, -η, -ον	seventh
ἔλαιον, -ου, τό	(olive) oil
ἕξ	six
καθάπερ	just as
καταπέτασμα, -ατος, τό	curtain
κριός, -οῦ, ὁ	ram
μόσχος, -ου, ὁ	calf, young bull
νεφέλη, -ης, ἡ	cloud
πλησίον	(+*gen*) near, close; (*subst*) neighbor
ῥάβδος, -ου, ἡ	rod, staff, scepter
στολή, -ῆς, ἡ	robe, cloak
τελευτάω	to die
χάλαζα, -ης, ἡ	hail

▹ List 4 — 18 to 15×

ἀποτίνω	to repay, compensate
ἀργυροῦς, -ᾶ, -οῦν	(made of) silver
δέρρις, -εως, ἡ	(item made of) animal skin, hide
εἴκοσι	twenty
ἑκατόν	one hundred
ἔναντι	(+*gen*) opposite, before, in the presence of
ἥμισυς, -εια, -υ	half
θυμίαμα, -ατος, τό	incense
θύω	to sacrifice, slaughter
καθά	as, just as
κεφαλίς, -ίδος, ἡ	capital (of a pillar); volume (of a book)
λατρεύω	to serve, perform cultic duties (for)
λογεῖον, -ου, τό	oracular breastpiece
λυχνία, -ας, ἡ	lampstand
τράπεζα, -ης, ἡ	table

▷ List 5 — 15 to 13×

ἄζυμος, -ος, -ον	unleavened (bread)
ἄσηπτος, -ος, -ον	not susceptible to rot
ἀφαίρεμα, -ατος, τό	deduction, contribution
γαμβρός, -οῦ, ὁ	son-in-law, father-in-law
εἰσάγω	to bring in, lead in, introduce
ἡνίκα	when
ἱλαστήριον, -ου, τό	place *or* means of propitiation
καλαμίσκος, -ου, ὁ	branch of a candlestick, tube
καλύπτω	to cover, conceal
μῆκος, -ους, τό	length, end-to-end measurement
πεντήκοντα	fifty
πλάξ, πλακός, ἡ	tablet, flat stone
σκληρύνω	to harden, make stubborn
ταῦρος, -ου, ὁ	bull, ox
χερουβ, τό (*translit*)	cherub

▷ List 6 — 13 to 11×

ἀγκύλη, -ης, ἡ	loop, hook
ἄκρος, -α, -ον	(far) end, tip, top
ἅρμα, -ατος, τό	chariot
αὔριον	tomorrow
βάτραχος, -ου, ὁ	frog
βοῦς, βοός, ὁ/ἡ	ox, cow
δέρμα, -ατος, τό	skin, hide
εἰσπορεύομαι	to go in, enter
ἑορτή, -ῆς, ἡ	feast, festival
ἐπάγω	to bring (up)on
εὖρος, -ους, τό	breadth, width
ἱστίον, -ου, τό	curtain, sail
καταλείπω	to leave (behind), abandon; (*pas*) to remain
καταχρυσόω	to gild, overlay with gold
συντρίβω	to break, crush, wreck

▹ List 7 — 11 to 10×

διπλοῦς, -ῆ, -οῦν	double
εἰσφέρω	to lead in, bring in
ἐνιαυτός, -οῦ, ὁ	year
ἱερατεύω	to minister as priest
καταπαύω	to bring to an end, stop, cease
κρέας, κρέως, τό	meat
λύχνος, -ου, ὁ	lamp
μοχλός, -οῦ, ὁ	bolt, bar (of a door)
προσάγω	to bring to, approach
ῥίπτω	to throw (away), defeat, reject
στίχος, -ου, ὁ	row, line
τρόπος, -ου, ὁ	manner, way, conduct
ὑποζύγιον, -ου, τό	beast of burden (donkey, mule)
χρίω	to anoint, smear
ὡσεί	as (if), like, approximately

▹ List 8 — 10 to 9×

ἀναφέρω	to bring up, offer, bear
ἀφαιρέω	to separate, remove; (*mid*) to deprive, seize, take away
βαδίζω	to go, proceed, walk
διάνοια, -ας, ἡ	mind, thought, understanding
ἑσπέρα, -ας, ἡ	evening
ἵππος, -ου, ὁ	horse
κρίκος, -ου, ὁ	eyelet, ring, loop
λειτουργέω	to serve (as priest), minister
μήποτε	lest, in order that . . . not
μνημόσυνον, -ου, τό	memory, memorial, reminder
νήθω	to spin (thread or cloth)
παρέρχομαι	to go past, pass by, move on
πεδίον, -ου, τό	plain, field, level area
περιαιρέω	to take away, remove
ὑπολείπω	to leave remaining; (*mid*) to remain

▷ List 9 — 9 to 8×

ἁγίασμα, -ατος, τό	sanctuary, sacred offering
ἀναγγέλλω	to report, announce, publicize
ἀπαρχή, -ῆς, ἡ	first portion, firstfruits
ἄχυρον, -ου, τό	straw, chaff
ἐντεῦθεν	from here; on this side . . . on that side
λυτρόω	(*mid*) to redeem, ransom
προσήλυτος, -ου, ὁ	immigrant, foreign guest
σίκλος, -ου, ὁ	shekel
συλλέγω	to collect, gather
σύνθεσις, -εως, ἡ	composition, collection, mixture
τίκτω	to give birth to, bear, produce
ὑακίνθινος, -η, -ον	hyacinth-colored, blue
ὑποδύτης, -ου, ὁ	(priestly) undergarment
ὑφαντός, -ή, -όν	woven
ὕψος, -ους, τό	height, summit

▷ List 10 — 8 to 7×

ἀναβάτης, -ου, ὁ	horse rider, charioteer
ἀναβιβάζω	to bring up, raise up
ἀναιρέω	to get rid of, destroy; (*mid*) to take up
ἀναλαμβάνω	to take up, carry, assume
ἄνωθεν	from above, from on high
ἀρσενικός, -ή, -όν	male
ἑβδομήκοντα	seventy
ἐμβάλλω	to throw in, put inside
ἐπονομάζω	to (give a) name, call (a name)
εὔχομαι	to pray, vow
ζύμη, -ης, ἡ	yeast, leaven
κάλυμμα, -ατος, τό	veil, covering
ὁλοκαύτωμα, -ατος, τό	whole burnt offering
χαλκός, -οῦ, ὁ	bronze, brass, copper
χιτών, -ῶνος, ὁ	tunic, shirt

▷ List 11 7×

κάρπωμα, -ατος, τό	cultic offering
κατακαίω	to burn up, consume
κλέπτω	to steal, carry off
κυνόμυια, -ας, ἡ	dog-fly
λῶμα, -ατος, τό	fringe, hem (of a robe)
μαῖα, -ας, ἡ	midwife
νίπτω	to wash
νόμιμος, -η/ος, -ον	lawful; (*subst*) ordinance, statute
νότος, -ου, ὁ	south (wind)
ξηρός, -ά, -όν	dry, withered, arid
πάσσαλος, -ου, ὁ	peg, pin
περιαργυρόω	to overlay with silver
πίμπλημι	to fill, satisfy
πληθύνω	to increase, multiply
παρίστημι	*to place near, present;* (intr) *to stand near, be present to serve*

▷ List 12 7 to 6×

ἀκοή, -ῆς, ἡ	report, news
ἀκρίς, -ίδος, ἡ	locust, swarm of locusts
ἀνάγω	to lead up, bring up, raise up
ἀπέναντι *or* ἀπεναντίον	(+*gen*) opposite, contrary to, against
ἄρσην, -εν	male
βραχίων, -ονος, ὁ	arm, (strength)
γάλα, -ακτος, τό	milk
συμβολή, -ῆς, ἡ	joint, meeting, sharing
σφραγίς, -ῖδος, ἡ	seal
τάλαντον, -ου, τό	talent (*monetary unit*)
τεσσαράκοντα	forty
τριάκοντα	thirty
χρῖσμα, -ατος, τό	anointing (with oil)
ὦμος, -ου, ὁ	shoulder
ὡσαύτως	in the same way, similarly

▷ List 13 — 6×

διανοίγω	to open up, spread apart
δικαίωμα, -ατος, τό	ordinance, decree, rightful claim
δουλεύω	to serve (as a slave)
ἐμπί(μ)πλημι	to fill up, satisfy; [ἐ. τὰς χεῖρας] to consecrate as priest
ἐνδύω	to dress, clothe
ἔνθεν	from here; on one side . . . on the other side
ἐξαίρω	to raise up, remove, pack up camp and go
ἐπιβάλλω	to lay upon, throw upon
ἐχθές	yesterday
θανατόω	to kill, put to death
καθήκω	to belong to, be proper, be due to
καθότι	as, insofar as, since
κακόω	to do wrong, mistreat
κέρας, κέρατος, τό	horn, flank (of an army)
κόλπος, -ου, ὁ	bosom, chest

▷ List 14 — 6×

κορυφή, -ῆς, ἡ	top, highest point
κραταιός, -ά, -όν	powerful, forceful, severe
μήτρα, -ας, ἡ	womb
οἰκέτης, -ου, ὁ	household servant
πάσχα, τό	Passover, Passover lamb *or* meal
παύω	to stop, prevent; (*mid*) to cease, come to an end
προπορεύομαι	to proceed, go beforehand
προσέχω	to pay attention to, be concerned about
ῥύομαι	to rescue, save
σκεπάζω	to cover over, shelter, conceal
σοφός, -ή, -όν	wise, skilled, learned
στέαρ, στέατος, τό	fat, suet
συναντάω	to meet (with), fall upon, happen
συνάπτω	to join together, engage, border on
σφάζω	to slaughter, slay

▷ List 15 — 6 to 5×

ἀδελφή, -ῆς, ἡ	sister, beloved woman
ἀμνός, -οῦ, ὁ	lamb
ἀφορίζω	to separate, mark out; (*mid*) to split
βαρύνω	to make heavy, burden
γερουσία, -ας, ἡ	council, senate
ἕνεκα *or* ἕνεκεν/εἵνεκεν	(+*gen*) on account of, because of
ἐξαιρέω	to take out, remove; (*mid*) to set free
ἐξολεθρεύω	to utterly destroy, eradicate
ἔξωθεν	outside; (+*gen*) from outside
ἐπισκέπτομαι	to visit, examine, account for
ἐρυθρός, -ή, -όν	red
θυμιάω	to burn incense (as an offering)
τέρας, -ατος, τό	wonder, omen, remarkable sight
τέταρτος, -η, -ον	fourth
χεῖλος, -ους, τό	lip, language, edge

▷ List 16 — 5×

καίω	to light (a flame), burn
κατεσθίω	to eat up, devour
κατισχύω	to strengthen, overpower; (*intr*) to be encouraged, become powerful
κοιμάω	(*mid*) to lie (down), sleep; [κ. +μετά] to have sexual intercourse
μέλι, -ιτος, τό	honey
νέος, -α, -ον	new, young; (*subst*) child
ὀδούς, -όντος, ὁ	tooth
ὄμνυμι *or* ὀμνύω	to swear, take an oath
ὀρθρίζω	to get up early
παιδίσκη, -ης, ἡ	young woman, female servant
παρεμβάλλω	to set up, pitch (a tent), encamp
συνάντησις, -εως, ἡ	meeting
τεῖχος, -ους, τό	(city) wall
τύπτω	to beat, strike (dead), afflict
πειρά(ζ)ω	*to tempt, test, try*

LEVITICUS

▷ List 1	61 to 34×
ἁγιάζω	to make holy, consecrate, sanctify
ἁφή, -ῆς, ἡ	infection, injury
δέρμα, -ατος, τό	skin, hide
δῶρον, -ου, τό	gift, offering
ἔλαιον, -ου, τό	(olive) oil
ἔναντι	(+*gen*) opposite, before, in the presence of
ἐξιλάσκομαι	to propitiate, make atonement
καθαρός, -ά, -όν	pure, clean
μαρτύριον, -ου, τό	proof, testimony, witness
μόσχος, -ου, ὁ	calf, young bull
ὁλοκαύτωμα, -ατος, τό	whole burnt offering
πλύνω	to wash, cleanse
προσάγω	to bring to, approach
στέαρ, στέατος, τό	fat, suet
σφάζω	to slaughter, slay

▷ List 2	34 to 22×
ἀκαθαρσία, -ας, ἡ	uncleanness, impurity
ἄμωμος, -ος, -ον	unblemished, spotless
ἀναφέρω	to bring up, offer, bear
ἀποκαλύπτω	to uncover, reveal, disclose
ἀσχημοσύνη, -ης, ἡ	indecency, privates, disgrace
ἄφεσις, -εως, ἡ	forgiveness, release (from debt), outlet (of water)
ἑσπέρα, -ας, ἡ	evening
κάρπωμα, -ατος, τό	cultic offering
κριός, -οῦ, ὁ	ram
κτῆνος, -ους, τό	(domesticated) animal; (*pl*) herd, cattle
λέπρα, -ας, ἡ	skin disease
λούω	to wash; (*mid*) to bathe
μιαίνω	to make unclean, defile, pollute
νόμιμος, -η/ος, -ον	lawful; (*subst*) ordinance, statute
σωτήριον, -ου, τό	salvation, (offering for) deliverance

▷ List 3 — 22 to 17×

ἄρσην, -εν	male
ἀφορίζω	to separate, mark out; (*mid*) to split
βεβηλόω	to profane, desecrate
ἕβδομος, -η, -ον	seventh
εὐωδία, -ας, ἡ	aroma, fragrance
θνησιμαῖον, -ου, τό	carcass, corpse, dead body
κατακαίω	to burn up, consume
καταλείπω	to leave (behind), abandon; (*pas*) to remain
κοίτη, -ης, ἡ	bed; sexual intercourse, ejaculation
λυτρόω	(*mid*) to redeem, ransom
ὀσμή, -ῆς, ἡ	fragrance, scent, smell
πλημμέλεια, -ας, ἡ	(sinful) error, mistake
προσήλυτος, -ου, ὁ	immigrant, foreign guest
χίμαρος, -ου, ὁ	young male goat
τιμή, -ῆς, ἡ	*honor, value, price*

▷ List 4 — 17 to 14×

βδέλυγμα, -ατος, τό	abomination, detestable object
βιβρώσκω	to consume, eat
ἐνιαυτός, -οῦ, ὁ	year
θραῦσμα, -ατος, τό	destruction, break(ing)
θρίξ, τριχός, ἡ	hair
κατάσχεσις, -εως, ἡ	possession
κοιμάω	(*mid*) to lie (down), sleep; [κ. +μετά] to have sexual intercourse
κρέας, κρέως, τό	meat
κύκλῳ	(*dat of* κύκλος) (all) around, surrounding
λευκός, -ή, -όν	white
λοβός, -οῦ, ὁ	lobe (of ear or liver)
πλησίον	(+*gen*) near, close; (*subst*) neighbor
ῥύσις, -εως, ἡ	flow, stream, discharge
σεμίδαλις, -εως, ἡ	fine flour
τρόπος, -ου, ὁ	manner, way, conduct

▷ List 5 — 14 to 12×

ἄκρος, -α, -ον	(far) end, tip, top
ἀμνός, -οῦ, ὁ	lamb
γονορρυής, -ής, -ές	(suffering of) involuntary discharge
δάκτυλος, -ου, ὁ	finger
δέκατος, -η, -ον	tenth; (*subst*) tithe
διαχέω	to spread, scatter, dissolve
ἐνδύω	to dress, clothe
ἑπτάκις	seven times
θανατόω	to kill, put to death
θῆλυς, -εια, -υ	female
νεφρός, -οῦ, ὁ	kidney, heart (as seat of emotions)
ὀρνίθιον, -ου, τό	little bird
ὄψις, -εως, ἡ	appearance, face, perception
πρόσταγμα, -ατος, τό	ordinance, command
χρώς, χρωτός, ὁ	(surface of the) body, skin

▷ List 6 — 12 to 10×

ἀδελφή, -ῆς, ἡ	sister, beloved woman
ἄζυμος, -ος, -ον	unleavened (bread)
αἴξ, αἰγός, ὁ	goat
ἄφεδρος, -ου, ἡ	menstruation
βάσις, -εως, ἡ	base, pedestal, foot
γένημα, -ατος, τό	fruit, yield, produce, (offspring)
ἐκχέω	to pour out, spill
ἑρπετόν, -οῦ, τό	reptile, creeping thing
κλητός, -ή, -όν	called, invited; (*subst*) guest
κοιλία, -ας, ἡ	belly, stomach, womb
περιαιρέω	to take away, remove
πλημμελέω	to trespass, err, offend
προσχέω	to pour out, pour on
στολή, -ῆς, ἡ	robe, cloak
συντάσσω	to command, prescribe, set in order

▷ **List 7**	**10 to 9×**
ἀφαιρέω	to separate, remove; (*mid*) to deprive, seize, take away
βοῦς, βοός, ὁ/ἡ	ox, cow
δίδραχμον, -ου, τό	two-drachma coin
ἐξάγω	to lead out, take out, bring out
ἐξολεθρεύω	to utterly destroy, eradicate
ἧπαρ, -ατος, τό	liver
κρόκη, -ης, ἡ	(the thread for the) woof
κτάομαι	to get, acquire
λινοῦς, -ῆ, -οῦν	(made of) linen
μεταβάλλω	to turn, change, alter
μῶμος, -ου, ὁ	defect, blemish
ὄγδοος, -η, -ον	eighth
πετεινός, -ή, -όν	winged; (*subst*) bird
σημασία, -ας, ἡ	signal, symbol
στήμων, -ονος, ὁ	warp (of a loom)

▷ **List 8**	**9 to 8×**
ἀμφότεροι, -αι, -α	both
ἀνάπαυσις, -εως, ἡ	rest, stopping
ἀφαίρεμα, -ατος, τό	deduction, contribution
βραχίων, -ονος, ὁ	arm, (strength)
δεκτός, -ή, -όν	acceptable
ἐξανθέω	to flower, blossom, bloom
ἐξαποστέλλω	to dispatch, dismiss, permit to leave
ἑορτή, -ῆς, ἡ	feast, festival
ἐπιχέω	to pour over, apply
ἔσθω	to eat
θερισμός, -οῦ, ὁ	harvest
περιστερά, -ᾶς, ἡ	dove, pigeon
ῥαίνω	to sprinkle, splatter
τρυγών, -όνος, ἡ	turtledove
ὅμοιος, -α, -ον	*like, similar to*

▷ List 9 — 8 to 7×

ἀλλάσσω	to alter, substitute, (take in) exchange
ἀνάγω	to lead up, bring up, raise up
ἀπέναντι *or* ἀπεναντίον	(+*gen*) opposite, contrary to, against
καίω	to light (a flame), burn
κέρας, -ατος, τό	horn, flank (of an army)
νεοσσός, -οῦ, ὁ	young bird, chick
ξυράω	to shave
ὁπλή, -ῆς, ἡ	hoof
πάροικος, -ος, -ον	strange, alien; (*subst*) foreigner
πλάγιος, -α, -ον	sideways, crooked; (*subst*) side, flank
πρόσκειμαι	to lie near, be attached to
προσοχθίζω	to be irritated, be offended
πρωί	in the morning; (*subst*) morning
στηθύνιον, -ου, τό	breast (of a sacrificed animal)
ταπεινός, -ή, -όν	humble, abject, oppressed

▷ List 10 — 7×

αὐγάζω	to shine, appear white *or* bright
βάπτω	to dip, plunge
βδελύσσω	to make detestable; (*mid*) to detest
διχηλέω	to have a divided hoof
ἐνιαύσιος, -α, -ον	year
ἐπίπεμπτος, -ου, ὁ	a fifth
θύω	to sacrifice, slaughter
ἱλαστήριον, -ου, τό	place *or* means of propitiation
καθάπερ	just as
καταπέτασμα, -ατος, τό	curtain
κατοικία, -ας, ἡ	dwelling place, settlement
μηρυκισμός, -οῦ, ὁ	(chewing the) cud
ὁλοκαύτωσις, -εως, ἡ	whole burnt offering
οὐλή, -ῆς, ἡ	scar, mark
παλαιός, -ά, -όν	old, ancient

▷ List 11 — 7 to 6×

διαστέλλω	to distinguish, separate, state precisely; (*mid*) to command
εἰσφέρω	to lead in, bring in
ἐκπορνεύω	to commit sexual immorality
ἐκφέρω	to bring out, produce
εὐχή, -ῆς, ἡ	prayer, vow
θυμίαμα, -ατος, τό	incense
κρίμα, -ατος, τό	decision, judgment, punishment
μνημόσυνον, -ου, τό	memory, memorial, reminder
πιπράσκω	to sell
πρᾶσις, -εως, ἡ	sale, transaction
τελείωσις, -εως, ἡ	completion, validation, perfection
τιμάω	to honor; (*mid*) to value (at a price)
φυράω	to knead, mix
χρῖσις, -εως, ἡ	anointing
χρίω	to anoint, smear

▷ List 12 — 6 to 5×

ἀνομία, -ας, ἡ	lawlessness, wrongful conduct
γένος, -ους, τό	kind, people group, family (lineage)
εἰσπορεύομαι	to go in, enter
ἕξ	six
ἐφίστημι	to cast over, place on
καθότι	as, insofar as, since
κόκκινος, -η, -ον	scarlet, dark red
κτῆσις, -εως, ἡ	acquisition, property
πεδίον, -ου, τό	plain, field, level area
προστάσσω	to command, order
ῥέω	to flow, stream
συντρίβω	to break, crush, wreck
ταπεινόω	to bring down, humiliate, humble
ὑπεροράω	to disregard, ignore
χιτών, -ῶνος, ὁ	tunic, shirt

NUMBERS

▷ LIST 1	151 TO 35×
ἀμνός, -οῦ, ὁ	lamb
ἀπαίρω	to remove, take away
βοῦς, βοός, ὁ/ἡ	ox, cow
δῆμος, -ου, ὁ	crowd, populace, district
δῶρον, -ου, τό	gift, offering
ἔναντι	(+*gen*) opposite, before, in the presence of
ἐνιαύσιος, -α, -ον	year
ἐπισκέπτομαι	to visit, examine, account for
ἐπίσκεψις, -εως, ἡ	numbering, investigation, inspection
κριός, -οῦ, ὁ	ram
μαρτύριον, -ου, τό	proof, testimony, witness
μόσχος, -ου, ὁ	calf, young bull
ὁλοκαύτωμα, -ατος, τό	whole burnt offering
παρεμβάλλω	to set up, pitch (a tent), encamp
πατριά, -ᾶς, ἡ	paternal lineage, family line

▷ LIST 2	35 TO 27×
αἴξ, αἰγός, ὁ	goat
ἀναποιέω	to prepare, mix, make up
ἀργυροῦς, -ᾶ, -οῦν	(made of) silver
ἀριθμός, -οῦ, ὁ	number, total
δέκατος, -η, -ον	tenth; (*subst*) tithe
ἔλαιον, -ου, τό	(olive) oil
ἐξαίρω	to raise up, remove, pack up camp and go
ἐπάνω	over, more than; (+*gen*) above, higher than
εὐχή, -ῆς, ἡ	prayer, vow
κληρονομία, -ας, ἡ	inheritance, possession(s)
κτῆνος, -ους, τό	(domesticated) animal; (*pl*) herd, cattle
σίκλος, -ου, ὁ	shekel
σπονδή, -ῆς, ἡ	drink offering
συντάσσω	to command, prescribe, set in order
τριάκοντα	thirty

▹ List 3 27 to 20×

ἄμωμος, -ος, -ον	unblemished, spotless
ἀρσενικός, -ή, -όν	male
ἑβδομήκοντα	seventy
ἑκατόν	one hundred
εὐωδία, -ας, ἡ	aroma, fragrance
θυμίαμα, -ατος, τό	incense
καθά	as, just as
λειτουργέω	to serve (as priest), minister
πεντήκοντα	fifty
πλήρης, -ης, -ες	full, complete
προσάγω	to bring to, approach
πρωτότοκος, -ος, -ον	firstborn
ῥάβδος, -ου, ἡ	rod, staff, scepter
σεμίδαλις, -εως, ἡ	fine flour
χίμαρος, -ου, ὁ	young male goat

▹ List 4 20 to 16×

ἁγιάζω	to make holy, consecrate, sanctify
ἀφαιρέω	to separate, remove; (*mid*) to deprive, seize, take away
δάμαλις, -εως, ἡ	young cow, heifer
εἰκοσαετής, -ής, -ές	(of) twenty years (old)
ἐξιλάσκομαι	to propitiate, make atonement
κλῆρος, -ου, ὁ	lot, share, portion
λειτουργία, -ας, ἡ	(cultic) ministry, (religious) service
νεφέλη, -ης, ἡ	cloud
ὁλοκαύτωσις, -εως, ἡ	whole burnt offering
ὄνος, -ου, ὁ	donkey
ὀσμή, -ῆς, ἡ	fragrance, scent, smell
πεντακόσιοι, -αι, -α	five hundred
σωτήριον, -ου, τό	salvation, (offering for) deliverance
τεσσαράκοντα	forty
χρυσοῦς, -ῆ, -οῦν / χρύσεος, -α, -ον	golden; (*subst*) golden coin

▹ List 5 — 16 to 14×

ἀμνάς, -άδος, ἡ	ewe lamb
ἀμφότεροι, -αι, -α	both
ἀφαίρεμα, -ατος, τό	deduction, contribution
εἰσπορεύομαι	to go in, enter
ἑξακόσιοι, -αι, -α	six hundred
εὔχομαι	to pray, vow
θυίσκη, -ης, ἡ	censer
κάρπωμα, -ατος, τό	cultic offering
κατασκέπτομαι	to view closely, spy, survey, inspect
κατάσχεσις, -εως, ἡ	possession
κύκλῳ	(*dat of* κύκλος) (all) around, surrounding
μιαίνω	to make unclean, defile, pollute
τρόπος, -ου, ὁ	manner, way, conduct
τρύβλιον, -ου, τό	bowl, dish
φιάλη, -ης, ἡ	(shallow) bowl, cup

▹ List 6 — 14 to 12×

ἀνατολή, -ῆς, ἡ	sprouting, rising; morning; (*pl*) east
ἀπαρχή, -ῆς, ἡ	first portion, firstfruits
ἕβδομος, -η, -ον	seventh
εἴκοσι	twenty
ἑσπέρα, -ας, ἡ	evening
καθαρός, -ά, -όν	pure, clean
καταράομαι	to curse
κληρονομέω	to inherit, become heir to, give as inheritance
παρέρχομαι	to go past, pass by, move on
συγγένεια, -ας, ἡ	relations, kin, family
τετρακόσιοι, -αι, -α	four hundred
τράγος, -ου, ὁ	(male) goat
ὑακίνθινος, -η, -ον	hyacinth-colored, blue
φονεύω	to kill, murder
ὡσεί	as (if), like, approximately

▷ List 7 — 12 to 10×

ἀγχιστεύω	to be *or* act as a kinsman *or* relative
ἀπέναντι *or* ἀπεναντίον	(+*gen*) opposite, contrary to, against
διακόσιοι, -αι, -α	two hundred
ἕξ	six
ἑξήκοντα	sixty
ἥμισυς, -εια, -υ	half
ιν (*translit*)	hin (liquid measure)
κάλυμμα, -ατος, τό	veil, covering
καλύπτω	to cover, conceal
κρέας, κρέως, τό	meat
ὁλκή, -ῆς, ἡ	weight
ὁρισμός, -οῦ, ὁ	oath, decree, obligation
προσήλυτος, -ου, ὁ	immigrant, foreign guest
πυρεῖον, -ου, τό	censer, incense burner
τάγμα, -ατος, τό	group, rank, unit

▷ List 8 — 10 to 8×

ἀναλαμβάνω	to take up, carry, assume
βωμός, -οῦ, ὁ	altar (typically pagan)
δεῦρο	come!, go!
εἰσάγω	to bring in, lead in, introduce
ἐπιβάλλω	to lay upon, throw upon
ἐπικαταράομαι	to call down curses upon
μηνιαῖος, -α, -ον	of one month (in age)
ὁρίζω	to determine, set limits
πάσχα, τό	Passover, Passover lamb *or* meal
πέραν	beyond; (+*gen*) on the other side
πρωί	in the morning; (*subst*) morning
σαλπίζω	to blow (a trumpet), trumpet (a sound)
στῦλος, -ου, ὁ	pillar, column
σύγκρισις, -εως, ἡ	interpretation, assessment, decision
τέταρτος, -η, -ον	fourth

▷ List 9 8×

ἀναφορεύς, -έως, ὁ	carrying pole
ἀφαγνίζω	to purify, consecrate
δισχίλιοι, -αι, -α	two thousand
ἐμβάλλω	to throw in, put inside
ἐξάγω	to lead out, take out, bring out
ἔπαυλις, -εως, ἡ	residence, settlement
θανατόω	to kill, put to death
θνῄσκω	to die
λίψ, λιβός, ὁ	south, southwest wind
λύτρον, -ου, τό	ransom, redemption price
παραβαίνω	to deviate, turn away
πλύνω	to wash, cleanse
σημασία, -ας, ἡ	signal, symbol
συνάντησις, -εως, ἡ	meeting
φονευτής, -οῦ, ὁ	murderer, killer

▷ List 10 7×

ἄζυμος, -ος, -ον	unleavened (bread)
ἀνανεύω	to refuse, deny
ἀποσκευή, -ῆς, ἡ	household member, belongings
ἀρχηγός, -οῦ, ὁ	chief, ruler, prince; beginning
ἀφίστημι	to keep away, remove; (*mid*) to depart, withdraw
βάσις, -εως, ἡ	base, pedestal, foot
δερμάτινος, -η, -ον	(made of) leather
διαβαίνω	to go through, cross (over)
δόμα, -ατος, τό	gift
ἐκκλίνω	to bend, turn away; (*intr*) to avoid, deviate
ἐπίκλητος, -ος, -ον	called, designated, appointed
ἑπτακόσιοι, -αι, -α	seven hundred
κακόω	to do wrong, mistreat
κορυφή, -ῆς, ἡ	top, highest point
νόμιμος, -η/ος, -ον	lawful; (*subst*) ordinance, statute

▷ List 11 — 7 to 6×

ἁγνίζω	to purify, cleanse
ἀλλογενής, -ής, -ές	foreign born
ὄφις, -εως, ὁ	snake
παρατάσσω	to form a battle line, battle
πεντεκαιεικοσαετής, -ής, -ές	twenty-five years old
πεντηκονταετής, -ής, -ές	fifty years old
περιαιρέω	to take away, remove
πληγή, -ῆς, ἡ	blow, wound, misfortune, plague
πρόσταγμα, -ατος, τό	ordinance, command
φεύγω	to flee, escape, vanish
φυγαδευτήριον, -ου, τό	refuge, sanctuary
χίλιοι, -αι, -α	one thousand
χρίω	to anoint, smear
χρυσίον, -ου, τό	gold
παρίστημι	*to place near, present;* (intr) *to stand near, be present to serve*

▷ List 12 — 6×

αὐλή, -ῆς, ἡ	court, courtyard
βορέας, -ου, ἡ / βορρᾶς, -ᾶ, ἡ	north
δικαίωμα, -ατος, τό	ordinance, decree, rightful claim
δυσμή, -ῆς, ἡ	(*always pl*) setting (of the sun), west
εἶδος, -ους, τό	form, appearance
ἑορτή, -ῆς, ἡ	feast, festival
ἐπισκοπή, -ῆς, ἡ	inspection, consideration, visitation
ζηλόω	to be jealous of *or* for, envy, strive for
κατακαίω	to burn up, consume
καταλείπω	to leave (behind), abandon; (*pas*) to remain
κιβωτός, -οῦ, ἡ	box, chest, ark
λυχνία, -ας, ἡ	lampstand
ὄμνυμι *or* ὀμνύω	to swear, take an oath
πέτρα, -ας, ἡ	rock, stone, cave
πολεμιστής, -οῦ, ὁ	combatant, warrior

DEUTERONOMY

▹ List 1	49 to 19×
βδέλυγμα, -ατος, τό	abomination, detestable object
διαβαίνω	to go through, cross (over)
δικαίωμα, -ατος, τό	ordinance, decree, rightful claim
εἰσακούω	to hear, listen to, obey
εἰσπορεύομαι	to go in, enter
ἐξάγω	to lead out, take out, bring out
ἐξολεθρεύω	to utterly destroy, eradicate
εὐφραίνω	to make happy, cheer; (*pas*) to rejoice
κληρονομέω	to inherit, become heir to, give as inheritance
κλῆρος, -ου, ὁ	lot, share, portion
λατρεύω	to serve, perform cultic duties (for)
ὄμνυμι *or* ὀμνύω	to swear, take an oath
πλησίον	(+*gen*) near, close; (*subst*) neighbor
προσήλυτος, -ου, ὁ	immigrant, foreign guest
τρόπος, -ου, ὁ	manner, way, conduct

▹ List 2	19 to 14×
ἀναγγέλλω	to report, announce, publicize
βοῦς, βοός, ὁ/ἡ	ox, cow
γένημα, -ατος, τό	fruit, yield, produce, (offspring)
γερουσία, -ας, ἡ	council, senate
εἰσάγω	to bring in, lead in, introduce
ἔναντι	(+*gen*) opposite, before, in the presence of
ἐπικατάρατος, -ος, -ον	cursed
εὖ	well, good
κατακληρονομέω	to give as inheritance, become owner, dispossess
κοιμάω	(*mid*) to lie (down), sleep; [κ. +μετά] to have sexual intercourse
κτῆνος, -ους, τό	(domesticated) animal; (*pl*) herd, cattle
μιμνῄσκομαι	to remember, recall
παρέρχομαι	to go past, pass by, move on
πλάξ, πλακός, ἡ	tablet, flat stone
ὑψηλός, -ή, -όν	elevated, proud; (*subst*) high place

▷ List 3 — 14 to 12×

βραχίων, -ονος, ὁ	arm, (strength)
ἐμπί(μ)πλημι	to fill up, satisfy; [ἐ. τὰς χεῖρας] to consecrate as priest
ἐξαίρω	to raise up, remove, pack up camp and go
ἐξαποστέλλω	to dispatch, dismiss, permit to leave
ἐπιλανθάνω	(*mid*) to forget, overlook, ignore
εὐλογία, -ας, ἡ	praise, blessing
θύω	to sacrifice, slaughter
καθά	as, just as
καθίστημι	to place, appoint, establish; (*mid*) to stand against
καθότι	as, insofar as, since
κρίμα, -ατος, τό	decision, judgment, punishment
πέραν	beyond; (+*gen*) on the other side
πληθύνω	to increase, multiply
προσέχω	to pay attention to, be concerned about
τεσσαράκοντα	forty

▷ List 4 — 12 to 10×

ἀλλότριος, -α, -ον	foreign, strange, unfamiliar
διατίθημι	to treat; (*mid*) to grant, arrange
ἔκγονος, -ος, -ον	born of; (*subst*) descendant
ἔλαιον, -ου, τό	(olive) oil
ἐνιαυτός, -οῦ, ὁ	year
καταλείπω	to leave (behind), abandon; (*pas*) to remain
κατάρα, -ας, ἡ	curse
κραταιός, -ά, -όν	powerful, forceful, severe
κρέας, κρέως, τό	meat
κριτής, -οῦ, ὁ	judge
ὁμοίωμα, -ατος, τό	similarity, likeness, representation
ὀρφανός, -ή, -όν	orphaned (person)
παροξύνω	to sharpen; to provoke, defy
χείμαρρος/ους, -ου, ὁ	stream, (seasonal) brook
χήρα, -ας, ἡ	widow

▷ List 5 — 10 to 9×

ἄκρος, -α, -ον	(far) end, tip, top
γάλα, -ακτος, τό	milk
ἐκκλίνω	to bend, turn away; (*intr*) to avoid, deviate
ἐκτρίβω	to rub firmly, destroy completely
ἐπιβάλλω	to lay upon, throw upon
μαρτύριον, -ου, τό	proof, testimony, witness
μέλι, -ιτος, τό	honey
μόσχος, -ου, ὁ	calf, young bull
οἰκέτης, -ου, ὁ	household servant
παιδίσκη, -ης, ἡ	young woman, female servant
πρωτότοκος, -ος, -ον	firstborn
τέρας, -ατος, τό	wonder, omen, remarkable sight
φάραγξ, -αγγος, ἡ	ravine, valley
ὡσεί	as (if), like, approximately
μάρτυς, -υρος, ὁ	*witness*

▷ List 6 — 9 to 8×

ἀμπελών, -ῶνος, ὁ	vineyard
ἀντιλογία, -ας, ἡ	dispute, (counter)argument
ἀπαίρω	to remove, take away
ἀπαρχή, -ῆς, ἡ	first portion, firstfruits
ἀπώλεια, -ας, ἡ	destruction, ruin, loss
δαν(ε)ίζω	to lend, borrow
ἐγκαταλείπω	to abandon, leave behind
ἐκζητέω	to search for, seek out, demand
ἑορτή, -ῆς, ἡ	feast, festival
κιβωτός, -οῦ, ἡ	box, chest, ark
μερίς, -ίδος, ἡ	share, part, portion
νεᾶνις, -ιδος, ἡ	girl, young woman
προπορεύομαι	to proceed, go beforehand
πρότερος, -α, -ον	former, earlier, before
σῖτος, -ου, ὁ	grain

▷ List 7 — 7 to 6×

ἁγιάζω	to make holy, consecrate, sanctify
ἀναφέρω	to bring up, offer, bear
ἀνθίστημι	to resist, oppose
ἀνταποδίδωμι	to give back, repay
γλυπτός, -ή, -όν	carved, graven; [τὸ γλύπτον] graven image
ἐπιθυμέω	to desire, yearn for
ἐπίσταμαι	to know, be acquainted with
εὔχομαι	to pray, vow
λίθινος, -η, -ον	(made of) stone
μανθάνω	to learn, find out
πληγή, -ῆς, ἡ	blow, wound, misfortune, plague
ῥέω	to flow, stream
συντρίβω	to break, crush, wreck
ὑπακούω	to obey, comply (with)
ὑποκάτω	(+*gen*) under, below

▷ List 8 — 6×

ἄνω	(from) above
ἀπειθέω	to be disobedient, refuse
ἀρά, -ᾶς, ἡ	curse, imprecation, oath
ἀρεστός, -ή, -όν	pleasing, acceptable
ἀριθμός, -οῦ, ὁ	number, total
ἄφεσις, -εως, ἡ	forgiveness, release (from debt), outlet (of water)
ἀφίστημι	to keep away, remove; (*mid*) to depart, withdraw
δουλεία, -ας, ἡ	slavery, servitude
δυσμή, -ῆς, ἡ	(*always pl*) setting (of the sun), west
ἐμβάλλω	to throw in, put inside
ἐξαναλίσκω	to utterly destroy, consume
ἐπιδέκατος, -η, -ον	tenth; (*subst*) tithe
ἐπιδέομαι	to need, lack, be in want of
θυμόω	to anger; (*pas*) to be(come) angry
ἰσχυρός, -ά, -όν	strong, powerful

▷ List 9 6×

ἰσχύω	to be strong, be capable; (*trans*) to intensify
καθαρός, -ά, -όν	pure, clean
κατακαίω	to burn up, consume
κατεσθίω	to eat up, devour
κληρονομία, -ας, ἡ	inheritance, possession(s)
κοιλία, -ας, ἡ	belly, stomach, womb
κορυφή, -ῆς, ἡ	top, highest point
λυτρόω	(*mid*) to redeem, ransom
μάχαιρα, -ας, ἡ	sword, dagger
ὁλοκαύτωμα, -ατος, τό	whole burnt offering
παιδεύω	to instruct, discipline
παραβαίνω	to deviate, turn away
πρᾶγμα, -ατος, τό	thing, matter, affair, deed
συντελέω	to finish, complete, accomplish
παρίστημι	*to place near, present;* (intr) *to stand near, be present to serve*

▷ List 10 6 to 5×

ἀκοή, -ῆς, ἡ	report, news
ἀνάθεμα, -ατος, τό	accursed, devoted to destruction
ἀνατολή, -ῆς, ἡ	sprouting, rising; morning; (*pl*) east
ἀριστερός, -ά, -όν	left
ἀσέβεια, -ας, ἡ	ungodliness, wickedness
διαμαρτύρομαι	to testify, warn, inform
δῶρον, -ου, τό	gift, offering
ἐγκάθημαι	to lie in wait, dwell, encamp
ἐκφέρω	to bring out, produce
ἐκχέω	to pour out, spill
ἐπονομάζω	to (give a) name, call (a name)
ὑετός, -οῦ, ὁ	rain
φείδομαι	to spare, refrain, hold back
ᾠδή, -ῆς, ἡ	song, ode
ἐγγύς	(+gen) *near, close to*

▷ List 11 — 5×

ἑσπέρα, -ας, ἡ	evening
εὐχή, -ῆς, ἡ	prayer, vow
ἥκω	to have come, reach, be present
θλίβω	to press, oppress, afflict
καθάπερ	just as
καταπαύω	to bring to an end, stop, cease
κάτω	down(ward), below, under
λιθοβολέω	to stone (to death)
μακράν	far away, distant
μνηστεύω	to betroth, become engaged
ὁπλή, -ῆς, ἡ	hoof
παρθένια, -ων, τά	virginity, proof of virginity
πεδίον, -ου, τό	plain, field, level area
πειρασμός, -οῦ, ὁ	test, temptation
ὅμοιος, -α, -ον	*like, similar to*

▷ List 12 — 5 to 4×

ἄδικος, -ος, -ον	unjust, unrighteous; (*subst*) wrongdoing
ἅμα	at once, together
ἄμητος, -ου, ὁ	harvest, reaping
ἀναίτιος, -ος/α, -ον	blameless, innocent
ἀνομέω	to act lawlessly, be wicked
ἀπέναντι *or* ἀπεναντίον	(+*gen*) opposite, contrary to, against
ἀρσενικός, -ή, -όν	male
ἁφή, -ῆς, ἡ	infection, injury
πρόσταγμα, -ατος, τό	ordinance, command
σκῦλον, -ου, τό	plunder, spoils
σοφός, -ή, -όν	wise, skilled, learned
τελευτάω	to die
τραυματίας, -ου, ὁ	wounded person, casualty
ὑπεροράω	to disregard, ignore
φεύγω	to flee, escape, vanish

▷ List 13	4×
βοηθέω	to help, aid
βουκόλιον, -ου, τό	herd (of cattle)
δάμαλις, -εως, ἡ	young cow, heifer
δέομαι	to ask (for), pray (for)
διάνοια, -ας, ἡ	mind, thought, understanding
διασπείρω	to scatter, spread around
διαστέλλω	to distinguish, separate, state precisely; (*mid*) to command
διχηλέω	to have a divided hoof
δορκάς, -άδος, ἡ	gazelle, deer
ἑβδομάς, -άδος, ἡ	period of seven days *or* years; seven-member grouping
ἕβδομος, -η, -ον	seventh
ἐκκόπτω	to cut off, do away with
ἐκπειράζω	to tempt, test, put to trial
ἔλαφος, -ου, ὁ	deer
ἐλεύθερος, -α, -ον	free, noble

▷ List 14	4×
ἐνδεής, -ής, -ές	lacking in, in need of
ἕξ	six
ἐξαλείφω	to wipe out, erase, obliterate
ἐπάγω	to bring (up)on
ἐπιβαίνω	to get on, walk over, fall upon
ἐρυθρός, -ή, -όν	red
ἡνίκα	when
θεράπων, -οντος, ὁ	servant, aide
ἰάομαι	to heal, cure, restore
ἵππος, -ου, ὁ	horse
καίω	to light (a flame), burn
κακόω	to do wrong, mistreat
καταδιώκω	to seek eagerly, chase down
κατοικίζω	to settle (a group), establish (residency)
ἐπιθυμία, -ας, ἡ	*desire, lust*

▷ List 15 — 4×

κολλάω	to join together, adhere to
κύκλῳ	(*dat of* κύκλος) (all) around, surrounding
λειτουργέω	to serve (as priest), minister
μέτρον, -ου, τό	measurement, dimension, rule
νέος, -α, -ον	new, young; (*subst*) child
ὄνος, -ου, ὁ	donkey
ὅραμα, -ατος, τό	vision, (object of) sight
ὀργίζω	to make angry; (*pas*) to be angry
ὄρνεον, -ου, τό	bird
παραπορεύομαι	to pass by, travel along, overlook
παρθένος, -ου, ἡ	unmarried woman, virgin
παροργίζω	to anger, provoke
πάσχα, τό	Passover, Passover lamb *or* meal
ποίμνιον, -ου, τό	flock
προνομεύω	to plunder, despoil

▷ List 16 — 4×

πρωί	in the morning; (*subst*) morning
σίδηρος, -ου, ὁ	iron (tool)
σιδηροῦς, -ᾶ, -οῦν	(made of) iron
σκληρός, -ά, -όν	difficult, harsh, rough
σταφυλή, -ῆς, ἡ	bunch of grapes
συνάντησις, -εως, ἡ	meeting
συνάπτω	to join together, engage, border on
ταπεινόω	to bring down, humiliate, humble
τάχος, -ους, τό	swiftness, quickness
τίκτω	to give birth to, bear, produce
τράχηλος, -ου, ὁ	neck, throat
φοβερός, -ά, -όν	intimidating, fearful, terrible
φονεύω	to kill, murder
φυτεύω	to plant
χεῖλος, -ους, τό	lip, language, edge

JOSHUA (A & B)

▷ List 1 — 41 to 19×

ἀνατολή, -ῆς, ἡ	sprouting, rising; morning; (*pl*) east
ἀφορίζω	to separate, mark out; (*mid*) to split
βορέας, -ου, ἡ / βορρᾶς, -ᾶ, ἡ	north
δῆμος, -ου, ὁ	crowd, populace, district
διαβαίνω	to go through, cross (over)
ἐξολεθρεύω	to utterly destroy, eradicate
ἥμισυς, -εια, -υ	half
καταλείπω	to leave (behind), abandon; (*pas*) to remain
κιβωτός, -οῦ, ἡ	box, chest, ark
κληρονομία, -ας, ἡ	inheritance, possession(s)
κλῆρος, -ου, ὁ	lot, share, portion
κώμη, -ης, ἡ	village, small town
λίψ, λιβός, ὁ	south, southwest wind
πέραν	beyond; (+*gen*) on the other side
τρόπος, -ου, ὁ	manner, way, conduct

▷ List 2 — 19 to 10×

ἀνάθεμα, -ατος, τό	accursed, devoted to destruction
ἀπέναντι *or* ἀπεναντίον	(+*gen*) opposite, contrary to, against
διέξοδος, -ου, ἡ	going out, outlet (of a stream)
καταδιώκω	to seek eagerly, chase down
κατακληρονομέω	to give as inheritance, become owner, dispossess
κληρονομέω	to inherit, become heir to, give as inheritance
λατρεύω	to serve, perform cultic duties (for)
μερίς, -ίδος, ἡ	share, part, portion
ξίφος, -ους, τό	sword
ὄμνυμι *or* ὀμνύω	to swear, take an oath
ὀρεινός, -ή, -όν	mountainous; (*subst*) hill country
περισπόρια, -ων, τά	(*always pl*) surrounding country, suburbs
πηγή, -ῆς, ἡ	spring, fountain
φάραγξ, -αγγος, ἡ	ravine, valley
φονεύω	to kill, murder

▹ List 3 10 to 8×

αὔριον	tomorrow
βωμός, -οῦ, ὁ	altar (typically pagan)
διασῴζω	to preserve, keep safe; (*pas*) to be spared, escape
διεκβάλλω	to move through, terminate at
δυσμή, -ῆς, ἡ	(*always pl*) setting (of the sun), west
εἰσπορεύομαι	to go in, enter
ἐμπνέω	to breathe, blow
ἐξάγω	to lead out, take out, bring out
ἔπαυλις, -εως, ἡ	residence, settlement
καθά	as, just as
κύκλῳ	(*dat of* κύκλος) (all) around, surrounding
παρέρχομαι	to go past, pass by, move on
πεδίον, -ου, τό	plain, field, level area
προσάγω	to bring to, approach
συντάσσω	to command, prescribe, set in order

▹ List 4 8 to 7×

ἀναιρέω	to get rid of, destroy; (*mid*) to take up
ἀφίστημι	to keep away, remove; (*mid*) to depart, withdraw
διατίθημι	to treat; (*mid*) to grant, arrange
ἐμπίπρημι	to set on fire
ἔναντι	(+*gen*) opposite, before, in the presence of
ἰσχύω	to be strong, be capable; (*trans*) to intensify
καθότι	as, insofar as, since
καταπαύω	to bring to an end, stop, cease
κατασκοπεύω	to observe closely, spy out
μαρτύριον, -ου, τό	proof, testimony, witness
νῶτος/ον, -ου, ὁ/τό	back, rear surface
περιέρχομαι	to travel about, come *or* go around
ποταμός, -οῦ, ὁ	river, stream
πρόσταγμα, -ατος, τό	ordinance, command
σπήλαιον, -ου, τό	cave

▷ LIST 5	7 TO 6×
ἔνεδρον, -ου, τό	ambush, trap
ἐννέα	nine
ἵππος, -ου, ὁ	horse
καθάπερ	just as
καθίστημι	to place, appoint, establish; (*mid*) to stand against
κατάσχεσις, -εως, ἡ	possession
κρύπτω	to hide, conceal
κτῆνος, -ους, τό	(domesticated) animal; (*pl*) herd, cattle
μάχαιρα, -ας, ἡ	sword, dagger
νεανίσκος, -ου, ὁ	young man
οὐθείς, οὐθέν	no one, none, nothing
περιτέμνω	to circumcise
πρότερος, -α, -ον	former, earlier, before
συνάπτω	to join together, engage, border on
φυγαδευτήριον, -ου, τό	refuge, sanctuary

▷ LIST 6	6 TO 5×
ἅμα	at once, together
ἀνάγω	to lead up, bring up, raise up
ἀναστρέφω	to return, change course; (*mid*) to conduct oneself, live
ἀνδρίζομαι	to be courageous, play the man
ἐκλείπω	to abandon, neglect; (*intr*) to fail, run out, cease
ἐκπολεμέω	to wage war (against)
ἕνεκα *or* ἕνεκεν/εἵνεκεν	(+*gen*) on account of, because of
καταλαμβάνω	to take hold of, overtake, capture
μάχιμος, -η, -ον	trained for battle; (*subst*) soldier
ὁρίζω	to determine, set limits
πατριά, -ας, ἡ	paternal lineage, family line
πολεμιστής, -οῦ, ὁ	combatant, warrior
προσαναβαίνω	to go up, ascend, proceed
σάλπιγξ, -ιγγος, ἡ	trumpet, horn
φεύγω	to flee, escape, vanish

▹ List 7 — 5 to 4×

ἀναγγέλλω	to report, announce, publicize
ἄνω	(from) above
ἀπαίρω	to remove, take away
ἀρέσκω	to please, gain favor
ἅρμα, -ατος, τό	chariot
γράμμα, -ατος, τό	letter (of the alphabet), writing
διαφεύγω	to escape, get away (from)
περικαθίζω	to besiege
πλημμελέω	to trespass, err, offend
πλησίον	(+*gen*) near, close; (*subst*) neighbor
σαλπίζω	to blow (a trumpet), trumpet (a sound)
σίδηρος, -ου, ὁ	iron (tool)
συγκαλέω	to call together, invite, summon
συντελέω	to finish, complete, accomplish
ὑπολείπω	to leave remaining; (*mid*) to remain

▹ List 8 — 4×

ἐνδείκνυμι	to show, display
ἐξαιρέω	to take out, remove; (*mid*) to set free
ἐξαποστέλλω	to dispatch, dismiss, permit to leave
ἐπακολουθέω	to follow, come after, tend to
ἐπεί	when, after, since, inasmuch as
ἐπισιτισμός, -οῦ, ὁ	provisions, (supply of) food
ἐπίσταμαι	to know, be acquainted with
ἐρυθρός, -ή, -όν	red
ἑσπέρα, -ας, ἡ	evening
ἐφίστημι	to cast over, place on
ἥκω	to have come, reach, be present
ἡνίκα	when
ἰσχυρός, -ά, -όν	strong, powerful
κάρπωμα, -ατος, τό	cultic offering
κατενώπιον	(+*gen*) before, in front of

▷ LIST 9 4×

κάτω	down(ward), below, under
κληρωτί	(done) by lot
μακράν	far away, distant
μητρόπολις, -εως, ἡ	metropolis, capital city
ξηρός, -ά, -όν	dry, withered, arid
ξυλοκόπος, -ου, ὁ	woodcutter
ὅρκος, -ου, ὁ	oath
παραβαίνω	to deviate, turn away
παραπορεύομαι	to pass by, travel along, overlook
πεδ(ε)ινός, -ή, -όν	flat, level; (*subst*) plain
πέτρινος, -η, -ον	of stone, of rock
πλημμέλεια, -ας, ἡ	(sinful) error, mistake
πολεμέω	to wage war, fight
πόρνη, -ης, ἡ	prostitute, harlot
προβαίνω	to move on, advance

▷ LIST 10 4 TO 3×

ἀθῷος, -ος, -ον	guiltless, innocent
ἅλς, ἁλός, ὁ	salt
ἀναβιβάζω	to bring up, raise up
ἀναβοάω	to cry out
ἀνθίστημι	to resist, oppose
ἀπερίτμητος, -ος, -ον	uncircumcised
προπορεύομαι	to proceed, go beforehand
πρωί	in the morning; (*subst*) morning
πρωτότοκος, -ος, -ον	firstborn
ῥομφαία, -ας, ἡ	sword
συνάντησις, -εως, ἡ	meeting
συντρίβω	to break, crush, wreck
σωτήριον, -ου, τό	salvation, (offering for) deliverance
ὑποχείριος, -ος, -ον	controlled, under authority, subordinate
ὡσεί	as (if), like, approximately

▷ List 11 3×

βιβρώσκω	to consume, eat
βοηθέω	to help, aid
διαιρέω	to divide, split, dispense
δρυμός, -οῦ, ὁ	forest, thicket
ἕβδομος, -η, -ον	seventh
ἐγκαταλείπω	to abandon, leave behind
ἐκτείνω	to stretch out, reach out, extend
ἐκφέρω	to bring out, produce
ἐναντίος, -α, -ον	against, opposed, opposite
ἕξ	six
ἐξανίστημι	to raise, bring about; (*intr*) to arise, emerge
ἐπιβαίνω	to get on, walk over, fall upon
εὐλογία, -ας, ἡ	praise, blessing
θάπτω	to bury
θεράπων, -οντος, ὁ	servant, aide

▷ List 12 3×

κατισχύω	to strengthen, overpower; (*intr*) to be encouraged, become powerful
κυριεύω	to rule over, dominate, control
μερίζω	to divide, distribute
οἰκέτης, -ου, ὁ	household servant
ὀρθρίζω	to get up early
προνομεύω	to plunder, despoil
προνομή, -ῆς, ἡ	spoils (of war), plunder
προσήλυτος, -ου, ὁ	immigrant, foreign guest
σπεύδω	to hasten, hurry
συνίημι	to understand, notice, ponder
τάχος, -ους, τό	swiftness, quickness
τεσσαράκοντα	forty
χείμαρρος/ους, -ου, ὁ	stream, (seasonal) brook
χρυσίον, -ου, τό	gold
ὡσαύτως	in the same way, similarly

JUDGES (A & B)

▷ **LIST 1**	**31 TO 12×**
αὐλίζομαι	to lodge overnight, stay
βοάω	to cry out, shout
γέ	(*emphatic particle*) indeed, really
γλυπτός, -ή, -όν	carved, graven; [τὸ γλύπτον] graven image
ἐξαίρω	to raise up, remove, pack up camp and go
ἐξαποστέλλω	to dispatch, dismiss, permit to leave
παιδάριον, -ου, τό	child, little boy, servant
παράταξις, -εως, ἡ	battle, line of battle
παρατάσσω	to form a battle line, battle
παρέρχομαι	to go past, pass by, move on
πολεμέω	to wage war, fight
ῥομφαία, -ας, ἡ	sword
τριάκοντα	thirty
φεύγω	to flee, escape, vanish
δέω	*to bind, constrain*

▷ **LIST 2**	**12 TO 10×**
ἀναφέρω	to bring up, offer, bear
ἅπαξ	once
διαβαίνω	to go through, cross (over)
δουλεύω	to serve (as a slave)
ἑβδομήκοντα	seventy
εἴκοσι	twenty
ἐκκλίνω	to bend, turn away; (*intr*) to avoid, deviate
ἔνεδρον, -ου, τό	ambush, trap
κεράτινος, -η, -ον	(made of) horn
κληρονομέω	to inherit, become heir to, give as inheritance
οἰκέω	to inhabit, live
ὄνος, -ου, ὁ	donkey
παλλακή, -ῆς, ἡ	concubine, mistress
παρεμβάλλω	to set up, pitch (a tent), encamp
πέτρα, -ας, ἡ	rock, stone, cave

▷ List 3 — 10 to 8×

ἀναγγέλλω	to report, announce, publicize
ἀνατολή, -ῆς, ἡ	sprouting, rising; morning; (*pl*) east
ἀπάντησις, -εως, ἡ	meeting
ἅρμα, -ατος, τό	chariot
ἑκατόν	one hundred
θάπτω	to bury
κοιλάς, -άδος, ἡ	valley
λατρεύω	to serve, perform cultic duties (for)
πρωί	in the morning; (*subst*) morning
πύργος, -ου, ὁ	tower
σπάω	to draw (a sword)
συνάντησις, -εως, ἡ	meeting
τίκτω	to give birth to, bear, produce
χίλιοι, -αι, -α	one thousand
ὡσεί	as (if), like, approximately

▷ List 4 — 8×

δεῦρο	come!, go!
διαφθείρω	to utterly destroy, ruin
εἰσακούω	to hear, listen to, obey
ἐκτείνω	to stretch out, reach out, extend
ἔναντι	(+*gen*) opposite, before, in the presence of
ἐνισχύω	to strengthen, grow strong(er), prevail (over)
ἐξεγείρω	to awake, rouse, raise
ἡνίκα	when
θανατόω	to kill, put to death
κληρονομία, -ας, ἡ	inheritance, possession(s)
ὄμνυμι *or* ὀμνύω	to swear, take an oath
ὀρθρίζω	to get up early
παροικέω	to dwell as a foreigner
πονηρία, -ας, ἡ	evil, vice
πρόβλημα, -ατος, τό	riddle, challenge

▷ List 5 — 8 to 7×

ἕλκω	to draw, pull, drag
ἡσυχάζω	to be quiet, rest
καθαιρέω	to take down, overpower, destroy
κακία, -ας, ἡ	evil, harm, misfortune
καταλαμβάνω	to take hold of, overtake, capture
κατασκάπτω	to destroy, burn to the ground
μάχαιρα, -ας, ἡ	sword, dagger
νεανίας, -ου, ὁ	young man
νεᾶνις, -ιδος, ἡ	girl, young woman
ὁλοκαύτωμα, -ατος, τό	whole burnt offering
ὀργίζω	to make angry; (*pas*) to be angry
σαλπίζω	to blow (a trumpet), trumpet (a sound)
σιαγών, -όνος, ἡ	jaw(bone), cheek
ταπεινόω	to bring down, humiliate, humble
τριακόσιοι, -αι, -α	three hundred

▷ List 6 — 7 to 6×

ἀγαθύνω	to do good, be glad; to give favor
ἀμπελών, -ῶνος, ὁ	vineyard
γαμβρός, -οῦ, ὁ	son-in-law, father-in-law
διασῴζω	to preserve, keep safe; (*pas*) to be spared, escape
ἐγκαταλείπω	to abandon, leave behind
ἐμπίπρημι	to set on fire
ἐνεδρεύω	to lie in wait for, set an ambush
πάσσαλος, -ου, ὁ	peg, pin
πόκος, -ου, ὁ	wool, fleece
σατράπης, -ου, ὁ	governor, satrap
συγγένεια, -ας, ἡ	relations, kin, family
τεσσαράκοντα	forty
τρόπος, -ου, ὁ	manner, way, conduct
ὑποζύγιον, -ου, τό	beast of burden (donkey, mule)
χείμαρρος/ους, -ου, ὁ	stream, (seasonal) brook

▹ List 7 6×

ἐξάγω	to lead out, take out, bring out
ἐξαιρέω	to take out, remove; (*mid*) to set free
ἐπιλαμβάνω	to catch, grab, obtain
ἐπισκέπτομαι	to visit, examine, account for
εφουδ (*translit*)	ephod
θλίβω	to press, oppress, afflict
ἰσχυρός, -ά, -όν	strong, powerful
κλίνω	to incline, lean, turn over, bend
κριτής, -οῦ, ὁ	judge
μήποτε	lest, in order that . . . not
μηρός, -οῦ, ὁ	thigh, flank
μόσχος, -ου, ὁ	calf, young bull
νέος, -α, -ον	new, young; (*subst*) child
πλησίον	(+*gen*) near, close; (*subst*) neighbor
προκαταλαμβάνω	to capture first, seize swiftly

▹ List 8 6 to 5×

αἴξ, αἰγός, ὁ	goat
ἄκρος, -α, -ον	(far) end, tip, top
ἄλσος, -ους, τό	grove, sacred area
ἀνάβασις, -εως, ἡ	ascent, going up
ἀποκλείω	to shut, lock up, exclude
ἀρέσκω	to please, gain favor
ἀριθμός, -οῦ, ὁ	number, total
γαστήρ, γαστρός, ἡ	belly, womb
δῆμος, -ου, ὁ	crowd, populace, district
δρόσος, -ου, ἡ	dew
δῶρον, -ου, τό	gift, offering
σκῦλον, -ου, τό	plunder, spoils
φόρος, -ου, ὁ	levy, tax, tribute
χωνευτός, -ή, -όν	molten, cast (of metal)
ἀσθενέω	*to be weak, become less functional*

▷ List 9 — 5×

ἐκλείπω	to abandon, neglect; (*intr*) to fail, run out, cease
ἐναντίος, -α, -ον	against, opposed, opposite
ἑξακόσιοι, -αι, -α	six hundred
ἔριφος, -ου, ὁ	young goat, kid
ἑσπέρα, -ας, ἡ	evening
εὐδοκέω	to consent, accept, be pleased
εὐφραίνω	to make happy, cheer; (*pas*) to rejoice
καταλείπω	to leave (behind), abandon; (*pas*) to remain
καταλύω	to lodge, bring down, destroy
κόπτω	to cut, strike; (*mid*) to mourn
λαμπάς, -άδος, ἡ	torch, lamp
λέων, -οντος, ὁ	lion
νότος, -ου, ὁ	south (wind)
ὀκτώ	eight
πέραν	beyond; (+*gen*) on the other side

▷ List 10 — 5 to 4×

ἄζυμος, -ος, -ον	unleavened (bread)
ἀναστρέφω	to return, change course; (*mid*) to conduct oneself, live
ἀριστερός, -ά, -όν	left
ἀρχηγός, -οῦ, ὁ	chief, ruler, prince; beginning
ἀφίστημι	to keep away, remove; (*mid*) to depart, withdraw
ἀφροσύνη, -ης, ἡ	foolishness
βορέας, -ου, ἡ / βορρᾶς, -ᾶ, ἡ	north
γόνυ, γόνατος, τό	knee
εἰσάγω	to bring in, lead in, introduce
εἰσφέρω	to lead in, bring in
ῥίπτω	to throw (away), defeat, reject
ῥύομαι	to rescue, save
συνάπτω	to join together, engage, border on
χρυσοῦς, -ῆ, -οῦν / χρύσεος, -α, -ον	golden; (*subst*) golden coin
φαίνω	*to shine;* (mid) *to appear, seem*

▹ List 11	4×
ἐκφέρω	to bring out, produce
ἐξολεθρεύω	to utterly destroy, eradicate
ἐπιβλέπω	to look at (attentively), observe, anticipate
κάμηλος, -ου, ὁ/ἡ	camel
καταδιώκω	to seek eagerly, chase down
κατακληρονομέω	to give as inheritance, become owner, dispossess
κατεσθίω	to eat up, devour
κατευθύνω	to direct, guide; (*pas*) to prosper
κινέω	to move, disturb
κοιλία, -ας, ἡ	belly, stomach, womb
κορυφή, -ῆς, ἡ	top, highest point
κρέας, κρέως, τό	meat
κυκλόω	to encircle, surround
κυριεύω	to rule over, dominate, control
καινός, -ή, -όν	*new*

▹ List 12	4×
νεανίσκος, -ου, ὁ	young man
ὀχύρωμα, -ατος, τό	stronghold, fortress
περιζώννυμι *or* περιζωννύω	to wrap around, put on
πλατύς, -εῖα, -ύ	wide, broad; [*fem subst* πλατεῖα] street, square
πρεσβύτης, -ου, ὁ	old man, elder
στολή, -ῆς, ἡ	robe, cloak
στῦλος, -ου, ὁ	pillar, column
συλλαμβάνω	to capture, catch; to become pregnant
συναντάω	to meet (with), fall upon, happen
συντρίβω	to break, crush, wreck
ταμιεῖον, -ου, τό	storeroom, private chamber
τάσσω	to position, appoint; (*mid*) to indicate
τραυματίας, -ου, ὁ	wounded person, casualty
φλόξ, φλογός, ἡ	flame
πειρά(ζ)ω	*to tempt, test, try*

1 ESDRAS AND 2 ESDRAS (EZRA-NEHEMIAH)

▹ List 1 — 52 to 22×

ᾄδω	to sing
αἰχμαλωσία, -ας, ἡ	captivity, (group of) captives
διακόσιοι, -αι, -α	two hundred
ἑβδομήκοντα	seventy
εἴκοσι	twenty
ἑκατόν	one hundred
ὀκτώ	eight
πατριά, -ᾶς, ἡ	paternal lineage, family line
πεντήκοντα	fifty
ποταμός, -οῦ, ὁ	river, stream
τεῖχος, -ους, τό	(city) wall
τεσσαράκοντα	forty
τριακόσιοι, -αι, -α	three hundred
χίλιοι, -αι, -α	one thousand
χρυσίον, -ου, τό	gold

▹ List 2 — 21 to 15×

γνώμη, -ης, ἡ	intent, will, decree, decision
δισχίλιοι, -αι, -α	two thousand
ἐκφέρω	to bring out, produce
ἕξ	six
ἑξακόσιοι, -αι, -α	six hundred
ἑξήκοντα	sixty
ἐπιστολή, -ῆς, ἡ	letter, epistle
ἑπτακόσιοι, -αι, -α	seven hundred
κατάλοιπος, -ος, -ον	rest, remainder, leftover
μιμνῄσκομαι	to remember, recall
πάσχα, τό	Passover, Passover lamb *or* meal
πυλωρός, -οῦ, ὁ	gatekeeper, porter, jailer
τετρακόσιοι, -αι, -α	four hundred
τριάκοντα	thirty
χώρα, -ας, ἡ	country, land, region

▷ List 3 — 14 to 11×

ἀλλογενής, -ής, -ές	foreign born
ἀργυροῦς, -ᾶ, -οῦν	(made of) silver
ἀρσενικός, -ή, -όν	male
γαζοφυλάκιον, -ου, τό	treasury
ἕβδομος, -η, -ον	seventh
ἐγκαταλείπω	to abandon, leave behind
ἔπαρχος, -ου, ὁ	governor, prefect
ἐπισκέπτομαι	to visit, examine, account for
ἥμισυς, -εια, -υ	half
ἱερός, -ά, -όν	holy, sacred; (*subst*) temple, sanctuary
κτῆνος, -ους, τό	(domesticated) animal; (*pl*) herd, cattle
πέραν	beyond; (+*gen*) on the other side
τάλαντον, -ου, τό	talent (*monetary unit*)
χρυσοῦς, -ῆ, -οῦν / χρύσεος, -α, -ον	golden; (*subst*) golden coin
ἀναγινώσκω	*to read (aloud)*

▷ List 4 — 11 to 9×

ἁγιάζω	to make holy, consecrate, sanctify
ἀλλότριος, -α, -ον	foreign, strange, unfamiliar
δουλεία, -ας, ἡ	slavery, servitude
ἐνιαυτός, -οῦ, ὁ	year
ἑορτή, -ῆς, ἡ	feast, festival
εὐφροσύνη, -ης, ἡ	joy, gladness
ἡγέομαι	to go before, guide, act as leader; think, consider
καταλείπω	to leave (behind), abandon; (*pas*) to remain
κριός, -οῦ, ὁ	ram
ναθινιμ, ὁ (*translit*)	temple servant(s)
νουμηνία, -ας, ἡ	new moon, beginning of the month
πρόσταγμα, -ατος, τό	ordinance, command
προστάσσω	to command, order
πύργος, -ου, ὁ	tower
ὑπερισχύω	to prevail (over), be very strong

▹ **List 5**	**9×**
ἀναφέρω	to bring up, offer, bear
ἀνομία, -ας, ἡ	lawlessness, wrongful conduct
ἀποικία, -ας, ἡ	exile, (place of) captivity
ἀποφέρω	to carry off
ἀριθμός, -οῦ, ὁ	number, total
δέκατος, -η, -ον	tenth; (*subst*) tithe
ἔλαιον, -ου, τό	(olive) oil
ἐνενήκοντα	ninety
ἐπιμελῶς	diligently, intentionally, meticulously
ἐπιτελέω	to complete, perform, finish
εὔχομαι	to pray, vow
ἰσχυρός, -ά, -όν	strong, powerful
κρίμα, -ατος, τό	decision, judgment, punishment
οἰκέω	to inhabit, live
χωρίζω	to separate, remove; (*pas*) to depart, exclude

▹ **List 6**	**8 to 7×**
ἄδικος, -ος, -ον	unjust, unrighteous; (*subst*) wrongdoing
ἀκαθαρσία, -ας, ἡ	uncleanness, impurity
ἅμα	at once, together
βασιλικός, -ή, -όν	royal, belonging to the king
γνωρίζω	to make known, publicize
ἵππος, -ου, ὁ	horse
μεγιστάν, -ᾶνος, ὁ	noble, magistrate, influential person
μέχρι(ς)	(+*gen*) until, as far as; (*conj*) until
μόσχος, -ου, ὁ	calf, young bull
ὁλοκαύτωσις, -εως, ἡ	whole burnt offering
περίχωρος, -ος, -ον	nearby region, surrounding area
σάλπιγξ, -ιγγος, ἡ	trumpet, horn
σύνδουλος, -ου, ὁ	fellow servant
συνίημι	to understand, notice, ponder
τελέω	to finish, perfect

▷ List 7 — 7×

ἀνάβασις, -εως, ἡ	ascent, going up
ἐννακόσιοι, -αι, -α	nine hundred
ἔντιμος, -ος, -ον	precious, valuable
εὐφραίνω	to make happy, cheer; (*pas*) to rejoice
θησαυρός, -οῦ, ὁ	treasure, treasury, storehouse
θυρωρός, -οῦ, ὁ	gatekeeper, porter
ἱερόδουλος, -ου, ὁ	temple servant
καταρτίζω	to set in order, ready, complete
μερίς, -ίδος, ἡ	share, part, portion
νεανίσκος, -ου, ὁ	young man
οἰκοδομή, -ῆς, ἡ	(process of) building, construction
παραβαίνω	to deviate, turn away
πλατύς, -εῖα, -ύ	wide, broad; [*fem subst* πλατεῖα] street, square
ῥομφαία, -ας, ἡ	sword
σῖτος, -ου, ὁ	grain

▷ List 8 — 7 to 6×

αἴνεσις, -εως, ἡ	praise
ἀμπελών, -ῶνος, ὁ	vineyard
ἀναγνώστης, -ου, ὁ	(public) reader
ἀναδείκνυμι	to disclose, display, appoint
ἀπέναντι *or* ἀπεναντίον	(+*gen*) opposite, contrary to, against
γνωστός, -ή, -όν	known; (*subst*) friend
ἑκουσιάζομαι	to volunteer, offer willingly
ἐννέα	nine
ἐξαποστέλλω	to dispatch, dismiss, permit to leave
ἐπισυνάγω	to bring together, gather up
ἐπιτάσσω	to command, provide instruction
ἐρημόω	to make desolate, dry up
εὐχή, -ῆς, ἡ	prayer, vow
στρατηγός, -οῦ, ὁ	commander, captain
συντελέω	to finish, complete, accomplish

▷ List 9	6×
ἐφημερία, -ας, ἡ	class (of priests), division (of a group)
ἡνίκα	when
ἱεροψάλτης, -ου, ὁ	temple singer
κληρονομέω	to inherit, become heir to, give as inheritance
κραταιός, -ά, -όν	powerful, forceful, severe
μέτρον, -ου, τό	measurement, dimension, rule
μνᾶ, μνᾶς, ἡ	mina (coin)
μυριάς, -άδος, ἡ	ten thousand, countless number
πενθέω	to grieve, mourn
πεντακισχίλιοι, -αι, -α	five thousand
πλημμέλεια, -ας, ἡ	(sinful) error, mistake
πονηρία, -ας, ἡ	evil, vice
πρᾶγμα, -ατος, τό	thing, matter, affair, deed
τράχηλος, -ου, ὁ	neck, throat
τρισχίλιοι, -αι, -α	three thousand

▷ List 10	6 to 5×
αἰνέω	to praise
ἀκολούθως	accordingly, in accordance with
ἀνατολή, -ῆς, ἡ	sprouting, rising; morning; (*pl*) east
ἀπαρχή, -ῆς, ἡ	first portion, firstfruits
ἀποστάτης, -ου, ὁ	rebel, traitor
ἀρήν, ἀρνός, ὁ	lamb, sheep
αὐλή, -ῆς, ἡ	court, courtyard
ἀφίστημι	to keep away, remove; (*mid*) to depart, withdraw
βίβλος, -ου, ἡ	scroll, book, record
βοηθέω	to help, aid
βουλή, -ῆς, ἡ	plan, advice, council
διαρ(ρ)ήγνυμι *or* διαρ(ρ)ήσσω	to tear, divide, break through
ὑψόω	to lift up, raise high, exalt
φόρος, -ου, ὁ	levy, tax, tribute
ἅπας, ἅπασα, ἅπαν	*all, every*

▷ List 11 — 5×

διαστέλλω	to distinguish, separate, state precisely; (*mid*) to command
ἑκούσιος, -α, -ον	voluntary
ἐκτείνω	to stretch out, reach out, extend
ἐκτινάσσω	to shake off, scatter, expel
ἐναντίος, -α, -ον	against, opposed, opposite
ἐπάνω	over, more than; (+*gen*) above, higher than
θεμελιόω	to establish, build a foundation
θλίβω	to press, oppress, afflict
καθαιρέω	to take down, overpower, destroy
καθίστημι	to place, appoint, establish; (*mid*) to stand against
κριτής, -οῦ, ὁ	judge
κυριεύω	to rule over, dominate, control
οἰκτιρμός, -οῦ, ὁ	compassion, pity
ὁρκίζω	to cause to swear, bind by oath
παιδίσκη, -ης, ἡ	young woman, female servant

▷ List 12 — 5×

πέμπτος, -η, -ον	fifth
πῆχυς, -εως, ὁ	cubit, (length of the) forearm
προηγέομαι	to lead, precede
προσέχω	to pay attention to, be concerned about
πυλών, -ῶνος, ὁ	gate, porch
πυρός, -οῦ, ὁ	wheat
σατράπης, -ου, ὁ	governor, satrap
σύμβουλος, -ου, ὁ	adviser, counselor
τοπάρχης, -ου, ὁ	toparch, regional governor
ὕψιστος, -η, -ον	highest, most high (God)
φύλλον, -ου, τό	leaf
φωτίζω	to brighten, shine, illuminate
φαίνω	*to shine;* (mid) *to appear, seem*

RUTH AND ESTHER (INCL. ADDITIONS)

▹ List 1 — 20 to 8×

ἀγχιστεύω	to be *or* act as a kinsman *or* relative
αὐλή, -ῆς, ἡ	court, courtyard
βασίλισσα, -ης, ἡ	queen
ἐκτίθημι	to distribute, turn over, expose
εὐνοῦχος, -ου, ὁ	eunuch
εὐφροσύνη, -ης, ἡ	joy, gladness
κοράσιον, -ου, τό	girl, young female servant
κρεμάννυμι *or* κρεμάζω	to hang (upon)
μερίς, -ίδος, ἡ	share, part, portion
πενθερά, -ᾶς, ἡ	mother-in-law
συλλέγω	to collect, gather
τεσσαρεσκαιδέκατος, -η, -ον	fourteenth
φίλος, -η, -ον	friendly; (*subst*) friend, associate
χράω	to use, employ; (*mid*) to treat (in a certain way)
χώρα, -ας, ἡ	country, land, region

▹ List 2 — 8 to 7×

ἀγχιστεύς, -έως, ὁ	close relative, kinsman
γράμμα, -ατος, τό	letter (of the alphabet), writing
δωδέκατος, -η, -ον	twelfth
ἐπιστολή, -ῆς, ἡ	letter, epistle
θερίζω	to reap
καθίστημι	to place, appoint, establish; (*mid*) to stand against
κληρονομία, -ας, ἡ	inheritance, possession(s)
κλῆρος, -ου, ὁ	lot, share, portion
κοιμάω	(*mid*) to lie (down), sleep; [κ. +μετά] to have sexual intercourse
μνημόσυνον, -ου, τό	memory, memorial, reminder
νύμφη, -ης, ἡ	bride, daughter-in-law
πότος, -ου, ὁ	drinking party
πρᾶγμα, -ατος, τό	thing, matter, affair, deed
ταράσσω	to trouble, disturb
ὑποδείκνυμι *or* ὑποδεικνύω	to demonstrate, inform, point out

▷ **List 3**	**7 to 5×**
ἅβρα, -ας, ἡ	companion, faithful servant
ἀντίγραφον, -ου, τό	copy (of a document)
ἀρέσκω	to please, gain favor
βασιλικός, -ή, -όν	royal, belonging to the king
γέ	(*emphatic particle*) indeed, really
δοχή, -ῆς, ἡ	banquet, entertaining reception
ἑκατόν	one hundred
θνῄσκω	to die
καταλείπω	to leave (behind), abandon; (*pas*) to remain
κριθή, -ῆς, ἡ	barley
κτάομαι	to get, acquire
παιδάριον, -ου, τό	child, little boy, servant
πρόσταγμα, -ατος, τό	ordinance, command
προστάσσω	to command, order
χρυσοῦς, -ῆ, -οῦν / χρύσεος, -α, -ον	golden; (*subst*) golden coin

▷ **List 4**	**5×**
ἀμφότεροι, -αι, -α	both
ἀξιόω	to deem worthy, place a request upon, entreat
ἀφανίζω	to cause to vanish, destroy
γένος, -ους, τό	kind, people group, family (lineage)
δακτύλιος, -ου, ὁ	ring
δούλη, -ης, ἡ	female slave
εἴκοσι	twenty
ἕξ	six
ἐξαποστέλλω	to dispatch, dismiss, permit to leave
ἐπιτάσσω	to command, provide instruction
μιμνῄσκομαι	to remember, recall
ῥύομαι	to rescue, save
συντελέω	to finish, complete, accomplish
τίκτω	to give birth to, bear, produce
τρισκαιδέκατος, -η, -ον	thirteenth

▷ List 5 4×

ἀγχιστεία, -ας, ἡ	duty of redeeming (as next of kin)
ἀναπαύω	to stop, refresh, rest; to give rest
ἀναπληρόω	to fill up, make complete, finish
ἀξίωμα, -ατος, τό	assessment, request, rank
ἀπώλεια, -ας, ἡ	destruction, ruin, loss
αὔριον	tomorrow
ἀφαιρέω	to separate, remove; (*mid*) to deprive, seize, take away
βοηθέω	to help, aid
βύσσινος, -η, -ον	(made of) fine linen
γυναικών, -ῶνος, ὁ	harem, women's quarters
διάκονος, -ου, ὁ	(court) servant
διαρπάζω	to seize property, plunder
εἰσπορεύομαι	to go in, enter
ἔνδοξος, -ος, -ον	reputable, honored, distinguished
ἐνύπνιον, -ου, τό	dream

▷ List 6 4×

ἐπαίρω	to lift up, raise, magnify
ἐπικρατέω	to rule over, prevail, hold power
ἡμέτερος, -α, -ον	our
ἵππος, -ου, ὁ/ἡ	horse
παρακούω	to refuse to listen, pay no attention
πένθος, -ους, τό	grief, mourning
πεντεκαιδέκατος, -η, -ον	fifteenth
περιβάλλω	to put around, cover, clothe
περιτίθημι	to put on, put around
πλησίον	(+*gen*) near, close; (*subst*) neighbor
πλοῦτος, ου, ὁ	wealth, riches
πολεμέω	to wage war, fight
σάκκος, -ου, ὁ	sackcloth
σποδός, -οῦ, ἡ	ashes
θεραπεύω	*to serve, care for, heal*

▷ **List 7**	**4 to 3×**
ἀνάπαυσις, -εως, ἡ	rest, stopping
ἀποκαλύπτω	to uncover, reveal, disclose
ἀργυροῦς, -ᾶ, -οῦν	(made of) silver
αὐλίζομαι	to lodge overnight, stay
βδελύσσω	to make detestable; (*mid*) to detest
βοάω	to cry out, shout
διηγέομαι	to describe in detail, relate fully
εἶδος, -ους, τό	form, appearance
ἐνδύω	to dress, clothe
στολή, -ῆς, ἡ	robe, cloak
στολίζω	to clothe, dress
σφραγίζω	to seal, authenticate (with a seal)
ὑπερηφανία, -ας, ἡ	arrogance, pride
φύλαξ, -ακος, ὁ	guard, watchman
ἐγγύς	(+gen) *near, close to*

▷ **List 8**	**3×**
ἕτοιμος, -η/ος, -ον	ready, prepared
εὐφραίνω	to make happy, cheer; (*pas*) to rejoice
λυπέω	to vex, displease; (*mid/pas*) to be distressed, grieve
παιδίσκη, -ης, ἡ	young woman, female servant
ποταμός, -οῦ, ὁ	river, stream
προσδέχομαι	to accept, receive favorably, anticipate
πρωΐ	in the morning; (*subst*) morning
ῥάβδος, -ου, ἡ	rod, staff, scepter
σατράπης, -ου, ὁ	governor, satrap
σπεύδω	to hasten, hurry
στρέφω	to change, turn; (*mid*) to rotate, flip
τάλαντον, -ου, τό	talent (*monetary unit*)
ταπεινόω	to bring down, humiliate, humble
μάρτυς, -υρος, ὁ	*witness*
ὑποτάσσω	*to subdue;* (mid/pas) *to (be) subject, submit*

1–2 SAMUEL (1–2 KINGDOMS)

▷ List 1	96 to 21×
ἀναγγέλλω	to report, announce, publicize
ἀναστρέφω	to return, change course; (*mid*) to conduct oneself, live
γέ	(*emphatic particle*) indeed, really
διαβαίνω	to go through, cross (over)
δόρυ, δόρατος, τό	spear
δούλη, -ης, ἡ	female slave
ἐξαποστέλλω	to dispatch, dismiss, permit to leave
ἥκω	to have come, reach, be present
θανατόω	to kill, put to death
κιβωτός, -οῦ, ἡ	box, chest, ark
παιδάριον, -ου, τό	child, little boy, servant
πολεμέω	to wage war, fight
προσάγω	to bring to, approach
ῥομφαία, -ας, ἡ	sword
φεύγω	to flee, escape, vanish

▷ List 2	21 to 17×
ἀμφότεροι, -αι, -α	both
ἀναφέρω	to bring up, offer, bear
βοάω	to cry out, shout
δουλεύω	to serve (as a slave)
ἐξαιρέω	to take out, remove; (*mid*) to set free
ἐπισκέπτομαι	to visit, examine, account for
θνῄσκω	to die
καθίστημι	to place, appoint, establish; (*mid*) to stand against
κακία, -ας, ἡ	evil, harm, misfortune
καταδιώκω	to seek eagerly, chase down
ὄνος, -ου, ὁ	donkey
παρεμβάλλω	to set up, pitch (a tent), encamp
ποίμνιον, -ου, τό	flock
πρωί	in the morning; (*subst*) morning
τίκτω	to give birth to, bear, produce

▷ List 3 — 17 to 14×

ἀπάντησις, -εως, ἡ	meeting
ἀποκαλύπτω	to uncover, reveal, disclose
ἀφαιρέω	to separate, remove; (*mid*) to deprive, seize, take away
ἀφίστημι	to keep away, remove; (*mid*) to depart, withdraw
βουνός, -οῦ, ὁ	hill
βοῦς, βοός, ὁ/ἡ	ox, cow
θύω	to sacrifice, slaughter
καθεύδω	to (lie down to) sleep
κοιμάω	(*mid*) to lie (down), sleep; [κ. +μετά] to have sexual intercourse
κραταιόω	to make strong, support, prevail (over)
κρύπτω	to hide, conceal
σκῦλον, -ου, τό	plunder, spoils
τεῖχος, -ους, τό	(city) wall
τρέχω	to run, advance
χρίω	to anoint, smear

▷ List 4 — 14 to 12×

ἀδικία, -ας, ἡ	unrighteousness, wrongdoing, injustice
ἀνάγω	to lead up, bring up, raise up
δεῦρο	come!, go!
διαρ(ρ)ήγνυμι *or* διαρ(ρ)ήσσω	to tear, divide, break through
διαφθείρω	to utterly destroy, ruin
εἴκοσι	twenty
εἰσάγω	to bring in, lead in, introduce
ἐκκλίνω	to bend, turn away; (*intr*) to avoid, deviate
ἐνταῦθα	here; on one side . . . on the other side
ἐξολεθρεύω	to utterly destroy, eradicate
ἐπιβλέπω	to look at (attentively), observe, anticipate
μερίς, -ίδος, ἡ	share, part, portion
ὁλοκαύτωσις, -εως, ἡ	whole burnt offering
ὄμνυμι *or* ὀμνύω	to swear, take an oath
συντελέω	to finish, complete, accomplish

▷ List 5 — 12 to 10×

ἀδελφή, -ῆς, ἡ	sister, beloved woman
ἀποκλείω	to shut, lock up, exclude
ἅρμα, -ατος, τό	chariot
αὔριον	tomorrow
βουλή, -ῆς, ἡ	plan, advice, council
δικάζω	to judge, condemn; to plead a case
ἐναντίος, -α, -ον	against, opposed, opposite
ἐξουδ(θ)ενό(έ)ω	to disdain, reject
ἐπάνω	over, more than; (+*gen*) above, higher than
ὄπισθε(ν)	from behind; (+*gen*) behind, after
ὀστοῦν, -οῦ, τό	bone
πλησίον	(+*gen*) near, close; (*subst*) neighbor
σατράπης, -ου, ὁ	governor, satrap
σπεύδω	to hasten, hurry
συναθροίζω	to gather

▷ List 6 — 10 to 9×

ἅμαξα, -ης, ἡ	wagon
δικαίωμα, -ατος, τό	ordinance, decree, rightful claim
εἰσπορεύομαι	to go in, enter
ἐκλύω	to loosen; (*mid*) to grow weak, tire out
ἐξίστημι	to amaze, overwhelm, confuse
ἐχθές	yesterday
θάπτω	to bury
θυμόω	to anger; (*pas*) to be(come) angry
μεγαλύνω	to enlarge, increase, magnify
νότος, -ου, ὁ	south (wind)
σκῆπτρον, -ου, τό	staff, scepter
ταπεινόω	to bring down, humiliate, humble
τύπτω	to beat, strike (dead), afflict
ὑπολείπω	to leave remaining; (*mid*) to remain
χρυσοῦς, -ῆ, -οῦν / χρύσεος, -α, -ον	golden; (*subst*) golden coin

▹ List 7 — 9 to 8×

ἁγιάζω	to make holy, consecrate, sanctify
εφουδ (*translit*)	ephod
ἦ	surely, truly
ἡγέομαι	to go before, guide, act as leader, think, consider
καταλαμβάνω	to take hold of, overtake, capture
καταράομαι	to curse
κείρω	to shave, shear
ὀρθρίζω	to get up early
παλλακή, -ῆς, ἡ	concubine, mistress
παρέρχομαι	to go past, pass by, move on
προφητεύω	to prophesy
σίκλος, -ου, ὁ	shekel
σχίζα, -ης, ἡ	arrow, shaft, dart
τράπεζα, -ης, ἡ	table
χείμαρρος/ους, -ου, ὁ	stream, (seasonal) brook

▹ List 8 — 8×

ἀναβοάω	to cry out
ἅπαξ	once
βουκόλιον, -ου, τό	herd (of cattle)
διακόσιοι, -αι, -α	two hundred
διασῴζω	to preserve, keep safe; (*pas*) to be spared, escape
διατίθημι	to treat; (*mid*) to grant, arrange
ἐξάγω	to lead out, take out, bring out
κοιλάς, -άδος, ἡ	valley
κύκλῳ	(*dat of* κύκλος) (all) around, surrounding
μάχαιρα, -ας, ἡ	sword, dagger
μόσχος, -ου, ὁ	calf, young bull
οὐθείς, οὐθέν	no one, none, nothing
παράταξις, -εως, ἡ	battle, line of battle
πληγή, -ῆς, ἡ	blow, wound, misfortune, plague
πταίω	to fall down, stumble, make a mistake

▷ List 9 — 8 to 7×

ἀνίημι	to let go, release, ignore, give up, allow to do
ἀνταποδίδωμι	to give back, repay
ἀπαντάω	to receive (someone), encounter, befall
ἀπαντή, -ῆς, ἡ	meeting
ἀριθμός, -οῦ, ὁ	number, total
διασπείρω	to scatter, spread around
εἰρηνικός, -ή, -όν	peaceful, peaceable
ἕνεκα *or* ἕνεκεν/εἵνεκεν	(+*gen*) on account of, because of
ἐνιαυτός, -οῦ, ὁ	year
ἑξακόσιοι, -αι, -α	six hundred
ἐπιφέρω	to bring (on), put on, inflict
σκήνωμα, -ατος, τό	tent, temporary dwelling
σκοπός, -οῦ, ὁ	watchman, something the eye or attention is fixed upon
τριάκοντα	thirty
ὠτίον, -ου, τό	ear

▷ List 10 — 7×

εὐλογητός, -ή, -όν	praised, blessed
θερισμός, -οῦ, ὁ	harvest
καταλείπω	to leave (behind), abandon; (*pas*) to remain
κόπτω	to cut, strike; (*mid*) to mourn
λάκκος, -ου, ὁ	pit, cistern, cavity
λοιμός, -οῦ, ὁ	pestilence, (public) nuisance
μηδαμῶς	by no means, certainly not
νηστεύω	to fast (from food)
παρατάσσω	to form a battle line, battle
πενθέω	to grieve, mourn
πέραν	beyond; (+*gen*) on the other side
πέτρα, -ας, ἡ	rock, stone, cave
πλήσσω	to strike, wound, pierce
σπήλαιον, -ου, τό	cave
παρίστημι	*to place near, present;* (intr) *to stand near, be present to serve*

▷ **List 11**	**7 to 6×**
ἀκοή, -ῆς, ἡ	report, news
ἄκρος, -α, -ον	(far) end, tip, top
ἀπερίτμητος, -ος, -ον	uncircumcised
βαρύνω	to make heavy, burden
γεύω	to give to taste; (*mid*) to taste, eat
γνωρίζω	to make known, publicize
διπλοΐς, -ΐδος, ἡ	(double) robe
δῶμα, -ατος, τό	roof, housetop
ἕδρα, -ας, ἡ	seat, chair, (buttocks)
εἰσφέρω	to lead in, bring in
τάφος, -ου, ὁ	grave, tomb
τετρακόσιοι, -αι, -α	four hundred
τραυματίας, -ου, ὁ	wounded person, casualty
ὑποκάτω	(+*gen*) under, below
φείδομαι	to spare, refrain, hold back

▷ **List 12**	**6×**
ἑκατόν	one hundred
ἐκλείπω	to abandon, neglect; (*intr*) to fail, run out, cease
ἐκλεκτός, -ή, -όν	chosen, select, elite
ἐκτείνω	to stretch out, reach out, extend
ἐξαίρω	to raise up, remove, pack up camp and go
ἐπακούω	to hear, listen to, comply
ἐπιβαίνω	to get on, walk over, fall upon
ἑταῖρος, -ου, ὁ	friend, companion
εὐφραίνω	to make happy, cheer; (*pas*) to rejoice
ἡμίονος, -ου, ὁ/ἡ	mule
ἰσχυρός, -ά, -όν	strong, powerful
κατακληρόω	to choose *or* receive by casting lots
κληρονομία, -ας, ἡ	inheritance, possession(s)
κοίτη, -ης, ἡ	bed; sexual intercourse, ejaculation
καυχάομαι	*to boast (about)*

▷ List 13 — 6×

κοπιάω	to become tired, work hard, strive
κύων, κυνός, ὁ/ἡ	dog
λέων, -οντος, ὁ	lion
μήποτε	lest, in order that . . . not
μῦς, μυός, ὁ	mouse, rat
παίω	to strike, hit, wound
παραπορεύομαι	to pass by, travel along, overlook
περιζώννυμι *or* περιζωννύω	to wrap around, put on
περιοχή, -ῆς, ἡ	fortified enclosure
πληθύνω	to increase, multiply
ῥύομαι	to rescue, save
συνάντησις, -εως, ἡ	meeting
συνέχω	to constrain, enclose, afflict
σφάζω	to slaughter, slay
μάρτυς, -υρος, ὁ	*witness*

▷ List 14 — 6 to 5×

ἀθῷος, -ος, -ον	guiltless, innocent
ἀνομία, -ας, ἡ	lawlessness, wrongful conduct
βαδίζω	to go, proceed, walk
δρυμός, -οῦ, ὁ	forest, thicket
ἑβδομήκοντα	seventy
ἐκδικέω	to avenge, punish
ἐκχέω	to pour out, spill
ἔλαιον, -ου, τό	(olive) oil
ἐμπυρίζω	to set on fire, burn
ὑψόω	to lift up, raise high, exalt
φακός, -οῦ, ὁ	lentil
χαλκοῦς, -ῆ, -οῦν	(made of) bronze
χίλιοι, -αι, -α	one thousand
ψάλλω	to play music, sing praise with an instrument
ὡσεί	as (if), like, approximately

▷ List 15 — 5×

ἔνδοξος, -ος, -ον	reputable, honored, distinguished
ἕξ	six
ἐπαίρω	to lift up, raise, magnify
ἐπανίστημι	to oppose, attack, rise up against
εὐθής, -ής, -ές	right, correct
εὐχή, -ῆς, ἡ	prayer, vow
ἡνίκα	when
θλίβω	to press, oppress, afflict
κατάγω	to bring down, reduce
κατέχω	to prevent, restrain, gain control
κέρας, κέρατος, τό	horn, flank (of an army)
κλίνη, -ης, ἡ	bed, couch
κραυγή, -ῆς, ἡ	outcry, shouting
κτάομαι	to get, acquire
μιμνῄσκομαι	to remember, recall

▷ List 16 — 5×

ὀνειδίζω	to insult, criticize, taunt
παρατίθημι	to set before, present; (*mid*) to entrust
περιαιρέω	to take away, remove
περιποιέω	to keep alive, preserve; to acquire
ποιμαίνω	to shepherd, tend
πολεμιστής, -οῦ, ὁ	combatant, warrior
πότος, -ου, ὁ	drinking party
πρωτότοκος, -ος, -ον	firstborn
πυρός, -οῦ, ὁ	wheat
σαβαωθ (*translit*)	sabaoth, of hosts
σαλπίζω	to blow (a trumpet), trumpet (a sound)
σίδηρος, -ου, ὁ	iron (tool)
σκληρός, -ά, -όν	difficult, harsh, rough
σοφός, -ή, -όν	wise, skilled, learned
συλλαμβάνω	to capture, catch; to become pregnant

1–2 KINGS (3–4 KINGDOMS)

▷ List 1	56 to 25×
ἅρμα, -ατος, τό	chariot
ἀφίστημι	to keep away, remove; (*mid*) to depart, withdraw
εἴκοσι	twenty
ἐνιαυτός, -οῦ, ὁ	year
ἐξαμαρτάνω	to do wrong, sin, miss
θανατόω	to kill, put to death
θάπτω	to bury
ἵππος, -ου, ὁ	horse
κοιμάω	(*mid*) to lie (down), sleep; [κ. +μετά] to have sexual intercourse
παιδάριον, -ου, τό	child, little boy, servant
πεντήκοντα	fifty
πῆχυς, -εως, ὁ	cubit, (length of the) forearm
στῦλος, -ου, ὁ	pillar, column
ὑψηλός, -ή, -όν	elevated, proud; (*subst*) high place
χρυσίον, -ου, τό	gold

▷ List 2	22 to 17×
ἀναγγέλλω	to report, announce, publicize
ἀπαντή, -ῆς, ἡ	meeting
βοῦς, βοός, ὁ/ἡ	ox, cow
γέ	(*emphatic particle*) indeed, really
δεῦρο	come!, go!
ἑκατόν	one hundred
ἐξαίρω	to raise up, remove, pack up camp and go
ἐξαποστέλλω	to dispatch, dismiss, permit to leave
θνῄσκω	to die
θυμιάω	to burn incense (as an offering)
μεχωνωθ, ἡ (*translit*)	stand, platform
πολεμέω	to wage war, fight
φεύγω	to flee, escape, vanish
χαλκοῦς, -ῆ, -οῦν	(made of) bronze
χρυσοῦς, -ῆ, -οῦν / χρύσεος, -α, -ον	golden; (*subst*) golden coin

▷ List 3 — 17 to 15×

ἄλσος, -ους, τό	grove, sacred area
ἀμφότεροι, -αι, -α	both
ἀναστρέφω	to return, change course; (*mid*) to conduct oneself, live
βοάω	to cry out, shout
διαρ(ρ)ήγνυμι *or* διαρ(ρ)ήσσω	to tear, divide, break through
ἐγκαταλείπω	to abandon, leave behind
ἐπάνωθεν	(from) above, on top
καταλείπω	to leave (behind), abandon; (*pas*) to remain
παροργίζω	to anger, provoke
ῥομφαία, -ας, ἡ	sword
συντελέω	to finish, complete, accomplish
τεσσαράκοντα	forty
τριάκοντα	thirty
χείμαρρος/ους, -ου, ὁ	stream, (seasonal) brook
χερουβ, τό (*translit*)	cherub

▷ List 4 — 15 to 13×

ἀμπελών, -ῶνος, ὁ	vineyard
δουλεύω	to serve (as a slave)
εἰσακούω	to hear, listen to, obey
ἔλαιον, -ου, τό	(olive) oil
ἐξάγω	to lead out, take out, bring out
ἐξολεθρεύω	to utterly destroy, eradicate
εὐθής, -ής, -ές	right, correct
κατεσθίω	to eat up, devour
κιβωτός, -οῦ, ἡ	box, chest, ark
λέων, -οντος, ὁ	lion
ῥίπτω	to throw (away), defeat, reject
συλλαμβάνω	to capture, catch; to become pregnant
τοῖχος, -ου, ὁ	wall
ὑπολείπω	to leave remaining; (*mid*) to remain
ὕψος, -ους, τό	height, summit

▹ List 5 — 13 to 12×

ἀθετέω	to refuse, reject, breach
ἀποικίζω	to carry off to exile, send away
εἰσπορεύομαι	to go in, enter
θησαυρός, -οῦ, ὁ	treasure, treasury, storehouse
θύω	to sacrifice, slaughter
καθίστημι	to place, appoint, establish; (*mid*) to stand against
κακία, -ας, ἡ	evil, harm, misfortune
κρίμα, -ατος, τό	decision, judgment, punishment
κυκλόθεν	all around, from all sides
ὁλοκαύτωσις, -εως, ἡ	whole burnt offering
ὄνος, -ου, ὁ	donkey
πίμπλημι	to fill, satisfy
ποταμός, -οῦ, ὁ	river, stream
τάλαντον, -ου, τό	talent (*monetary unit*)
παρίστημι	*to place near, present;* (intr) *to stand near, be present to serve*

▹ List 6 — 12 to 11×

αιλαμ, τό (*translit*)	porch
δικαίωμα, -ατος, τό	ordinance, decree, rightful claim
δυναστεία, -ας, ἡ	power, dominance
ἕβδομος, -η, -ον	seventh
εἰσφέρω	to lead in, bring in
ἡγέομαι	to go before, guide, act as leader, think, consider
θυσιάζω	to sacrifice
κύκλῳ	(*dat of* κύκλος) (all) around, surrounding
μερίς, -ίδος, ἡ	share, part, portion
ὀστοῦν, -οῦ, τό	bone
πρωί	in the morning; (*subst*) morning
τάφος, -ου, ὁ	grave, tomb
τεῖχος, -ους, τό	(city) wall
φρόνησις, -εως, ἡ	insight, understanding
χρίω	to anoint, smear

▷ LIST 7	11 TO 10×
ἀνάγω	to lead up, bring up, raise up
ἀναφέρω	to bring up, offer, bear
αὐλή, -ῆς, ἡ	court, courtyard
διατίθημι	to treat; (*mid*) to grant, arrange
ἐκκλίνω	to bend, turn away; (*intr*) to avoid, deviate
ἐπιβλέπω	to look at (attentively), observe, anticipate
ἱππεύς, -έως, ὁ	rider, cavalryman
κραταιόω	to make strong, support, prevail (over)
κύων, κυνός, ὁ/ἡ	dog
σκήνωμα, -ατος, τό	tent, temporary dwelling
σκῆπτρον, -ου, τό	staff, scepter
στίχος, -ου, ὁ	row, line
συντρίβω	to break, crush, wreck
συστρέφω	to gather up, unite
τίκτω	to give birth to, bear, produce

▷ LIST 8	10 TO 9×
βδέλυγμα, -ατος, τό	abomination, detestable object
εἴδωλον, -ου, τό	image (of a god), idol
ἕξ	six
ἐξαιρέω	to take out, remove; (*mid*) to set free
ἥμισυς, -εια, -υ	half
καθαιρέω	to take down, overpower, destroy
κατάγω	to bring down, reduce
κέδρος, -ου, ἡ	cedar
κλίνη, -ης, ἡ	bed, couch
κλοιός, -οῦ, ὁ	collar
κρύπτω	to hide, conceal
ὑετός, -οῦ, ὁ	rain
ὑποκάτω	(+*gen*) under, below
χεῖλος, -ους, τό	lip, language, edge
χώρα, -ας, ἡ	country, land, region

▷ List 9 — 9 to 8×

ἀρρωστέω	to be unwell, become sick
δέησις, -εως, ἡ	supplication, request
δέομαι	to ask (for), pray (for)
δεῦτε	come here!, come on!
εἴσοδος, -ου, ἡ	entering, entryway, area of entrance
ἐπακούω	to hear, listen to, comply
κυκλόω	to encircle, surround
ναῦς, νεώς, ἡ	ship
ὄμνυμι *or* ὀμνύω	to swear, take an oath
ὀσφύς, -ύος, ἡ	loins, waist
παρατρέχω	to run (along), pass by, accompany
πλάτος, -ους, τό	breadth, width
σίκλος, -ου, ὁ	shekel
τέταρτος, -η, -ον	fourth
ὠμία, -ας, ἡ	shoulder, corner (of a building)

▷ List 10 — 8×

ἐπίθεμα, -ατος, τό	cover, top (of a column), surplus, addition
ἐπισκέπτομαι	to visit, examine, account for
εὐνοῦχος, -ου, ὁ	eunuch
κληρονομία, -ας, ἡ	inheritance, possession(s)
κόπτω	to cut, strike; (*mid*) to mourn
λέβης, -ητος, ὁ	cauldron, kettle
μονόζωνος, -ος, -ον	lightly armed
μόσχος, -ου, ὁ	calf, young bull
πεντηκόνταρχος, -ου, ὁ	commander of fifty men
περιβάλλω	to put around, cover, clothe
περιέχω	to surround, encircle, contain
πρόσταγμα, -ατος, τό	ordinance, command
πτέρυξ, -υγος, ἡ	wing
σάκκος, -ου, ὁ	sackcloth
σταθμός, -οῦ, ὁ	lodgings; doorpost; scales

▷ List 11 — 8 to 7×

ἁγιάζω	to make holy, consecrate, sanctify
ἀλλότριος, -α, -ον	foreign, strange, unfamiliar
ἀπάγω	to lead away, divert
αὔριον	tomorrow
γόνυ, γόνατος, τό	knee
εἰσάγω	to bring in, lead in, introduce
ἐκφέρω	to bring out, produce
ἐναντίος, -α, -ον	against, opposed, opposite
ἑξήκοντα	sixty
στήλη, -ης, ἡ	pillar, stele, monument
ταμιεῖον, -ου, τό	storeroom, private chamber
τετρακόσιοι, -αι, -α	four hundred
τόξον, -ου, τό	bow (to shoot arrows)
ὑποκάτωθεν	from beneath; (+*gen*) under
χοῦς, χοός, ὁ	dust, dry soil

▷ List 12 — 7×

ἔξοδος, ου, ἡ	departure, way out
ἐπάγω	to bring (up)on
ἐπαίρω	to lift up, raise, magnify
ἥκω	to have come, reach, be present
κατακαίω	to burn up, consume
κῆπος, -ου, ὁ	garden
λιμός, -οῦ, ὁ	hunger, famine
μεθίστημι	to remove, deprive of, change
μέτρον, -ου, τό	measurement, dimension, rule
ὄγδοος, -η, -ον	eighth
ὁλοκαύτωμα, -ατος, τό	whole burnt offering
συγκλείω	to close off, shut in, encase, prevent
συμβουλεύω	to advise; (*mid*) to consult, take counsel
συναθροίζω	to gather
ὅμοιος, -α, -ον	*like, similar to*

▷ List 13 — 7 to 6×

ἀποδιδράσκω	to run away, escape
βαρύς, -εῖα, -ύ	heavy, difficult
βέλος, -ους, τό	arrow, dart
βουνός, -οῦ, ὁ	hill
εἰρηνικός, -ή, -όν	peaceful, peaceable
ἐκλεκτός, -ή, -όν	chosen, select, elite
ἐκχέω	to pour out, spill
ἔνατος, -η, -ον	ninth
ἔνθεν	from here; on one side . . . on the other side
ἑορτή, -ῆς, ἡ	feast, festival
τίμιος, -α, -ον	reputable, valuable, expensive
τράπεζα, -ης, ἡ	table
φόρος, -ου, ὁ	levy, tax, tribute
χαλκός, -οῦ, ὁ	bronze, brass, copper
ἀναγινώσκω	*to read (aloud)*

▷ List 14 — 6×

ἀδελφή, -ῆς, ἡ	sister, beloved woman
καθά	as, just as
κέρας, κέρατος, τό	horn, flank (of an army)
λατρεύω	to serve, perform cultic duties (for)
μῆκος, -ους, τό	length, end-to-end measurement
ὀχυρός, -ά, -όν	secure, fortified, firm
πλησίον	(+*gen*) near, close; (*subst*) neighbor
πυλών, -ῶνος, ὁ	gate, porch
ῥήγνυμι *or* ῥήσσω	to tear, burst, break in pieces
συνάντησις, -εως, ἡ	meeting
συνέχω	to constrain, enclose, afflict
τρέχω	to run, advance
τριακόσιοι, -αι, -α	three hundred
φιάλη, -ης, ἡ	(shallow) bowl, cup
φρόνιμος, -ος, -ον	thoughtful, prudent, wise

▷ List 15 5×

ἀλλάσσω	to alter, substitute, (take in) exchange
ἀναβοάω	to cry out
ἀνατολή, -ῆς, ἡ	sprouting, rising; morning; (*pl*) east
ἀποκλείω	to shut, lock up, exclude
ἀρέσκω	to please, gain favor
ἀριστερός, -ά, -όν	left
βαρύνω	to make heavy, burden
βουλή, -ῆς, ἡ	plan, advice, council
διαβαίνω	to go through, cross (over)
διαπορεύομαι	to go through, pass by, walk about
διαφθείρω	to utterly destroy, ruin
δρυμός, -οῦ, ὁ	forest, thicket
δῶρον, -ου, τό	gift, offering
ἑβδομήκοντα	seventy
ἐμπίπρημι	to set on fire

▷ List 16 5×

ἐπιλαμβάνω	to catch, grab, obtain
ἐσώτερος, -α, -ον	inner; inside
ζηλόω	to be jealous of *or* for, envy, strive for
ἰάομαι	to heal, cure, restore
ἵλεως, -ως, -ων	gracious, merciful
κληρονομέω	to inherit, become heir to, give as inheritance
κολλάω	to join together, adhere to
κόλπος, -ου, ὁ	bosom, chest
λειτουργέω	to serve (as priest), minister
λούω	to wash; (*mid*) to bathe
μαρτύριον, -ου, τό	proof, testimony, witness
νεᾶνις, -ιδος, ἡ	girl, young woman
οἰκέω	to inhabit, live
ὅπλον, -ου, τό	weapon; (*pl*) arms, armor
προσάγω	to bring to, approach

1–2 CHRONICLES (1–2 PARALIPOMENA)

▷ List 1	65 to 25×
ἀναφέρω	to bring up, offer, bear
ἀριθμός, -οῦ, ὁ	number, total
ἅρμα, -ατος, τό	chariot
διαίρεσις, -εως, ἡ	division, distribution
εἴκοσι	twenty
ἑκατόν	one hundred
ἡγέομαι	to go before, guide, act as leader, think, consider
κατισχύω	to strengthen, overpower; (*intr*) to be encouraged, become powerful
κιβωτός, -οῦ, ἡ	box, chest, ark
μόσχος, -ου, ὁ	calf, young bull
πατριά, -ᾶς, ἡ	paternal lineage, family line
περισπόρια, -ων, τά	(*always pl*) surrounding country, suburbs
πῆχυς, -εως, ὁ	cubit, (length of the) forearm
πρωτότοκος, -ος, -ον	firstborn
χρυσίον, -ου, τό	gold

▷ List 2	25 to 20×
ἀφίστημι	to keep away, remove; (*mid*) to depart, withdraw
ἐγκαταλείπω	to abandon, leave behind
εἰσφέρω	to lead in, bring in
ἕξ	six
θύω	to sacrifice, slaughter
καθίστημι	to place, appoint, establish; (*mid*) to stand against
κώμη, -ης, ἡ	village, small town
λειτουργέω	to serve (as priest), minister
λειτουργία, -ας, ἡ	(cultic) ministry, (religious) service
ὁλοκαύτωμα, -ατος, τό	whole burnt offering
ὁλοκαύτωσις, -εως, ἡ	whole burnt offering
πολεμέω	to wage war, fight
τίκτω	to give birth to, bear, produce
τριάκοντα	thirty
χρυσοῦς, -ῆ, -οῦν / χρύσεος, -α, -ον	golden; (*subst*) golden coin

▷ List 3 — 20 to 17×

ἁγνίζω	to purify, cleanse
αἰνέω	to praise
ἐκζητέω	to search for, seek out, demand
ἐξολεθρεύω	to utterly destroy, eradicate
ἐργασία, -ας, ἡ	work, occupation, product
ἐφημερία, -ας, ἡ	class (of priests), division (of a group)
θάπτω	to bury
θησαυρός, -οῦ, ὁ	treasure, treasury, storehouse
σάλπιγξ, -ιγγος, ἡ	trumpet, horn
συντελέω	to finish, complete, accomplish
τάλαντον, -ου, τό	talent (*monetary unit*)
τέταρτος, -η, -ον	fourth
ὑψηλός, -ή, -όν	elevated, proud; (*subst*) high place
φασεχ/εκ, τό (*translit*)	Passover
χίλιοι, -αι, -α	one thousand

▷ List 4 — 16 to 14×

ἁγιάζω	to make holy, consecrate, sanctify
αὐλή, -ῆς, ἡ	court, courtyard
διακόσιοι, -αι, -α	two hundred
ἑξακόσιοι, -αι, -α	six hundred
ἐξομολογέω	to acknowledge, admit, confess
ἑορτή, -ῆς, ἡ	feast, festival
ἐπακούω	to hear, listen to, comply
εὐοδόω	to lead safely, ensure success, grant; (*pas*) to prosper
ἥμισυς, -εια, -υ	half
θυμιάω	to burn incense (as an offering)
καταλείπω	to leave (behind), abandon; (*pas*) to remain
κατέναντι	(+*gen*) in front of, opposite, against
κρίμα, -ατος, τό	decision, judgment, punishment
πρόσταγμα, -ατος, τό	ordinance, command
φεύγω	to flee, escape, vanish

▷ List 5 — 14 to 12×

ἀνατολή, -ῆς, ἡ	sprouting, rising; morning; (*pl*) east
βοάω	to cry out, shout
γένεσις, -εως, ἡ	beginning, birth, family origin
εὐφραίνω	to make happy, cheer; (*pas*) to rejoice
ἡγεμών, -όνος, ὁ	leader
κατάλοιπος, -ος, -ον	rest, remainder, leftover
κλῆρος, -ου, ὁ	lot, share, portion
ὀκτώ	eight
πεντήκοντα	fifty
πυλωρός, -οῦ, ὁ	gatekeeper, porter, jailer
ῥομφαία, -ας, ἡ	sword
σκῦλον, -ου, τό	plunder, spoils
ταπεινόω	to bring down, humiliate, humble
ὕψος, -ους, τό	height, summit
χερουβ, τό (*translit*)	cherub

▷ List 6 — 12 to 11×

βοηθέω	to help, aid
διατίθημι	to treat; (*mid*) to grant, arrange
δουλεύω	to serve (as a slave)
ἕβδομος, -η, -ον	seventh
εἴδωλον, -ου, τό	image (of a god), idol
εἰκοστός, -ή, -όν	twentieth
ἐνιαυτός, -οῦ, ὁ	year
εὐθής, -ής, -ές	right, correct
θυρεός, -οῦ, ὁ	(oblong) shield
ἰσχύω	to be strong, be capable; (*trans*) to intensify
ὄργανον, -ου, τό	part (of the body); (musical) instrument; contraption
παρατάσσω	to form a battle line, battle
πέμπτος, -η, -ον	fifth
τεῖχος, -ους, τό	(city) wall
χαλκός, -οῦ, ὁ	bronze, brass, copper

▷ List 7 — 11 to 10×

ἀδελφή, -ῆς, ἡ	sister, beloved woman
δόρυ, δόρατος, τό	spear
ἔναντι	(+*gen*) opposite, before, in the presence of
ἑξήκοντα	sixty
ἐπάνω	over, more than; (+*gen*) above, higher than
εὐφροσύνη, -ης, ἡ	joy, gladness
ἰσχυρός, -ά, -όν	strong, powerful
κατασπάω	to pull down, tear down
κινύρα, -ας, ἡ	kinnor (stringed instrument)
κοιμάω	(*mid*) to lie (down), sleep; [κ. +μετά] to have sexual intercourse
κύκλῳ	(*dat of* κύκλος) (all) around, surrounding
κύμβαλον, -ου, τό	cymbal
νάβλα, -ης, ἡ	harp
πτέρυξ, -υγος, ἡ	wing
τριακόσιοι, -αι, -α	three hundred

▷ List 8 — 10 to 9×

ἄλσος, -ους, τό	grove, sacred area
ἀριθμέω	to number, count
δῶρον, -ου, τό	gift, offering
εἰσπορεύομαι	to go in, enter
ἕκτος, -η, -ον	sixth
ἐξάγω	to lead out, take out, bring out
ἵππος, -ου, ὁ	horse
κυκλόθεν	all around, from all sides
μαρτύριον, -ου, τό	proof, testimony, witness
ὀγδοήκοντα	eighty
ὄγδοος, -η, -ον	eighth
ὀχυρός, -ά, -όν	secure, fortified, firm
στρατιά, -ᾶς, ἡ	army, large company (of people)
χαλκοῦς, -ῆ, -οῦν	(made of) bronze
ψαλτῳδός, -οῦ, ὁ	psalm singer

▷ List 9 — 9 to 8×

ᾄδω	to sing
αἰχμαλωσία, -ας, ἡ	captivity, (group of) captives
ἀνάγω	to lead up, bring up, raise up
ἀπάντησις, -εως, ἡ	meeting
ἀριστερός, -ά, -όν	left
βουλεύω	to consider, resolve, counsel
εἰσακούω	to hear, listen to, obey
παράταξις, -εως, ἡ	battle, line of battle
πληθύνω	to increase, multiply
πλήρης, -ης, -ες	full, complete
πολεμιστής, -οῦ, ὁ	combatant, warrior
ποταμός, -οῦ, ὁ	river, stream
σταθμός, -οῦ, ὁ	lodgings; doorpost; scales
στῦλος, -ου, ὁ	pillar, column
σύνεσις, -εως, ἡ	understanding, intelligence

▷ List 10 — 8×

ἑκατόνταρχος/ης, -ου, ὁ	captain of a hundred
ἔλαιον, -ου, τό	(olive) oil
ἐντρέπομαι	to show respect to; to feel shame about
ἐξεκκλησιάζω	to summon to an assembly
θανατόω	to kill, put to death
ἱππεύς, -έως, ὁ	rider, cavalryman
καθαρός, -ά, -όν	pure, clean
κριτής, -οῦ, ὁ	judge
μάχαιρα, -ας, ἡ	sword, dagger
πλοῦτος, -ου, ὁ	wealth, riches
προθυμέομαι	to be willing, be eager, be ardent
πρωί	in the morning; (*subst*) morning
σίδηρος, -ου, ὁ	iron (tool)
σκυλεύω	to plunder, spoil, strip (of goods)
σωτήριον, -ου, τό	salvation, (offering for) deliverance

▷ List 11 8 to 7×

ἁγίασμα, -ατος, τό	sanctuary, sacred offering
γίγας, -αντος, ὁ	giant, mighty person
δέησις, -εως, ἡ	supplication, request
δυσμή, -ῆς, ἡ	(*always pl*) setting (of the sun), west
εἴσοδος, -ου, ἡ	entering, entryway, area of entrance
ἔνατος, -η, -ον	ninth
ἐνδύω	to dress, clothe
ἔξοδος, -ου, ἡ	departure, way out
ἑπτακόσιοι, -αι, -α	seven hundred
ζυγός/ζυγόν, -οῦ, ὁ/τό	yoke; balance scale
θυμίαμα, -ατος, τό	incense
καταπαύω	to bring to an end, stop, cease
τόξον, -ου, τό	bow (to shoot arrows)
χιλίαρχος, -ου, ὁ	commander of a thousand
ᾠδή, -ῆς, ἡ	song, ode

▷ List 12 7×

κατευθύνω	to direct, guide; (*pas*) to prosper
κοιλάς, -άδος, ἡ	valley
κριός, -οῦ, ὁ	ram
κτῆνος, -ους, τό	(domesticated) animal; (*pl*) herd, cattle
μερίς, -ίδος, ἡ	share, part, portion
μῆκος, -ους, τό	length, end-to-end measurement
παλλακή, -ῆς, ἡ	concubine, mistress
πύργος, -ου, ὁ	tower
σαλπίζω	to blow (a trumpet), trumpet (a sound)
σκήνωμα, -ατος, τό	tent, temporary dwelling
σοφός, -ή, -όν	wise, skilled, learned
στάσις, -εως, ἡ	standing, position, rebellion
τεσσαράκοντα	forty
τετρακόσιοι, -αι, -α	four hundred
τίμιος, -α, -ον	reputable, valuable, expensive

▷ List 13 — 7 to 6×

ἄζυμος, -ος, -ον	unleavened (bread)
αἴνεσις, -εως, ἡ	praise
αἰχμαλωτεύω	to take prisoner, deport
ἀλλότριος, -α, -ον	foreign, strange, unfamiliar
ἀντιλαμβάνομαι	to aid, assist
ἄνω	(from) above
ἀπατάω	to deceive, trick
ἀποσκευή, -ῆς, ἡ	household member, belongings
ἀργυροῦς, -ᾶ, -οῦν	(made of) silver
γωνία, -ας, ἡ	corner, angle; leader
ἐκκλίνω	to bend, turn away; (*intr*) to avoid, deviate
ἐξαίρω	to raise up, remove, pack up camp and go
ἐπίσκεψις, -εως, ἡ	numbering, investigation, inspection
τράπεζα, -ης, ἡ	table
ὑψόω	to lift up, raise high, exalt

▷ List 14 — 6×

ἀθετέω	to refuse, reject, breach
ἵλεως, -ως, -ων	gracious, merciful
κληρονομία, -ας, ἡ	inheritance, possession(s)
κοιλία, -ας, ἡ	belly, stomach, womb
λύχνος, -ου, ὁ	lamp
νέος, -α, -ον	new, young; (*subst*) child
πεδίον, -ου, τό	plain, field, level area
πληγή, -ῆς, ἡ	blow, wound, misfortune, plague
προκαταλαμβάνω	to capture first, seize swiftly
σπάω	to draw (a sword)
στολή, -ῆς, ἡ	robe, cloak
τοῖχος, -ου, ὁ	wall
τραυματίας, -ου, ὁ	wounded person, casualty
τρισχίλιοι, -αι, -α	three thousand
ὅμοιος, -α, -ον	*like, similar to*

▷ List 15 5×

ἀμνός, -οῦ, ὁ	lamb
ἀνθίστημι	to resist, oppose
βδέλυγμα, -ατος, τό	abomination, detestable object
βορέας, -ου, ἡ / βορρᾶς, -ᾶ, ἡ	north
βουλή, -ῆς, ἡ	plan, advice, council
γλυπτός, -ή, -όν	carved, graven; [τὸ γλύπτον] graven image
δέκατος, -η, -ον	tenth; (*subst*) tithe
διαρ(ρ)ήγνυμι *or* διαρ(ρ)ήσσω	to tear, divide, break through
δόμα, -ατος, τό	gift
ἑβδομήκοντα	seventy
εἰσάγω	to bring in, lead in, introduce
ἔνδοξος, -ος, -ον	reputable, honored, distinguished
ἐνισχύω	to strengthen, grow strong(er), prevail (over)
θυμόω	to anger; (*pas*) to be(come) angry
κάμηλος, -ου, ὁ/ἡ	camel

▷ List 16 5×

κατάσχεσις, -εως, ἡ	possession
κόπτω	to cut, strike; (*mid*) to mourn
κραταιόω	to make strong, support, prevail (over)
κυκλόω	to encircle, surround
μεγαλύνω	to enlarge, increase, magnify
παιδεύω	to instruct, discipline
παρεμβάλλω	to set up, pitch (a tent), encamp
πέραν	beyond; (+*gen*) on the other side
προφητεύω	to prophesy
πτοέω	to startle, alarm, terrify
πυλών, -ῶνος, ὁ	gate, porch
σῖτος, -ου, ὁ	grain
συνίημι	to understand, notice, ponder
συντρίβω	to break, crush, wreck
τέκτων, -ονος, ὁ	carpenter, craftsman

PSALMS AND PRAYER OF MANASSEH

▹ LIST 1	83 TO 41 ×
ἀγαλλιάομαι	to rejoice greatly, exult
αἰνέω	to praise
ἀνομία, -ας, ἡ	lawlessness, wrongful conduct
διάψαλμα, -ατος, τό	(*musical interlude, renders Heb* selāh)
εἰσακούω	to hear, listen to, obey
ἐξομολογέω	to acknowledge, admit, confess
εὐφραίνω	to make happy, cheer; (*pas*) to rejoice
κρίμα, -ατος, τό	decision, judgment, punishment
μιμνῄσκομαι	to remember, recall
ῥύομαι	to rescue, save
ὑψόω	to lift up, raise high, exalt
ψάλλω	to play music, sing praise with an instrument
ψαλμός, -οῦ, ὁ	psalm, song of praise
ᾠδή, -ῆς, ἡ	song, ode
ὡσεί	as (if), like, approximately

▹ LIST 2	36 TO 27 ×
ἀδικία, -ας, ἡ	unrighteousness, wrongdoing, injustice
αἴνεσις, -εως, ἡ	praise
δέησις, -εως, ἡ	supplication, request
δικαίωμα, -ατος, τό	ordinance, decree, rightful claim
ἐκζητέω	to search for, seek out, demand
ἐκλείπω	to abandon, neglect; (*intr*) to fail, run out, cease
ἐπιλανθάνω	(*mid*) to forget, overlook, ignore
θαυμάσιος, -α, -ον	remarkable, amazing
μαρτύριον, -ου, τό	proof, testimony, witness
πένης, -ητος, ὁ	poor person, day laborer
σαλεύω	to shake, rock, disrupt
σωτήριον, -ου, τό	salvation, (offering for) deliverance
ταπεινόω	to bring down, humiliate, humble
ταράσσω	to trouble, disturb
χεῖλος, -ους, τό	lip, language, edge

▷ List 3 — 27 to 23×

ᾄδω	to sing
βοηθός, -οῦ, ὁ	help, helper
ἕνεκα *or* ἕνεκεν/εἵνεκεν	(+*gen*) on account of, because of
ἐπακούω	to hear, listen to, comply
θλίβω	to press, oppress, afflict
κληρονομία, -ας, ἡ	inheritance, possession(s)
λόγιον, -ου, τό	saying, teaching, oracle
λυτρόω	(*mid*) to redeem, ransom
ὁδηγέω	to lead, guide
ὅσιος, -α, -ον	holy, pious, devout
πληθύνω	to increase, multiply
προσέχω	to pay attention to, be concerned about
σκήνωμα, -ατος, τό	tent, temporary dwelling
συνίημι	to understand, notice, ponder
ὕψιστος, -η, -ον	highest, most high (God)

▷ List 4 — 22 to 19×

αλληλουια (*translit*)	hallelujah
ἀναγγέλλω	to report, announce, publicize
ἀσεβής, -ής, -ές	ungodly, wicked, sacrilegious
βοηθέω	to help, aid
διηγέομαι	to describe in detail, relate fully
ἐγκαταλείπω	to abandon, leave behind
ἐξαποστέλλω	to dispatch, dismiss, permit to leave
ἐξολεθρεύω	to utterly destroy, eradicate
καταδιώκω	to seek eagerly, chase down
καταισχύνω	to put to shame, disappoint
κατασκηνόω	to dwell, settle
κλίνω	to incline, lean, turn over, bend
παγίς, -ίδος, ἡ	trap, snare
πότε	when?, how long?
συντρίβω	to break, crush, wreck

▷ **List 5**	**19 to 17×**
ἀγαλλίασις, -εως, ἡ	great gladness, exultation
ᾅδης, -ου, ὁ	Hades, the underworld
αἰσχύνω	to dishonor; (*pas*) to be ashamed
ἀνταποδίδωμι	to give back, repay
βοήθεια, -ας, ἡ	help, support
δυναστεία, -ας, ἡ	power, dominance
ἐκκλίνω	to bend, turn away; (*intr*) to avoid, deviate
κραταιόω	to make strong, support, prevail (over)
κρύπτω	to hide, conceal
κυκλόω	to encircle, surround
μεγαλύνω	to enlarge, increase, magnify
μελετάω	to care for, think upon, pay attention
ῥομφαία, -ας, ἡ	sword
σύνεσις, -εως, ἡ	understanding, intelligence
ὑπομένω	to remain, endure, wait for

▷ **List 6**	**17 to 16×**
ἀντιλήμπτωρ, -ορος, ὁ	protector, helper
ἀπωθέω	to thrust away, drive back, reject
βουλή, -ῆς, ἡ	plan, advice, council
ἐξάγω	to lead out, take out, bring out
ἐξαιρέω	to take out, remove; (*mid*) to set free
ἐξουδ(θ)ενό(έ)ω	to disdain, reject
ἐπιβλέπω	to look at (attentively), observe, anticipate
εὐλογητός, -ή, -όν	praised, blessed
κύκλῳ	(*dat of* κύκλος) (all) around, surrounding
οἰκουμένη, -ης, ἡ	(inhabited) world, realm
ὀστοῦν, -οῦ, τό	bone
πέρας, -ατος, τό	limit, end
ποταμός, -οῦ, ὁ	river, stream
ὑπερασπιστής, -οῦ, ὁ	protector, defender
χρηστότης, -ητος, ἡ	kindness, goodness, generosity

▷ List 7 — 15 to 13×

ἄβυσσος, -ος, -ον	deep; (*subst*) abyss, depths
ἄδικος, -ος, -ον	unjust, unrighteous; (*subst*) wrongdoing
ἀναβαθμός, -οῦ, ὁ	steps, (flight of) stairs
ἀντιλαμβάνομαι	to aid, assist
ἀφίστημι	to keep away, remove; (*mid*) to depart, withdraw
ἐκχέω	to pour out, spill
ἐξεγείρω	to awake, rouse, raise
ἐπαίρω	to lift up, raise, magnify
εὐδοκέω	to consent, accept, be pleased
καταφυγή, -ῆς, ἡ	refuge, shelter
κέρας, κέρατος, τό	horn, flank (of an army)
ματαιότης, -ητος, ἡ	purposelessness, futility, worthlessness
νεφέλη, -ης, ἡ	cloud
τρίβος, -ου, ἡ/ὁ	path, route
χρηστός, -ή, -όν	kind, fine (quality), pleasant

▷ List 8 — 13 to 12×

ἄμωμος, -ος, -ον	unblemished, spotless
βραχίων, -ονος, ὁ	arm, (strength)
ἐπαινέω	to praise
εὐθύτης, -ητος, ἡ	uprightness
ἥκω	to have come, reach, be present
κατευθύνω	to direct, guide; (*pas*) to prosper
μακρύνω	to lengthen, delay, be *or* make distant
οἰκτίρω	to show mercy (to), have compassion (on)
ὀργίζω	to make angry; (*pas*) to be angry
πέτρα, -ας, ἡ	rock, stone, cave
πονηρεύομαι	to act wickedly, behave evilly
πρωί	in the morning; (*subst*) morning
τόξον, -ου, τό	bow (to shoot arrows)
ὕμνος, -ου, ὁ	hymn, song of praise
φοβερός, -ά, -όν	intimidating, fearful, terrible

▷ List 9 — 12 to 11×

ἀδικέω	to do wrong, harm
ἀλλότριος, -α, -ον	foreign, strange, unfamiliar
αὐλή, -ῆς, ἡ	court, courtyard
βέλος, -ους, τό	arrow, dart
γνωρίζω	to make known, publicize
ἐπανίστημι	to oppose, attack, rise up against
κτῆνος, -ους, τό	(domesticated) animal; (*pl*) herd, cattle
μήποτε	lest, in order that . . . not
ὄμνυμι *or* ὀμνύω	to swear, take an oath
ὀνειδίζω	to insult, criticize, taunt
ὄνειδος, -ους, τό	disgrace, loss of esteem
παιδεύω	to instruct, discipline
παραπικραίνω	to provoke, infuriate
ὕψος, -ους, τό	height, summit
ἀσθενέω	*to be weak, become less functional*

▷ List 10 — 11×

δόλιος, -α, -ον	deceitful, treacherous
ἔλαιον, -ου, τό	(olive) oil
ἐνδύω	to dress, clothe
ἐνωτίζομαι	to pay attention to, listen to
εὐφροσύνη, -ης, ἡ	joy, gladness
θαυμαστός, -ή, -όν	remarkable, wonderful, astonishing
θεμελιόω	to establish, build a foundation
καλύπτω	to cover, conceal
κιθάρα, -ας, ἡ	kithara, lyre
κληρονομέω	to inherit, become heir to, give as inheritance
οἰκτιρμός, -οῦ, ὁ	compassion, pity
πίμπλημι	to fill, satisfy
πόνος, -ου, ὁ	toil, distress, pain
προφθάνω	to precede, come before, anticipate
ἐπιθυμία, -ας, ἡ	*desire, lust*

▷ List 11 — 11 to 10×

διάβημα, -ατος, τό	(foot)step
διασκορπίζω	to scatter, disperse
ἐκλεκτός, -ή, -όν	chosen, select, elite
ἐμπί(μ)πλημι	to fill up, satisfy; [ἐ. τὰς χεῖρας] to consecrate as priest
ἐφοράω	to scrutinize, survey, oversee
καταιγίς, -ίδος, ἡ	storm, squall, hurricane
καταρτίζω	to set in order, ready, complete
κόπος, -ου, ὁ	difficulty, trouble, toil
μεγαλοπρέπεια, -ας, ἡ	majesty, magnificence
μελέτη, -ης, ἡ	meditation, (object of) study
ὀνειδισμός, -οῦ, ὁ	disgrace, insult
πλάσσω	to form, mold
πτέρυξ, -υγος, ἡ	wing
ὑπερήφανος, -ος, -ον	arrogant, haughty, lofty
χόρτος, -ου, ὁ	grass, hay

▷ List 12 — 10 to 9×

ἀδολεσχέω	to chatter, to meditate
ἀθῷος, -ος, -ον	guiltless, innocent
ἀριθμός, -οῦ, ὁ	number, total
γαστήρ, γαστρός, ἡ	belly, womb
διαπορεύομαι	to go through, pass by, walk about
διαρ(ρ)ήγνυμι *or* διαρ(ρ)ήσσω	to tear, divide, break through
πλησίον	(+*gen*) near, close; (*subst*) neighbor
πλοῦτος, -ου, ὁ	wealth, riches
ποιμαίνω	to shepherd, tend
σκιά, -ᾶς, ἡ	shadow
ταπείνωσις, -εως, ἡ	low status, humiliation, humility
ὑψηλός, -ή, -όν	elevated, proud; (*subst*) high place
χοῦς, χοός, ὁ	dust, dry soil
ψαλτήριον, -ου, τό	stringed instrument, harp, lyre
τιμή, -ῆς, ἡ	*honor, value, price*

▹ List 13 9×

ἐξομολόγησις, -εως, ἡ	(confession of) thanksgiving
ἐπιτήδευμα, -ατος, τό	intentional pursuit, consistent practice
ἕτοιμος, -η/ος, -ον	ready, prepared
εὐλογία, -ας, ἡ	praise, blessing
κολλάω	to join together, adhere to
κραταιός, -ά, -όν	powerful, forceful, severe
λάρυγξ, -υγγος, ὁ	throat
νεότης, -ητος, ἡ	youth
ὁμοιόω	to be similar, make like, compare
συνετίζω	to instruct, make aware (of)
σωτήρ, -ῆρος, ὁ	savior, deliverer
ὑπερηφανία, -ας, ἡ	arrogance, pride
φωτίζω	to brighten, shine, illuminate
χορτάζω	to feed, fill up; (*pas*) to be satisfied
ὑποτάσσω	*to subdue;* (mid/pas) *to (be) subject, submit*

▹ List 14 9 to 8×

ἁγίασμα, -ατος, τό	sanctuary, sacred offering
αἰσχύνη, -ης, ἡ	shame, disgrace
αἰχμαλωσία, -ας, ἡ	captivity, (group of) captives
ἀκακία, -ας, ἡ	innocence, guiltlessness
ἀλαλάζω	to cry aloud, shout
ἀνάγω	to lead up, bring up, raise up
ἀνταναιρέω	to remove from, bring to an end
ἄνυδρος, -ος, -ον	dry, waterless
ἄφρων, -ων, -ον	foolish, senseless; (*subst*) fool
βδελύσσω	to make detestable; (*mid*) to detest
δάκρυον, -ου, τό	tear, drop
δεῦτε	come here!, come on!
διαμένω	to continue, persist, endure
διαφθείρω	to utterly destroy, ruin
δοκιμάζω	to prove, put to the test

▷ List 15 8×

δόλος, -ου, ὁ	deceit, dishonesty, craftiness
δουλεύω	to serve (as a slave)
δρυμός, -οῦ, ὁ	forest, thicket
ἐκκαίω	to inflame, kindle, burn
ἐντρέπομαι	to show respect to; to feel shame about
ἐξαγγέλλω	to make known, proclaim
ἐξερευνάω	to search out, investigate
ἐπισκέπτομαι	to visit, examine, account for
εὖγε	well done!, excellent!
εὐδοκία, -ας, ἡ	goodwill, approval; satisfaction
εὐχή, -ῆς, ἡ	prayer, vow
θύω	to sacrifice, slaughter
καθίστημι	to place, appoint, establish; (*mid*) to stand against
κατανοέω	to understand, consider, perceive
κατεσθίω	to eat up, devour

▷ List 16 8×

λέων, -οντος, ὁ	lion
μάτην	pointlessly, uselessly, in vain
ὀρφανός, -ή, -όν	orphaned (person)
παράνομος, -ος, -ον	unlawful, lawless
παροικέω	to dwell as a foreigner
πεδάω	to bind, tie up
πεδίον, -ου, τό	plain, field, level area
περιέχω	to surround, encircle, contain
περιζώννυμι *or* περιζωννύω	to wrap around, put on
πολεμέω	to wage war, fight
πρόσταγμα, -ατος, τό	ordinance, command
πυρόω	to burn (red hot), purify (in fire)
ῥάβδος, -ου, ἡ	rod, staff, scepter
σελήνη, -ης, ἡ	moon
σός, σή, σόν	your, yours

▹ List 17 — 8 to 7×

ἀλλοιόω	to change, alter
ἅμα	at once, together
ἀνάγκη, -ης, ἡ	constraint, distress
ἀπόκρυφος, -ος, -ον	hidden, concealed, obscure
ἁρπάζω	to snatch, carry off
δέομαι	to ask (for), pray (for)
διαλογίζομαι	to consider, think on, devise
διαλογισμός, -οῦ, ὁ	deliberation, thought, discussion
διαφθορά, -ᾶς, ἡ	destruction, decay, rot
στεναγμός, -οῦ, ὁ	groaning, moaning
συνταράσσω	to throw into confusion, send into panic
τήκω	to melt; to waste away
χείμαρρος/ους, -ου, ὁ	stream, (seasonal) brook
χρυσίον, -ου, τό	gold
ἄνεμος, -ου, ὁ	*wind*

▹ List 18 — 7×

δῶρον, -ου, τό	gift, offering
ἐκτείνω	to stretch out, reach out, extend
ἐλέγχω	to question, rebuke, reprove
ἐντείνω	to stretch tight, bend
ἔξοδος, -ου, ἡ	departure, way out
ἐπελπίζω	to place hope in, give hope to
ἐπιποθέω	to yearn for, desire greatly
ἐπιφαίνω	to appear, show forth, display
ἑσπέρα, -ας, ἡ	evening
ἰάομαι	to heal, cure, restore
καθαιρέω	to take down, overpower, destroy
κακόω	to do wrong, mistreat
κατακυριεύω	to gain mastery over, dominate
καταπίνω	to gulp down, swallow up
ἐγγύς	(+gen) *near, close to*

▹ List 19 7×

κέδρος, -ου, ἡ	cedar
κτίζω	to establish, build, create
λάκκος, -ου, ὁ	pit, cistern, cavity
μάστιξ, -ιγος, ἡ	whip, suffering
μάταιος, -α/ος, -ον	vain, pointless, worthless
μερίς, -ίδος, ἡ	share, part, portion
μόσχος, -ου, ὁ	calf, young bull
νέος, -α, -ον	new, young; (*subst*) child
νήπιος, -α/ος, -ον	infant, child
νομοθετέω	to instruct (in law), legislate
ξηραίνω	to dry up, make dry
ὀδούς, -όντος, ὁ	tooth
ὀδύνη, -ης, ἡ	pain, grief
οἰκτίρμων, -ων, -ον	merciful, compassionate
ὁλοκαύτωμα, -ατος, τό	whole burnt offering

▹ List 20 7×

παρέρχομαι	to go past, pass by, move on
παροξύνω	to sharpen; to provoke, defy
περιβάλλω	to put around, cover, clothe
πηγή, -ῆς, ἡ	spring, fountain
πίων, -ων, -ον	fat, wealthy, fertile, abounding
ποτίζω	to give drink to, water
πραῢς, πραεῖα, πραΰ	gentle, considerate, mild
σκάνδαλον, -ου, τό	obstacle, cause of offense, enticement to sin
σκέπη, -ης, ἡ	covering, shelter, hideout
συλλαμβάνω	to capture, catch; to become pregnant
ταλαιπωρία, -ας, ἡ	misery, hardship, distress
ταπεινός, -ή, -όν	humble, abject, oppressed
ταχύς, -εῖα, -ύ	quickly, soon
τροφή, -ῆς, ἡ	food, provisions
ὅμοιος, -α, -ον	*like, similar to*

▷ List 21 — 7 to 6×

ἀναλαμβάνω	to take up, carry, assume
ἀνατέλλω	to spring up, rise, appear
ἀνταπόδοσις, -εως, ἡ	repayment, reward
ἀντίλημψις, -εως, ἡ	help, aid
ἀντιλογία, -ας, ἡ	dispute, (counter)argument
ἀρχαῖος, -α, -ον	former, old, ancient
βεβηλόω	to profane, desecrate
βουνός, -οῦ, ὁ	hill
γείτων, -ονος, ὁ	neighbor
διέξοδος, -ου, ἡ	going out, outlet (of a stream)
δυσμή, -ῆς, ἡ	(*always pl*) setting (of the sun), west
δωρεά, -ᾶς, ἡ	gift; (*adv*) freely, without cause
ἐκδίκησις, -εως, ἡ	vengeance, punishment
ὑπνόω	to sleep, cause to sleep
φεύγω	to flee, escape, vanish

▷ List 22 — 6×

ἐλεήμων, -ων, -ον	merciful, showing pity
ἐντροπή, -ῆς, ἡ	shame, humiliation
ἐξαλείφω	to wipe out, erase, obliterate
ἐπιπίπτω	to fall upon, embrace, attack
θανατόω	to kill, put to death
θαυμαστόω	to magnify, express astonishment (with)
κακία, -ας, ἡ	evil, harm, misfortune
κατάγω	to bring down, reduce
καταπατέω	to walk all over, deal harshly with, oppress
καταράσσω	to hurl down, break in pieces
κατοικίζω	to settle (a group), establish (residency)
κράτος, -ους, τό	might, strength, power
κριτής, -οῦ, ὁ	judge
μέχρι(ς)	(+*gen*) until, as far as; (*conj*) until
καινός, -ή, -όν	*new*

▷ List 23 — 6×

μνημόσυνον, -ου, τό	memory, memorial, reminder
νῶτος/ον, -ου, ὁ/τό	back, rear surface
ὅπλον, -ου, τό	weapon; (*pl*) arms, armor
παρασιωπάω	to keep quiet, refrain from comment
πεινάω	to be hungry
πετεινός, -ή, -όν	winged; (*subst*) bird
πλατύνω	to enlarge, widen
πλήρης, -ης, -ες	full, complete
πονηρία, -ας, ἡ	evil, vice
σκεπάζω	to cover over, shelter, conceal
στηλογραφία, -ας, ἡ	inscription, title (of certain psalms)
στρέφω	to change, turn; (*mid*) to rotate, flip
τάφος, -ου, ὁ	grave, tomb
παρίστημι	*to place near, present;* (intr) *to stand near, be present to serve*
πειρά(ζ)ω	*to tempt, test, try*

▷ List 24 — 6 to 5×

ἀδίκως	wrongfully, unjustly, falsely
ἀθετέω	to refuse, reject, breach
αἱρετίζω	to choose
ἀκονάω	to sharpen
ἀλαλαγμός, -οῦ, ὁ	shout, loud sound
ἄμπελος, -ου, ἡ	vine, vineyard
ἀνατολή, -ῆς, ἡ	sprouting, rising; morning; (*pl*) east
ἀπορ(ρ)ίπτω	to throw away, discard, reject
ᾆσμα, -ατος, τό	song
ἀστραπή, -ῆς, ἡ	lightning, flashing
βουλεύω	to consider, resolve, counsel
τέρας, -ατος, τό	wonder, omen, remarkable sight
ὑπολαμβάνω	to say in response, take up, consider
φυτεύω	to plant
ψεύδομαι	to lie, speak deceitfully

▷ List 25 5×

βρῶμα, -ατος, τό	food, provisions
βρῶσις, -εως, ἡ	food, consuming
γλυπτός, -ή, -όν	carved, graven; [τὸ γλύπτον] graven image
γνῶσις, -εως, ἡ	knowledge, understanding
γνωστός, -ή, -όν	known; (*subst*) friend
δειλιάω	to be afraid (of), lack courage
δεσπόζω	to be master, rule over
διαμερίζω	to divide (up), distribute
διατίθημι	to treat; (*mid*) to grant, arrange
δίκη, -ης, ἡ	penalty, punishment, justice
δράκων, -οντος, ὁ	dragon, large serpent
ἐκδιώκω	to chase away, banish
ἐκθλίβω	to afflict, force, squeeze, press
ἐμπήγνυμι	to place firmly into, fix in
δικαιόω	*to justify, vindicate, pronounce righteous*

▷ List 26 5×

ἐνδιαβάλλω	to accuse falsely
ἐξουδένωσις, -εως, ἡ	scorn, contempt
ἐπιβαίνω	to get on, walk over, fall upon
ἐπιχαίρω	to rejoice maliciously, be glad at someone's expense
ἐρυθρός, -ή, -όν	red
εὐθής, -ής, -ές	right, correct
ἦχος, -ου/ους, ὁ/τό	noise, sound
θεμέλιον/ος, -ου, τό	foundation
ἵππος, -ου, ὁ	horse
καταβάλλω	to throw down, overthrow, ruin
καταλαμβάνω	to take hold of, overtake, capture
κατώτατος, -η, -ον	lowest
κενός, -ή, -όν	empty, worthless, pointless
κοιλία, -ας, ἡ	belly, stomach, womb
καυχάομαι	*to boast (about)*

▷ **List 27**	5×
κοιμάω	(*mid*) to lie (down), sleep; [κ. +μετά] to have sexual intercourse
κόλπος, -ου, ὁ	bosom, chest
κραυγή, -ῆς, ἡ	outcry, shouting
κριός, -οῦ, ὁ	ram
κρύφιος, -α, -ον	secret, hidden
κῦμα, -ατος, τό	wave, billow
κύων, κυνός, ὁ/ἡ	dog
μακρόθυμος, -ος, -ον	patient
μεταστρέφω	to turn (back), change, alter
νεφρός, -οῦ, ὁ	kidney, heart (as seat of emotions)
ὁπότε	when
ὄρθρος, -ου, ὁ	early morning, dawn
παιδεία, -ας, ἡ	training, discipline, instruction
παλαιόω	to age, be old, wear out
παρανομέω	to violate the law

▷ **List 28**	5×
παροικία, -ας, ἡ	residence as a foreigner
παροργίζω	to anger, provoke
πλήρωμα, -ατος, τό	contents, abundance, fullness
πολυέλεος, -ος, -ον	very merciful
πρώιος, -α, -ον	early morning, in the morning
πρωτότοκος, -ος, -ον	firstborn
πτωχεία, -ας, ἡ	poverty
σάλπιγξ, -ιγγος, ἡ	trumpet, horn
σιγάω	to be silent, become quiet
στέαρ, στέατος, τό	fat, suet
στερεόω	to make strong, establish
στερέωμα, -ατος, τό	firmness, strength; firmament
στρουθίον, -ου, τό	sparrow, ostrich
συγκλείω	to close off, shut in, encase, prevent
ποτήριον, -ου, τό	*cup*

PROVERBS

▷ LIST 1	90 TO 18×
ἄδικος, -ος, -ον	unjust, unrighteous; (*subst*) wrongdoing
αἴσθησις, -εως, ἡ	perception, awareness, discernment
ἀσεβής, -ής, -ές	ungodly, wicked, sacrilegious
ἄφρων, -ων, -ον	foolish, senseless; (*subst*) fool
βουλή, -ῆς, ἡ	plan, advice, council
ἐκκλίνω	to bend, turn away; (*intr*) to avoid, deviate
εὐφραίνω	to make happy, cheer; (*pas*) to rejoice
παιδεία, -ας, ἡ	training, discipline, instruction
παράνομος, -ος, -ον	unlawful, lawless
πλοῦτος, -ου, ὁ	wealth, riches
σός, σή, σόν	your, yours
σοφός, -ή, -όν	wise, skilled, learned
φίλος, -η, -ον	friendly; (*subst*) friend, associate
χεῖλος, -ους, τό	lip, language, edge
ψευδής, -ής, -ές	lying, false; (*subst*) liar

▷ LIST 2	17 TO 12×
ἀλλότριος, -α, -ον	foreign, strange, unfamiliar
ἀπώλεια, -ας, ἡ	destruction, ruin, loss
βδέλυγμα, -ατος, τό	abomination, detestable object
γνῶσις, -εως, ἡ	knowledge, understanding
ἔλεγχος, -ου, ὁ	reproof, conviction, refutation
ἐνδεής, -ής, -ές	lacking in, in need of
ἔννοια, -ας, ἡ	insight, reflection
ἐπέρχομαι	to come upon, happen upon, attack
κρύπτω	to hide, conceal
ὀρθός, -ή, -όν	straight, upright, just
πανοῦργος, -ος, -ον	shrewd, sly, clever
πηγή, -ῆς, ἡ	spring, fountain
πίμπλημι	to fill, satisfy
φρόνησις, -εως, ἡ	insight, understanding
φρόνιμος, -ος, -ον	thoughtful, prudent, wise

▹ List 3 — 12 to 10×

ᾅδης, -ου, ὁ	Hades, the underworld
ἀτιμία, -ας, ἡ	shame, dishonor
δεκτός, -ή, -όν	acceptable
δυνάστης, -ου, ὁ	ruler, master, official
ἐλέγχω	to question, rebuke, reprove
ἐμπί(μ)πλημι	to fill up, satisfy; [ἐ. τὰς χεῖρας] to consecrate as priest
κτάομαι	to get, acquire
νοέω	to understand, perceive
ὀκνηρός, -ά, -όν	lazy, idle
παγίς, -ίδος, ἡ	trap, snare
παιδεύω	to instruct, discipline
σκολιός, -ά, -όν	crooked, dishonest, perverse
τρίβος, -ου, ἡ/ὁ	path, route
ὕβρις, -εως, ἡ	arrogance, insult, insolence
μάρτυς, -υρος, ὁ	*witness*

▹ List 4 — 10 to 9×

ἀτιμάζω	to dishonor
ἀφαιρέω	to separate, remove; (*mid*) to deprive, seize, take away
ἀφροσύνη, -ης, ἡ	foolishness
δόλιος, -α, -ον	deceitful, treacherous
ἐμπίπτω	to fall into, fall on, attack
ἐρείδω	to fix firmly, reinforce, prop up
ἡνίκα	when
ἰσχυρός, -ά, -όν	strong, powerful
κατευθύνω	to direct, guide; (*pas*) to prosper
μάχη, -ης, ἡ	battle, quarrel, strife
ὄλλυμι	to destroy, kill
πλούσιος, -α, -ον	rich, wealthy, abundant
ῥύομαι	to rescue, save
τιμάω	to honor; (*mid*) to value (at a price)
ἐπιθυμία, -ας, ἡ	*desire, lust*

▷ **List 5**	**9 to 8×**
ἄκακος, -ος, -ον	innocent, ingenuous
ἄνομος, -ος, -ον	lawless, wicked
ἀσέβεια, -ας, ἡ	ungodliness, wickedness
βίος, -ου, ὁ	life, existence
κατορθόω	to arrange properly, repair, do correctly
μακράν	far away, distant
ὅσιος, -α, -ον	holy, pious, devout
πένης, -ητος, ὁ	poor person, day laborer
ῥῆσις, -εως, ἡ	saying, speech, report
συνετός, -ή, -όν	sensible, clever, intelligent
συντριβή, -ῆς, ἡ	breaking, damage
τίμιος, -α, -ον	reputable, valuable, expensive
ὑπακούω	to obey, comply (with)
φιλία, -ας, ἡ	friendship, love
πράσσω	*to act, do, accomplish*

▷ **List 6**	**8 to 7×**
ἀδίκως	wrongfully, unjustly, falsely
αἰσχύνω	to dishonor; (*pas*) to be ashamed
ἀνδρεῖος, -α, -ον	courageous, virtuous
ἔξοδος, -ου, ἡ	departure, way out
κακία, -ας, ἡ	evil, harm, misfortune
οἰκέτης, -ου, ὁ	household servant
πενία, -ας, ἡ	need, shortfall, lack, poverty
προσέχω	to pay attention to, be concerned about
συναντάω	to meet (with), fall upon, happen
συνέδριον, -ου, τό	council, assembly
σύνεσις, -εως, ἡ	understanding, intelligence
συνίημι	to understand, notice, ponder
τεκταίνω	to work, devise, plan, scheme
φρήν, φρενός, ἡ	mental faculty, mind, reason
ἄνεμος, -ου, ὁ	*wind*

▹ List 7 7×

ἀπαίδευτος, -ος, -ον	uneducated, untrained, ignorant
δόλος, -ου, ὁ	deceit, dishonesty, craftiness
ἐκτείνω	to stretch out, reach out, extend
ἐλεημοσύνη, -ης, ἡ	kind act, charitable giving, mercy
ἔνδεια, -ας, ἡ	need, lack, deficiency
καταλαμβάνω	to take hold of, overtake, capture
καταφρονέω	to scorn, disdain, show contempt
λέων, -οντος, ὁ	lion
λύπη, -ης, ἡ	sorrow, pain
νοήμων, -ων, -ον	understanding, thoughtful, discerning
ὀστοῦν, -οῦ, τό	bone
στέφανος, -ου, ὁ	crown, (victor's) garland
ὑψηλός, -ή, -όν	elevated, proud; (*subst*) high place
φείδομαι	to spare, refrain, hold back
φαίνω	*to shine;* (mid) *to appear, seem*

▹ List 8 7 to 6×

ἄμητος, -ου, ὁ	harvest, reaping
ἀμφότεροι, -αι, -α	both
ἀπέχω	to be far away, be unavailable, withdraw, receive payment; (*mid*) to stay away
ἀπωθέω	to thrust away, drive back, reject
διαστρέφω	to turn, divert, mislead, pervert
δῶρον, -ου, τό	gift, offering
ἐγκαταλείπω	to abandon, leave behind
εἰσακούω	to hear, listen to, obey
ἔκγονος, -ος, -ον	born of; (*subst*) descendant
εὐφροσύνη, -ης, ἡ	joy, gladness
ζηλόω	to be jealous of *or* for, envy, strive for
θησαυρός, -οῦ, ὁ	treasure, treasury, storehouse
ἴασις, -εως, ἡ	remedy, healing
κόλπος, -ου, ὁ	bosom, chest
χράω	to use, employ; (*mid*) to treat (in a certain way)

▷ List 9 — 6 to 5×

ἀδικία, -ας, ἡ	unrighteousness, wrongdoing, injustice
ἄκρος, -α, -ον	(far) end, tip, top
ἁλίσκομαι	to be captured, be caught
ἀνελεήμων, -ων, -ον	unmerciful
ἀσθενής, -ής, -ές	weak, helpless
μυκτηρίζω	to sneer at, treat disrespectfully
οἰκέω	to inhabit, live
ὄνειδος, -ους, τό	disgrace, loss of esteem
παραβάλλω	to throw alongside, set beside, expose (to risk)
πλατύς, -εῖα, -ύ	wide, broad; [*fem subst* πλατεῖα] street, square
πόνος, -ου, ὁ	toil, distress, pain
ταμιεῖον, -ου, τό	storeroom, private chamber
τροχιά, -ᾶς, ἡ	path, course, wheel track
χρυσίον, -ου, τό	gold
ψεῦδος, -ους, τό	lie, falsehood

▷ List 10 — 5×

βοηθέω	to help, aid
γεώργιον, -ου, τό	cultivation; tilled land, field
δεσπότης, -ου, ὁ	master, absolute ruler
ἐγγυάω	to pledge (in marriage), give surety for
ἐγκωμιάζω	to praise, extol, eulogize
ἐκκαίω	to inflame, kindle, burn
ἐκλείπω	to abandon, neglect; (*intr*) to fail, run out, cease
ἐπιλανθάνω	(*mid*) to forget, overlook, ignore
ἐπίσταμαι	to know, be acquainted with
εὐχή, -ῆς, ἡ	prayer, vow
ἔχθρα, -ας, ἡ	hatred, hostility
θρασύς, -εῖα, -ύ	bold, rash, insolent
θυμώδης, -ης, -ες	hot tempered, furious
καθαρός, -ά, -όν	pure, clean
καλύπτω	to cover, conceal

▷ List 11 5×

κοιλία, -ας, ἡ	belly, stomach, womb
κρίμα, -ατος, τό	decision, judgment, punishment
λογισμός, -οῦ, ὁ	thought, (line of) reasoning
λοιμός, -οῦ, ὁ	pestilence, (public) nuisance
λυμαίνομαι	to do harm to, discredit, outrage
μακρόθυμος, -ος, -ον	patient
μάταιος, -α/ος, -ον	vain, pointless, worthless
μάχαιρα, -ας, ἡ	sword, dagger
μελετάω	to care for, think upon, pay attention
μέλι, -ιτος, τό	honey
μέντοι	but, nevertheless
μήποτε	lest, in order that . . . not
νέφος, -ους, τό	cloud, cloud mass
ὄμμα, -ατος, τό	eye
ὄρνεον, -ου, τό	bird

▷ List 12 5 to 4×

ἁγνός, -ή, -όν	(morally) pure
ἀετός, -οῦ, ὁ	eagle, vulture
ὀχύρωμα, -ατος, τό	stronghold, fortress
παροξύνω	to sharpen; to provoke, defy
πεινάω	to be hungry
πολυτελής, -ής, -ές	expensive, costly
προίημι	to yield, give up, express (words)
ῥάβδος, -ου, ἡ	rod, staff, scepter
σῖτος, -ου, ὁ	grain
συντρίβω	to break, crush, wreck
ταπεινόω	to bring down, humiliate, humble
τίκτω	to give birth to, bear, produce
ὑψόω	to lift up, raise high, exalt
φαῦλος, -η, -ον	base, worthless, evil
φιλέω	to love, kiss

▷ List 13 4×

αἰσχύνη, -ης, ἡ	shame, disgrace
ἄμωμος, -ος, -ον	unblemished, spotless
ἀναστρέφω	to return, change course; (*mid*) to conduct oneself, live
ἀπειλή, -ῆς, ἡ	threat, anger
ἀπολείπω	to leave (behind), abandon; to cease
ἀτιμώρητος, -ος, -ον	unavenged, unpunished
ἀφανίζω	to cause to vanish, destroy
βαθύς, -εῖα, -ύ	deep, profound
βλέφαρα, -ων, τά	eyelids
γνωρίζω	to make known, publicize
γωνία, -ας, ἡ	corner, angle; leader
ἐκζητέω	to search for, seek out, demand
ἐλεήμων, -ων, -ον	merciful, showing pity
ἐμβάλλω	to throw in, put inside
ἐπαίρω	to lift up, raise, magnify

▷ List 14 4×

ἐπιγνώμων, -ονος, ὁ/ἡ	understanding; arbiter
ἐπιθυμέω	to desire, yearn for
ἐπιμέλεια, -ας, ἡ	care, attention, diligence
ἐπονείδιστος, -ος, -ον	deserving reproach, shameful
εὐλογία, -ας, ἡ	praise, blessing
ἐφίστημι	to cast over, place on
ζημιόω	to penalize (with a fine), punish
ἡγέομαι	to go before, guide, act as leader, think, consider
ἥκω	to have come, reach, be present
ἡσυχάζω	to be quiet, rest
θησαυρίζω	to store up, treasure
κακοποιέω	to harm, do wrong
καταπίνω	to gulp down, swallow up
κατασκάπτω	to destroy, burn to the ground
κοινός, -ή, -όν	common, impure

▷ **List 15**	4×
λαμπτήρ, -ῆρος, ὁ	lamp, torch, lantern
λυπηρός, -ά, -όν	grievous, distressful, sad
μαστιγόω	to flog, whip, torment
μερίζω	to divide, distribute
ὀδύνη, -ης, ἡ	pain, grief
οἰκτίρω	to show mercy (to), have compassion (on)
ὁμιλέω	to converse with, associate with
ὀχυρός, -ά, -όν	secure, fortified, firm
παρασκευάζω	to prepare, get ready
πάρειμι	to be near, be present, have arrived
πληθύνω	to increase, multiply
πνοή, -ῆς, ἡ	wind, blow, breath
ποιμαίνω	to shepherd, tend
πρᾶγμα, -ατος, τό	thing, matter, affair, deed
ὅμοιος, -α, -ον	*like, similar to*

▷ **List 16**	4×
σβέννυμι	to extinguish, smother
σκληρός, -ά, -όν	difficult, harsh, rough
στάθμιον, -ου, τό	(small stone as a standard of) weight
συντελέω	to finish, complete, accomplish
ταπεινός, -ή, -όν	humble, abject, oppressed
τελευταῖος, -α, -ον	final, last
τελευτάω	to die
τέταρτος, -η, -ον	fourth
τίνω	to render payment; (*mid*) to avenge oneself
τράχηλος, -ου, ὁ	neck, throat
τύπτω	to beat, strike (dead), afflict
ὕπαρξις, -εως, ἡ	possession, property
ὑφίστημι	to set up, stand (in place), resist
ψωμός, -οῦ, ὁ	morsel (of food), scrap
τιμή, -ῆς, ἡ	*honor, value, price*

ECCLESIASTES AND SONG OF SONGS

▷ List 1 — 61 to 10×

ἀδελφιδός, -οῦ, ὁ	kinsman, relative
ἀσεβής, -ής, -ές	ungodly, wicked, sacrilegious
ἄφρων, -ων, -ον	foolish, senseless; (*subst*) fool
γέ	(*emphatic particle*) indeed, really
γνῶσις, -εως, ἡ	knowledge, understanding
ἐξουσιάζω	to exercise authority (over), have power
εὐφραίνω	to make happy, cheer; (*pas*) to rejoice
κῆπος, ου, ὁ	garden
μαστός, -οῦ, ὁ	breast (of a woman)
ματαιότης, -ητος, ἡ	purposelessness, futility, worthlessness
μοχθέω	to become weary, toil
μόχθος, -ου, ὁ	toil, labor, hardship
περισσεία, -ας, ἡ	advantage, abundance, surplus
ποίημα, -ατος, τό	deed, act, work; created thing
σοφός, -ή, -όν	wise, skilled, learned

▷ List 2 — 10 to 7×

ἀγαθωσύνη, -ης, ἡ	kindness, goodness
ἀδελφή, -ῆς, ἡ	sister, beloved woman
ἀμπελών, -ῶνος, ὁ	vineyard
ἄρωμα, -ατος, τό	spice, herb
ἀφροσύνη, -ης, ἡ	foolishness
εὐφροσύνη, -ης, ἡ	joy, gladness
κρίνον, -ου, τό	lily
κυκλόω	to encircle, surround
μερίς, -ίδος, ἡ	share, part, portion
ὀσμή, -ῆς, ἡ	fragrance, scent, smell
πένης, -ητος, ὁ	poor person, day laborer
περισπασμός, -οῦ, ὁ	distraction, preoccupation
περιστερά, -ᾶς, ἡ	dove, pigeon
πλησίον	(+*gen*) near, close; (*subst*) neighbor
προαίρεσις, -εως, ἡ	choice, plan (of action), commitment

▹ List 3 — 7 to 5×

ἀγέλη, -ης, ἡ	herd, group
ἄμπελος, -ου, ἡ	vine, vineyard
ἀνθέω	to bloom, flourish
ἐμπί(μ)πλημι	to fill up, satisfy; [ἐ. τὰς χεῖρας] to consecrate as priest
ἐξεγείρω	to awake, rouse, raise
κακία, -ας, ἡ	evil, harm, misfortune
μῆλον, -ου, τό	apple, fruit; cheek
νεβρός, -οῦ, ὁ	fawn, young deer
νύμφη, -ης, ἡ	bride, daughter-in-law
πλοῦτος, -ου, ὁ	wealth, riches
ῥόα, -ας, ἡ	pomegranate (tree)
σκιά, -ᾶς, ἡ	shadow
σμύρνα, -ης, ἡ	myrrh, aromatic spice
συνάντημα, -ατος, τό	event, fate, calamity
χεῖλος, -ους, τό	lip, language, edge

▹ List 4 — 5 to 4×

ἀριθμός, -οῦ, ὁ	number, total
ἀρρωστία, -ας, ἡ	sickness
ᾆσμα, -ατος, τό	song
γέλως, -ωτος, ὁ	laughter, mockery
δεῦρο	come!, go!
δορκάς, -άδος, ἡ	gazelle, deer
εἰσάγω	to bring in, lead in, introduce
εὔχομαι	to pray, vow
θάμβος, -ους/ου, ὁ/τό	fearful astonishment, stupor
ὁρκίζω	to cause to swear, bind by oath
περισσός, -ή, -όν	more, remaining, excessive
ποιμαίνω	to shepherd, tend
φυτεύω	to plant
χίλιοι, -αι, -α	one thousand
ὡραῖος, -α, -ον	beautiful, lovely

▷ List 5 — 4×

καταράομαι	to curse
κτῆνος, -ους, τό	(domesticated) animal; (*pl*) herd, cattle
λαλιά, -ᾶς, ἡ	chat, (manner *or* subject of) speech
μιμνῄσκομαι	to remember, recall
μνήμη, -ης, ἡ	memory, remembrance
μύρον, -ου, τό	ointment, perfume
νεότης, -ητος, ἡ	youth
ὁμοιόω	to be similar, make like, compare
περιλαμβάνω	to embrace, surround
πλήρωμα, -ατος, τό	contents, abundance, fullness
πονηρία, -ας, ἡ	evil, vice
πρᾶγμα, -ατος, τό	thing, matter, affair, deed
πύργος, -ου, ὁ	tower
σοφίζω	to make wise; (*mid*) to be wise
ταμιεῖον, -ου, τό	storeroom, private chamber

▷ List 6 — 4 to 3×

ἀγορά, -ᾶς, ἡ	market(place)
ἀκρόδρυα, -ων, τό	fruit tree, fruit (with a hard shell)
ἀνάπαυσις, -εως, ἡ	rest, stopping
ἀνδρεία, -ας, ἡ	courage, virtue
βορέας, -ου, ἡ / βορρᾶς, -ᾶ, ἡ	north
βότρυς, -υος, ὁ	bunch of grapes
γάλα, -ακτος, τό	milk
γλυκύς, -εῖα, -ύ	sweet, pleasant
διαπνέω	to blow through, draw breath
διαστρέφω	to turn, divert, mislead, pervert
τράχηλος, -ου, ὁ	neck, throat
ὑστερέω	to come up short, fail, lack
ὑψηλός, -ή, -όν	elevated, proud; (*subst*) high place
φθάνω	to come before; to overtake, reach
χρυσίον, -ου, τό	gold

▹ **List 7**	3×
δόμα, -ατος, τό	gift
ἐκλεκτός, -ή, -όν	chosen, select, elite
ἐκτός	(+*gen*) out of
ἔλαιον, -ου, τό	(olive) oil
ἔλαφος, -ου, ὁ	deer
ἕλκω	to draw, pull, drag
ἐξουδ(θ)ενό(έ)ω	to disdain, reject
ἐπαινέω	to praise
ἑταῖρος, -ου, ὁ	friend, companion
εὐθύτης, -ητος, ἡ	uprightness
ζῆλος, -ου, ὁ	jealousy, zeal
κατασκέπτομαι	to view closely, spy, survey, inspect
κλείω	to shut, close
κοιλία, -ας, ἡ	belly, stomach, womb
κύκλῳ	(*dat of* κύκλος) (all) around, surrounding

▹ **List 8**	3×
λογισμός, -οῦ, ὁ	thought, (line of) reasoning
μακρύνω	to lengthen, delay, be *or* make distant
μεγαλύνω	to enlarge, increase, magnify
νάρδος, -ου, ἡ	oil of nard, costly ointment
νότος, -ου, ὁ	south (wind)
ὀδούς, -όντος, ὁ	tooth
παρέρχομαι	to go past, pass by, move on
πένθος, -ους, τό	grief, mourning
περασμός, -οῦ, ὁ	coming to an end, completing
περισπάω	to draw off, distract, preoccupy
περιφορά, -ᾶς, ἡ	madness, erroneous thinking
πηγή, -ῆς, ἡ	spring, fountain
πληθύνω	to increase, multiply
σιώπησις, -εως, ἡ	covering, veil
σπαρτίον, -ου, τό	small cord

▷ List 9 3×

στάζω	to trickle, drip, sprinkle
συκοφαντία, -ας, ἡ	extortion, oppression, sophistry
συλλαμβάνω	to capture, catch; to become pregnant
συναντάω	to meet (with), fall upon, happen
τάσσω	to position, appoint; (*mid*) to indicate
τεῖχος, -ους, τό	(city) wall
τίκτω	to give birth to, bear, produce
ὑετός, -οῦ, ὁ	rain
ὕψος, -ους, τό	height, summit
φιλέω	to love, kiss
φύλαξ, -ακος, ὁ	guard, watchman
χείμαρρος/ους, -ου, ὁ	stream, (seasonal) brook
χοῦς, χοός, ὁ	dust, dry soil
ὡραιόομαι	to be beautiful

JOB

▷ **List 1**	**37 to 15×**
ἄδικος, -ος, -ον	unjust, unrighteous; (*subst*) wrongdoing
ἀναγγέλλω	to report, announce, publicize
ἀσεβής, -ής, -ές	ungodly, wicked, sacrilegious
βροτός, -οῦ, ὁ	mortal (person)
ἔναντι	(+*gen*) opposite, before, in the presence of
ἐπέρχομαι	to come upon, happen upon, attack
ἦ	surely, truly
καθαρός, -ά, -όν	pure, clean
κενός, -ή, -όν	empty, worthless, pointless
κρίμα, -ατος, τό	decision, judgment, punishment
κρύπτω	to hide, conceal
νέφος, -ους, τό	cloud, cloud mass
ὀδύνη, -ης, ἡ	pain, grief
παντοκράτωρ, -ορος, ὁ	ruler of all, almighty
ὑπολαμβάνω	to say in response, take up, consider

▷ **List 2**	**15 to 11×**
ἀδύνατος, -ος, -ον	powerless, incapacitated
ἄμεμπτος, -ος, -ον	blameless
ἀποβαίνω	to turn out, happen, prove to be; to depart
βίος, -ου, ὁ	life, existence
γαστήρ, γαστρός, ἡ	belly, womb
δίαιτα, -ης, ἡ	dwelling place, daily regimen
εἶτα	then, further
ἐλέγχω	to question, rebuke, reprove
ἐπιστήμη, -ης, ἡ	skill, competence, understanding
ἴσος, -η, -ον	equal, same
ὁμοθυμαδόν	with one accord, together
πότερον	(*untranslatable particle*), whether
σύνεσις, -εως, ἡ	understanding, intelligence
ὑπομένω	to remain, endure, wait for
διάβολος, -ου, ὁ	*accuser, adversary*

▷ List 3 — 11 to 10×

ἀληθινός, -ή, -όν	true, genuine
ἀνομία, -ας, ἡ	lawlessness, wrongful conduct
ἄνομος, -ος, -ον	lawless, wicked
ἀπώλεια, -ας, ἡ	destruction, ruin, loss
δυνάστης, -ου, ὁ	ruler, master, official
ἐμπί(μ)πλημι	to fill up, satisfy; [ἐ. τὰς χεῖρας] to consecrate as priest
ἡγέομαι	to go before, guide, act as leader, think, consider
κοιμάω	(*mid*) to lie (down), sleep, [κ. +μετά] to have sexual intercourse
ὀστοῦν, -οῦ, τό	bone
ῥίζα, -ης, ἡ	root
σῖτος, -ου, ὁ	grain
σκιά, -ᾶς, ἡ	shadow
συνέχω	to constrain, enclose, afflict
φίλος, -η, -ον	friendly; (*subst*) friend, associate
χεῖλος, -ους, τό	lip, language, edge

▷ List 4 — 10 to 8×

ᾅδης, -ου, ὁ	Hades, the underworld
ἀδικία, -ας, ἡ	unrighteousness, wrongdoing, injustice
ἀνάγκη, -ης, ἡ	constraint, distress
ἄνευ	(+*gen*) without, far from
αὐλίζομαι	to lodge overnight, stay
βουλή, -ῆς, ἡ	plan, advice, council
εἰσακούω	to hear, listen to, obey
ἐξαίσιος, -ος, -ον	remarkable, marvelous
ἐπίσταμαι	to know, be acquainted with
θεράπων, -οντος, ὁ	servant, aide
συντελέω	to finish, complete, accomplish
τελευτάω	to die
ὑετός, -οῦ, ὁ	rain
φείδομαι	to spare, refrain, hold back
ἐμαυτοῦ, -ῆς, -οῦ	*myself*

▷ **List 5**	**8×**
ἀφαιρέω	to separate, remove; (*mid*) to deprive, seize, take away
δέομαι	to ask (for), pray (for)
ἐκκλίνω	to bend, turn away; (*intr*) to avoid, deviate
ἐπισκοπή, -ῆς, ἡ	inspection, consideration, visitation
ἡσυχάζω	to be quiet, rest
ἰσχυρός, -ά, -όν	strong, powerful
καταγελάω	to ridicule, laugh at
κοιλία, -ας, ἡ	belly, stomach, womb
νουθετέω	to warn, admonish
ὀρφανός, -ή, -όν	orphaned (person)
οὐθείς, οὐθέν	no one, none, nothing
παύω	to stop, prevent; (*mid*) to cease, come to an end
πέτρα, -ας, ἡ	rock, stone, cave
πλήρης, -ης, -ες	full, complete
πράσσω	*to act, do, accomplish*

▷ **List 6**	**8 to 7×**
ἄβυσσος, -ος, -ον	deep; (*subst*) abyss, depths
ἀναλαμβάνω	to take up, carry, assume
ἀναπαύω	to stop, refresh, rest; to give rest
ἀπαλλάσσω	to get rid of, remove, set free
ἀπόκρισις, -εως, ἡ	decision, answer
ἀριθμός, -οῦ, ὁ	number, total
πτῶμα, -ατος, τό	disaster, misfortune; corpse, carcass
ῥήγνυμι *or* ῥήσσω	to tear, burst, break in pieces
σβέννυμι	to extinguish, smother
σοφός, -ή, -όν	wise, skilled, learned
συναντάω	to meet (with), fall upon, happen
τιτρώσκω	to wound, injure
ὑπακούω	to obey, comply (with)
χράω	to use, employ; (*mid*) to treat (in a certain way)
χρυσίον, -ου, τό	gold

▷ List 7 7×

βοῦς, βοός, ὁ/ἡ	ox, cow
γυμνός, -ή, -όν	naked
δείδω	to fear, be anxious
καταστρέφω	to turn over, overthrow, ruin
μιμνῄσκομαι	to remember, recall
ὄνος, -ου, ὁ	donkey
παρέρχομαι	to go past, pass by, move on
περιτίθημι	to put on, put around
πηλός, -οῦ, ὁ	mud, clay
προσέχω	to pay attention to, be concerned about
σίδηρος, -ου, ὁ	iron (tool)
συνίημι	to understand, notice, ponder
ταπεινόω	to bring down, humiliate, humble
τρίβος, -ου, ἡ/ὁ	path, route
θαυμάζω	*to be astonished, marvel at*

▷ List 8 6×

ἀποποιέομαι	to reject, cast away, disown
ἀριθμέω	to number, count
ἀσεβέω	to act wickedly, be ungodly
ἄτοπος, -ος, -ον	out of place, inappropriate, wrong
ἀφίστημι	to keep away, remove; (*mid*) to depart, withdraw
βέλος, -ους, τό	arrow, dart
γέ	(*emphatic particle*) indeed, really
γνόφος, -ου, ὁ	darkness
δέρμα, -ατος, τό	skin, hide
δράκων, -οντος, ὁ	dragon, large serpent
ἐνωτίζομαι	to pay attention to, listen to
ἐπανίστημι	to oppose, attack, rise up against
ἐπιλανθάνω	(*mid*) to forget, overlook, ignore
ἐπιπίπτω	to fall upon, embrace, attack
καλύπτω	to cover, conceal

▷ List 9 — 6 to 5×

ἄγριος, -α, -ον	wild, fierce
ἀπέχω	to be far away, be unavailable, withdraw, receive payment; (*mid*) to stay away
ἄφρων, -ων, -ον	foolish, senseless; (*subst*) fool
βοάω	to cry out, shout
βραχίων, -ονος, ὁ	arm, (strength)
κοίτη, -ης, ἡ	bed; sexual intercourse, ejaculation
κύκλῳ	(*dat of* κύκλος) (all) around, surrounding
κωφεύω	to keep quiet, be silent
λέων, -οντος, ὁ	lion
μέχρι(ς)	(+*gen*) until, as far as; (*conj*) until
οἴομαι	to suppose, think, reckon
σαπρία, -ας, ἡ	decay, rot
σπουδάζω	to hurry, strive
ὑψόω	to lift up, raise high, exalt
ψεύδομαι	to lie, speak deceitfully

▷ List 10 — 5×

γεννητός, -ή, -όν	born; (*subst*) human being
δέησις, -εως, ἡ	supplication, request
διακρίνω	to evaluate, judge, decide
διασῴζω	to preserve, keep safe; (*pas*) to be spared, escape
ἐάω	to permit, pass over, allow
εἰρηνεύω	to be at peace
ἐκλείπω	to abandon, neglect; (*intr*) to fail, run out, cease
ἔλεγχος, -ου, ὁ	reproof, conviction, refutation
ἐξάγω	to lead out, take out, bring out
ἐξαποστέλλω	to dispatch, dismiss, permit to leave
ἐξιχνιάζω	to explore, search around, track down
ἐπάγω	to bring (up)on
καίω	to light (a flame), burn
κακόω	to do wrong, mistreat
δέω	*to bind, constrain*

▷ List 11 5×

καταράομαι	to curse
λάρυγξ, -υγγος, ὁ	throat
μερίς, -ίδος, ἡ	share, part, portion
ξηραίνω	to dry up, make dry
ὀδούς, -όντος, ὁ	tooth
παίω	to strike, hit, wound
παλαιόω	to age, be old, wear out
πήγνυμι	to put up, pitch (a tent), fasten
πικρία, -ας, ἡ	bitterness
πνοή, -ῆς, ἡ	wind, blow, breath
πόθεν	from where?
πόνος, -ου, ὁ	toil, distress, pain
ῥύομαι	to rescue, save
σιωπάω	to be quiet, keep silent
στενάζω	to groan, mourn, sigh

▷ List 12 5 to 4×

ἀθῷος, -ος, -ον	guiltless, innocent
ἀποκαθίστημι	to restore, put back, pay
ἁρπάζω	to snatch, carry off
ἄστρον, -ου, τό	star
στολή, -ῆς, ἡ	robe, cloak
συντάσσω	to command, prescribe, set in order
συντρίβω	to break, crush, wreck
ταράσσω	to trouble, disturb
τήκω	to melt; to waste away
ὑψηλός, -ή, -όν	elevated, proud; (*subst*) high place
φέγγος, -ους, τό	light, splendor
χήρα, -ας, ἡ	widow
χῶμα, -ατος, τό	mound (of soil), heap
χώρα, -ας, ἡ	country, land, region
ἄνεμος, -ου, ὁ	*wind*

▷ List 13 4×

ἀφανίζω	to cause to vanish, destroy
βαρύς, -εῖα, -ύ	heavy, difficult
βδελύσσω	to make detestable; (*mid*) to detest
βοηθέω	to help, aid
δένδρον, -ου, τό	tree
διάνοια, -ας, ἡ	mind, thought, understanding
δόλος, -ου, ὁ	deceit, dishonesty, craftiness
δῶρον, -ου, τό	gift, offering
ἐκτείνω	to stretch out, reach out, extend
ἐνδύω	to dress, clothe
ἐξαιρέω	to take out, remove; (*mid*) to set free
ἐξίστημι	to amaze, overwhelm, confuse
ἐπακούω	to hear, listen to, comply
ἐπιλαμβάνω	to catch, grab, obtain
ἐγγύς	(+gen) *near, close to*

▷ List 14 4×

εὔχομαι	to pray, vow
ἐφοράω	to scrutinize, survey, oversee
ἥκω	to have come, reach, be present
κατεσθίω	to eat up, devour
κατέχω	to prevent, restrain, gain control
κολλάω	to join together, adhere to
κόπος, -ου, ὁ	difficulty, trouble, toil
κραυγή, -ῆς, ἡ	outcry, shouting
κτῆνος, -ους, τό	(domesticated) animal; (*pl*) herd, cattle
κυκλόω	to encircle, surround
λιμός, -οῦ, ὁ	hunger, famine
νεότης, -ητος, ἡ	youth
νεφέλη, -ης, ἡ	cloud
νήπιος, -α/ος, -ον	infant, child
λύω	*to loosen, release*

▷ **List 15**	**4×**
νοῦς, νοός, ὁ	mind, thought
ὅθεν	from where, consequently
οἴχομαι	to go, depart
ὀσφύς, -ύος, ἡ	loins, waist
πεδίον, -ου, τό	plain, field, level area
πλάσσω	to form, mold
πλοῦτος, -ου, ὁ	wealth, riches
ποταμός, -οῦ, ὁ	river, stream
πότε	when?, how long?
προσδέχομαι	to accept, receive favorably, anticipate
πρόσταγμα, -ατος, τό	ordinance, command
πρωΐ	in the morning; (*subst*) morning
πτέρυξ, -υγος, ἡ	wing
παρίστημι	*to place near, present;* (intr) *to stand near, be present to serve*
ποῖος, -α, -ον	*what (kind of)?, which?*

▷ **List 16**	**4 to 3×**
ἀδελφή, -ῆς, ἡ	sister, beloved woman
αἰνέω	to praise
αἰχμαλωτεύω	to take prisoner, deport
ἀναιρέω	to get rid of, destroy; (*mid*) to take up
ἀνατέλλω	to spring up, rise, appear
ἀνθίστημι	to resist, oppose
τάσσω	to position, appoint; (*mid*) to indicate
τόξον, -ου, τό	bow (to shoot arrows)
ὕβρις, -εως, ἡ	arrogance, insult, insolence
ὑποκάτω	(+ *gen*) under, below
ὕψιστος, -η, -ον	highest, most high (God)
χείμαρρος/ους, -ου, ὁ	stream, (seasonal) brook
χίλιοι, -αι, -α	one thousand
ὠδίν, -ῖνος, ἡ	pains of childbirth, birth pangs
τιμή, -ῆς, ἡ	*honor, value, price*

▷ List 17	3×
ἀπαντάω	to receive (someone), encounter, befall
ἀποφέρω	to carry off
ἀσπίς, -ίδος, ἡ	shield; asp, snake
ἀτιμία, -ας, ἡ	shame, dishonor
βιβρώσκω	to consume, eat
διανοίγω	to open up, spread apart
διψάω	to be thirsty, be arid
δουλεύω	to serve (as a slave)
δρόσος, -ου, ἡ	dew
ἐκκόπτω	to cut off, do away with
ἐκτρίβω	to rub firmly, destroy completely
ἐκχέω	to pour out, spill
ἕλκω	to draw, pull, drag
ἔνδοξος, -ος, -ον	reputable, honored, distinguished
ἄξιος, -α, -ον	*deserving, appropriate*

▷ List 18	3×
ἐνύπνιον, -ου, τό	dream
ἑσπέρα, -ας, ἡ	evening
εὐχή, -ῆς, ἡ	prayer, vow
ζυγός/ζυγόν, -οῦ, ὁ/τό	yoke; balance scale
θεμέλιον/ος, -ου, τό	foundation
θερισμός, -οῦ, ὁ	crop, harvest
θῆλυς, -εια, -υ	female
θησαυρός, -οῦ, ὁ	treasure, treasury, storehouse
ἴχνος, -ους, τό	footprint, track, sole (of the foot)
κακία, -ας, ἡ	evil, harm, misfortune
κάμηλος, -ου, ὁ/ἡ	camel
καταβάλλω	to throw down, overthrow, ruin
κόλπος, -ου, ὁ	bosom, chest
κοπιάω	to become tired, work hard, strive
ἱκανός, -ή, -όν	*sufficient, adequate, capable*

▷ **List 19**	3×
κραταιός, -ά, -όν	powerful, forceful, severe
κριτής, -οῦ, ὁ	judge
λύχνος, -ου, ὁ	lamp
μάχαιρα, -ας, ἡ	sword, dagger
μεταβάλλω	to turn, change, alter
μέτρον, -ου, τό	measurement, dimension, rule
νότος, -ου, ὁ	south (wind)
ὀργίζω	to make angry; (*pas*) to be angry
παγίς, -ίδος, ἡ	trap, snare
παράνομος, -ος, -ον	unlawful, lawless
πετεινός, -ή, -όν	winged; (*subst*) bird
πότος, -ου, ὁ	drinking party
πτοέω	to startle, alarm, terrify
σκέπη, -ης, ἡ	covering, shelter, hideout
ὅμοιος, -α, -ον	*like, similar to*

▷ **List 20**	3×
σός, σή, σόν	your, yours
σποδός, -οῦ, ἡ	ashes
στρέφω	to change, turn; (*mid*) to rotate, flip
συμβαίνω	to happen, come about, befall
τάφος, -ου, ὁ	grave, tomb
τρέχω	to run, advance
τρόπος, -ου, ὁ	manner, way, conduct
τυγχάνω	to happen, obtain, meet
ὕψος, -ους, τό	height, summit
χόρτος, -ου, ὁ	grass, hay
ὦμος, -ου, ὁ	shoulder

ISAIAH

▷ List 1 — 53 to 25×

ἅμα	at once, together
ἀναγγέλλω	to report, announce, publicize
ἀφαιρέω	to separate, remove; (*mid*) to deprive, seize, take away
βουλή, -ῆς, ἡ	plan, advice, council
εὐφραίνω	to make happy, cheer; (*pas*) to rejoice
εὐφροσύνη, -ης, ἡ	joy, gladness
ἥκω	to have come, reach, be present
καταλείπω	to leave (behind), abandon; (*pas*) to remain
ποταμός, -οῦ, ὁ	river, stream
ῥύομαι	to rescue, save
σαβαωθ (*translit*)	sabaoth, of hosts
ταπεινόω	to bring down, humiliate, humble
τρόπος, -ου, ὁ	manner, way, conduct
ὑψηλός, -ή, -όν	elevated, proud; (*subst*) high place
ὑψόω	to lift up, raise high, exalt

▷ List 2 — 25 to 17×

αἰσχύνω	to dishonor; (*pas*) to be ashamed
ἀναπαύω	to stop, refresh, rest; to give rest
ἀνομία, -ας, ἡ	lawlessness, wrongful conduct
ἄνομος, -ος, -ον	lawless, wicked
βοάω	to cry out, shout
βουλεύω	to consider, resolve, counsel
ἐμπί(μ)πλημι	to fill up, satisfy; [ἐ. τὰς χεῖρας] to consecrate as priest
ἐνοικέω	to inhabit, dwell in
ἰσχύω	to be strong, be capable; (*trans*) to intensify
μάχαιρα, -ας, ἡ	sword, dagger
μιμνῄσκομαι	to remember, recall
φάραγξ, -αγγος, ἡ	ravine, valley
φεύγω	to flee, escape, vanish
χώρα, -ας, ἡ	country, land, region
οὐαί	*woe!, ah!*

▹ LIST 3	17 TO 15×
ἀμπελών, -ῶνος, ὁ	vineyard
ἀσεβής, -ής, -ές	ungodly, wicked, sacrilegious
βραχίων, -ονος, ὁ	arm, (strength)
διψάω	to be thirsty, be arid
ἐγκαταλείπω	to abandon, leave behind
ἐκλείπω	to abandon, neglect; (*intr*) to fail, run out, cease
ἔνδοξος, -ος, -ον	reputable, honored, distinguished
ἐρημόω	to make desolate, dry up
καίω	to light (a flame), burn
κοπιάω	to become tired, work hard, strive
μάταιος, -α/ος, -ον	vain, pointless, worthless
οἰκουμένη, -ης, ἡ	(inhabited) world, realm
συντρίβω	to break, crush, wreck
τεῖχος, -ους, τό	(city) wall
τίκτω	to give birth to, bear, produce

▹ LIST 4	15 TO 13×
ἄκρος, -α, -ον	(far) end, tip, top
ἀνατέλλω	to spring up, rise, appear
ἀνίημι	to let go, release, ignore, give up, allow to do
ἀπειθέω	to be disobedient, refuse
βουνός, -οῦ, ὁ	hill
ἐπάγω	to bring (up)on
ἐπέρχομαι	to come upon, happen upon, attack
καταπατέω	to walk all over, deal harshly with, oppress
κληρονομέω	to inherit, become heir to, give as inheritance
νῆσος, -ου, ἡ	island
ξηραίνω	to dry up, make dry
ὀλολύζω	to wail, howl
παύω	to stop, prevent; (*mid*) to cease, come to an end
πεινάω	to be hungry
σωτήριον, -ου, τό	salvation, (offering for) deliverance

▷ List 5 13 to 12×

ἀθετέω	to refuse, reject, breach
αἰσχύνη, -ης, ἡ	shame, disgrace
δρυμός, -οῦ, ὁ	forest, thicket
ἐκλεκτός, -ή, -όν	chosen, select, elite
ἕνεκα *or* ἕνεκεν/εἵνεκεν	(+*gen*) on account of, because of
ἐξαιρέω	to take out, remove; (*mid*) to set free
ἐξίστημι	to amaze, overwhelm, confuse
ζυγός/ζυγόν, -οῦ, ὁ/τό	yoke; balance scale
ἡττάω	to overcome; (*pas*) to be defeated, be inferior
ἵππος, -ου, ὁ	horse
πενθέω	to grieve, mourn
πέτρα, -ας, ἡ	rock, stone, cave
πλάσσω	to form, mold
ὕψος, -ους, τό	height, summit
καινός, -ή, -όν	*new*

▷ List 6 12 to 11×

ᾅδης, -ου, ὁ	Hades, the underworld
ἀναιρέω	to get rid of, destroy; (*mid*) to take up
ἀνάπαυσις, -εως, ἡ	rest, stopping
δουλεύω	to serve (as a slave)
ἐνιαυτός, -οῦ, ὁ	year
θεμέλιον/ος, -ου, τό	foundation
καταιγίς, -ίδος, ἡ	storm, squall, hurricane
κατακαίω	to burn up, consume
λυτρόω	(*mid*) to redeem, ransom
παρέρχομαι	to go past, pass by, move on
πληγή, -ῆς, ἡ	blow, wound, misfortune, plague
πλοῦτος, -ου, ὁ	wealth, riches
πρίν	before
σκληρός, -ά, -όν	difficult, harsh, rough
ταπεινός, -ή, -όν	humble, abject, oppressed

▷ List 7 — 11 to 10×

ἀγαλλιάομαι	to rejoice greatly, exult
ἀκουστός, -ή, -όν	heard, audible
ἁλίσκομαι	to be captured, be caught
ἀνατολή, -ῆς, ἡ	sprouting, rising; morning; (*pl*) east
ἀφίστημι	to keep away, remove; (*mid*) to depart, withdraw
βοηθέω	to help, aid
εἰσακούω	to hear, listen to, obey
ἐπιλανθάνω	(*mid*) to forget, overlook, ignore
ἰάομαι	to heal, cure, restore
ἰσχυρός, -ά, -όν	strong, powerful
κατεσθίω	to eat up, devour
κοιλία, -ας, ἡ	belly, stomach, womb
λέων, -οντος, ὁ	lion
μανθάνω	to learn, find out
ταράσσω	to trouble, disturb

▷ List 8 — 10 to 9×

ἀγαλλίαμα, -ατος, τό	joy, gladness
ἀδικέω	to do wrong, harm
ἄμπελος, -ου, ἡ	vine, vineyard
ἀνακαλύπτω	to uncover, disclose
ἄνθος, -ους, τό	flower, blossom
ὀνειδίζω	to insult, criticize, taunt
πρότερος, -α, -ον	former, earlier, before
πρωί	in the morning; (*subst*) morning
σύνεσις, -εως, ἡ	understanding, intelligence
συντελέω	to finish, complete, accomplish
ὕβρις, -εως, ἡ	arrogance, insult, insolence
φλόξ, φλογός, ἡ	flame
χεῖλος, -ους, τό	lip, language, edge
χόρτος, -ου, ὁ	grass, hay
χρυσίον, -ου, τό	gold

▷ List 9 — 9×

ἀντιλαμβάνομαι	to aid, assist
ἀπώλεια, -ας, ἡ	destruction, ruin, loss
ἅρμα, -ατος, τό	chariot
βοῦς, βοός, ὁ/ἡ	ox, cow
ἐμβλέπω	to look at, evaluate
ἐξεγείρω	to awake, rouse, raise
ἐπακούω	to hear, listen to, comply
ἐπιβάλλω	to lay upon, throw upon
κοιμάω	(*mid*) to lie (down), sleep; [κ. +μετά] to have sexual intercourse
παροξύνω	to sharpen; to provoke, defy
πλήρης, -ης, -ες	full, complete
σάκκος, -ου, ὁ	sackcloth
σείω	to shake, sway, stir up
τρίβος, -ου, ἡ/ὁ	path, route
ὠδίνω	to be in labor, suffer pain

▷ List 10 — 9 to 8×

ἀδικία, -ας, ἡ	unrighteousness, wrongdoing, injustice
ἄδικος, -ος, -ον	unjust, unrighteous; (*subst*) wrongdoing
ἄκανθα, -ης, ἡ	thorn, thorny plant
ἀναβάτης, -ου, ὁ	horse rider, charioteer
βδέλυγμα, -ατος, τό	abomination, detestable object
βοήθεια, -ας, ἡ	help, support
βόσκω	to feed, graze
δῶρον, -ου, τό	gift, offering
εἴδωλον, -ου, τό	image (of a god), idol
ἔκγονος, -ος, -ον	born of; (*subst*) descendant
ἐνδύω	to dress, clothe
ἐντρέπομαι	to show respect to; to feel shame about
ἐπίσταμαι	to know, be acquainted with
ὡσεί	as (if), like, approximately
δικαιόω	*to justify, vindicate, pronounce righteous*

▹ List 11 8×

θλίβω	to press, oppress, afflict
νεανίσκος, -ου, ὁ	young man
νεφέλη, -ης, ἡ	cloud
ὀδύνη, -ης, ἡ	pain, grief
ὀχυρός, -ά, -όν	secure, fortified, firm
πολεμέω	to wage war, fight
πόνος, -ου, ὁ	toil, distress, pain
πόρρωθεν	from a distance
προνομεύω	to plunder, despoil
προνομή, -ῆς, ἡ	spoils (of war), plunder
ῥάβδος, -ου, ἡ	rod, staff, scepter
ῥήγνυμι *or* ῥήσσω	to tear, burst, break in pieces
σκέπη, -ης, ἡ	covering, shelter, hideout
σκῦλον, -ου, τό	plunder, spoils
συνίημι	to understand, notice, ponder

▹ List 12 8 to 7×

ἀληθινός, -ή, -όν	true, genuine
διασκεδάζω	to break, thwart, scatter
διασπείρω	to scatter, spread around
ἡνίκα	when
καθαρός, -ά, -όν	pure, clean
κληρονομία, -ας, ἡ	inheritance, possession(s)
κρίμα, -ατος, τό	decision, judgment, punishment
κυριεύω	to rule over, dominate, control
μακράν	far away, distant
μετέωρος, -ος, -ον	raised, upper, haughty
οἰκέω	to inhabit, live
ὄμνυμι *or* ὀμνύω	to swear, take an oath
σύντριμμα, -ατος, τό	fracture, wound, destruction
ὦμος, -ου, ὁ	shoulder
μάρτυς, -υρος, ὁ	*witness*

▹ **List 13**	**7 to 6×**
ἁγιάζω	to make holy, consecrate, sanctify
αἰχμάλωτος, -ος, -ον	captive, prisoner
ἀναφέρω	to bring up, offer, bear
ἄνθραξ, -ακος, ὁ	coal, precious dark red stone
ἀνταποδίδωμι	to give back, repay
ἀρήν, ἀρνός, ὁ	lamb, sheep
πατέω	to walk (on), trample
πηλός, -οῦ, ὁ	mud, clay
πονηρία, -ας, ἡ	evil, vice
ῥίζα, -ης, ἡ	root
σιωπάω	to be quiet, keep silent
στενάζω	to groan, mourn, sigh
ταχύς, -εῖα, -ύ	quickly, soon
φυτεύω	to plant
χειροποίητος, -ος, -ον	handmade, manufactured; (*subst*) idol

▹ **List 14**	**6×**
ἀριθμός, -οῦ, ὁ	number, total
ἀροτριάω	to plow
ἀρχαῖος, -α, -ον	former, old, ancient
ἀσπίς, -ίδος, ἡ	asp, snake
γλυπτός, -ή, -όν	carved, graven; [τὸ γλύπτον] graven image
δεῦτε	come here!, come on!
ἐκζητέω	to search for, seek out, demand
ἕλος, -ους, τό	marshland
ἔντιμος, -ος, -ον	precious, valuable
ἐπιθυμέω	to desire, yearn for
ζῆλος, -ου, ὁ	jealousy, zeal
θησαυρός, -οῦ, ὁ	treasure, treasury, storehouse
καπνός, -οῦ, ὁ	smoke
καταλαμβάνω	to take hold of, overtake, capture
θαυμάζω	*to be astonished, marvel at*

▹ List 15 — 6×

καταπάτημα, -ατος, τό	trampling down
κατισχύω	to strengthen, overpower; (*intr*) to be encouraged, become powerful
κέδρος, -ου, ἡ	cedar
κενός, -ή, -όν	empty, worthless, pointless
κλαυθμός, -ου, ὁ	weeping, crying
κόπτω	to cut, strike; (*mid*) to mourn
κρύπτω	to hide, conceal
κτίζω	to establish, build, create
κύκλῳ	(*dat of* κύκλος) (all) around, surrounding
κωφός, -ή, -όν	speechless, mute
λυπέω	to vex, displease; (*mid/pas*) to be distressed, grieve
μελετάω	to care for, think upon, pay attention
ὄνειδος, -ους, τό	disgrace, loss of esteem
ὀργίζω	to make angry; (*pas*) to be angry
ὀσφύς, -ύος, ἡ	loins, waist

▹ List 16 — 6×

περιβάλλω	to put around, cover, clothe
πλάνησις, -εως, ἡ	error, deception
πολιορκέω	to besiege
πρέσβυς, -εως, ὁ	elder, ambassador
προσέχω	to pay attention to, be concerned about
πύργος, -ου, ὁ	tower
σβέννυμι	to extinguish, smother
σίκερα, τό	liquor, fermented drink
στέαρ, στέατος, τό	fat, suet
στέφανος, -ου, ὁ	crown, (victor's) garland
συναντάω	to meet (with), fall upon, happen
τράχηλος, -ου, ὁ	neck, throat
ὑπεναντίος, -α, -ον	against, opposite; (*subst*) enemy
χήρα, -ας, ἡ	widow
ὠφελέω	to profit, benefit, be useful

▹ List 17 5×

αἴνεσις, -εως, ἡ	praise
ἀλλότριος, -α, -ον	foreign, strange, unfamiliar
ἄνευ	(+*gen*) without, far from
ἀνομέω	to act lawlessly, be wicked
ἄνω	(from) above
ἀποκαλύπτω	to uncover, reveal, disclose
βία, -ας, ἡ	violence, force
βορέας, -ου, ἡ / βορρᾶς, -ᾶ, ἡ	north
γένημα, -ατος, τό	fruit, yield, produce, (offspring)
γίγας, -αντος, ὁ	giant, mighty person
γυμνός, -ή, -όν	naked
δεκτός, -ή, -όν	acceptable
δένδρον, -ου, τό	tree
ἀσθενέω	*to be weak, become less functional*
δέω	*to bind, constrain*

▹ List 18 5×

διάνοια, -ας, ἡ	mind, thought, understanding
ἐμβάλλω	to throw in, put inside
ἐνωτίζομαι	to pay attention to, listen to
ἐξάγω	to lead out, take out, bring out
ἔπαυλις, -εως, ἡ	residence, settlement
ἐφίστημι	to cast over, place on
θεμελιόω	to establish, build a foundation
κατάγω	to bring down, reduce
καταπίνω	to gulp down, swallow up
κῆπος, -ου, ὁ	garden
κινέω	to move, disturb
κραυγή, -ῆς, ἡ	outcry, shouting
κρέας, κρέως, τό	meat
λύπη, -ης, ἡ	sorrow, pain
μεθύσκω	to make drunk; (*pas*) to be drunk

▷ List 19 5×

νηστεία, -ας, ἡ	fast (from eating)
ὁμοιόω	to be similar, make like, compare
ὀνειδισμός, -οῦ, ὁ	disgrace, insult
ὄνος, -ου, ὁ	donkey
ὅραμα, -ατος, τό	vision, (object of) sight
ὅρασις, -εως, ἡ	seeing, appearance, (prophetic) vision
ὄφις, -εως, ὁ	snake
πάρειμι	to be near, be present, have arrived
παρθένος, -ου, ἡ	unmarried woman, virgin
πηγή, -ῆς, ἡ	spring, fountain
πληθύνω	to increase, multiply
πλούσιος, -α, -ον	rich, wealthy, abundant
ποίμνιον, -ου, τό	flock
πτέρυξ, -υγος, ἡ	wing
σκεπάζω	to cover over, shelter, conceal

▷ List 20 5×

σκιά, -ᾶς, ἡ	shadow
σοφός, -ή, -όν	wise, skilled, learned
σπήλαιον, -ου, τό	cave
στερεόω	to make strong, establish
συνετός, -ή, -όν	sensible, clever, intelligent
σωτήρ, -ῆρος, ὁ	savior, deliverer
ταῦρος, -ου, ὁ	bull, ox
τέκτων, -ονος, ὁ	carpenter, craftsman
τοῖχος, -ου, ὁ	wall
τρόμος, -ου, ὁ	trembling, quaking
τροχός, -οῦ, ὁ	wheel
ὑετός, -οῦ, ὁ	rain
ὑπακούω	to obey, comply (with)
ὑπομένω	to remain, endure, wait for
τιμή, -ῆς, ἡ	*honor, value, price*

JEREMIAH (INCL. BAR., LAM., EP. JER.)

▹ **List 1**	**51 to 22×**
ἀδικία, -ας, ἡ	unrighteousness, wrongdoing, injustice
ἀναγγέλλω	to report, announce, publicize
βαδίζω	to go, proceed, walk
βορέας, -ου, ὁ / βορρᾶς, -ᾶ, ὁ	north
ἐκλείπω	to abandon, neglect; (*intr*) to fail, run out, cease
ἐπάγω	to bring (up)on
ἥκω	to have come, reach, be present
καταλείπω	to leave (behind), abandon; (*pas*) to remain
κύκλῳ	(*dat of* κύκλος) (all) around, surrounding
λιμός, -οῦ, ὁ	hunger, famine
μάχαιρα, -ας, ἡ	sword, dagger
μιμνῄσκομαι	to remember, recall
προφητεύω	to prophesy
συντρίβω	to break, crush, wreck
ψευδής, -ής, -ές	lying, false; (*subst*) liar

▹ **List 2**	**21 to 18×**
ἄβατος, -ος, -ον	desolate, untrodden, inaccessible
ἀλλότριος, -α, -ον	foreign, strange, unfamiliar
ἀποικία, -ας, ἡ	exile, (place of) captivity
αὐλή, -ῆς, ἡ	court, courtyard
ἀφανισμός, -οῦ, ὁ	disappearance, annihilation
ἐγκαταλείπω	to abandon, leave behind
ἐξαποστέλλω	to dispatch, dismiss, permit to leave
ἐπισκέπτομαι	to visit, examine, account for
θυμιάω	to burn incense (as an offering)
καταισχύνω	to put to shame, disappoint
κατάλοιπος, -ος, -ον	left over; (*subst*) rest, remainder
ὀνειδισμός, -οῦ, ὁ	disgrace, insult
ποιμήν, -ένος, ὁ	shepherd
συλλαμβάνω	to capture, catch; to become pregnant
ἀναγινώσκω	*to read (aloud)*

▹ **List 3**	**18 to 16×**
αἰχμαλωσία, -ας, ἡ	captivity, (group of) captives
δουλεύω	to serve (as a slave)
εἰσακούω	to hear, listen to, obey
ἐκδικέω	to avenge, punish
ἐξάγω	to lead out, take out, bring out
ἐξαιρέω	to take out, remove; (*mid*) to set free
ἐπιλανθάνω	(*mid*) to forget, overlook, ignore
ἵππος, -ου, ὁ	horse
κατεσθίω	to eat up, devour
κόπτω	to cut, strike; (*mid*) to mourn
νεανίσκος, -ου, ὁ	young man
πλησίον	(+*gen*) near, close; (*subst*) neighbor
ῥομφαία, -ας, ἡ	sword
φεύγω	to flee, escape, vanish
ἅπας, ἅπασα, ἅπαν	*all, every*

▹ **List 4**	**16 to 14×**
ἀφανίζω	to cause to vanish, destroy
ἀφίστημι	to keep away, remove; (*mid*) to depart, withdraw
διασκορπίζω	to scatter, disperse
ἐκδίκησις, -εως, ἡ	vengeance, punishment
ἐκχέω	to pour out, spill
κατακαίω	to burn up, consume
κρίμα, -ατος, τό	decision, judgment, punishment
κτῆνος, -ους, τό	(domesticated) animal; (*pl*) herd, cattle
ὄμνυμι *or* ὀμνύω	to swear, take an oath
παντοκράτωρ, -ορος, ὁ	ruler of all, almighty
παρθένος, -ου, ἡ	unmarried woman, virgin
πληθύνω	to increase, multiply
πολεμέω	to wage war, fight
τίκτω	to give birth to, bear, produce
τράχηλος, -ου, ὁ	neck, throat

▹ List 5 — 14 to 13×

ἀνάγω	to lead up, bring up, raise up
ἀποικίζω	to carry off to exile, send away
διαφθείρω	to utterly destroy, ruin
ἔξωθεν	outside; (+*gen*) from outside
εὐφροσύνη, -ης, ἡ	joy, gladness
ἡγεμών, -όνος, ὁ	leader
καθίστημι	to place, appoint, establish; (*mid*) to stand against
καίω	to light (a flame), burn
κακία, -ας, ἡ	evil, harm, misfortune
κραυγή, -ῆς, ἡ	outcry, shouting
κρύπτω	to hide, conceal
κτάομαι	to get, acquire
ὀστοῦν, -οῦ, τό	bone
τεῖχος, -ους, τό	(city) wall
ὑψηλός, -ή, -όν	elevated, proud; (*subst*) high place

▹ List 6 — 13 to 12×

αἰσχύνω	to dishonor; (*pas*) to be ashamed
ἀναιρέω	to get rid of, destroy; (*mid*) to take up
ἀπωθέω	to thrust away, drive back, reject
διασπείρω	to scatter, spread around
ἐπιτήδευμα, -ατος, τό	intentional pursuit, consistent practice
ἰσχυρός, -ά, -όν	strong, powerful
καθαιρέω	to take down, overpower, destroy
κληρονομία, -ας, ἡ	inheritance, possession(s)
λάκκος, -ου, ὁ	pit, cistern, cavity
λέων, -οντος, ὁ	lion
παύω	to stop, prevent; (*mid*) to cease, come to an end
πονηρία, -ας, ἡ	evil, vice
ῥίπτω	to throw (away), defeat, reject
συντελέω	to finish, complete, accomplish
χαρτίον, -ου, τό	papyrus roll

▷ List 7 — 12 to 10×

ἀνάπτω	to light up, set on fire
ἀναστρέφω	to return, change course; (*mid*) to conduct oneself, live
ἐκλεκτός, -ή, -όν	chosen, select, elite
ἐξωθέω	to drive out, thrust out, expel
ζυγός/ζυγόν, -οῦ, ὁ/τό	yoke; balance scale
ξύλινος, -η, -ον	wooden
οἴχομαι	to go, depart
πτοέω	to startle, alarm, terrify
συντάσσω	to command, prescribe, set in order
σύντριμμα, -ατος, τό	fracture, wound, destruction
ταπεινόω	to bring down, humiliate, humble
τόξον, -ου, τό	bow (to shoot arrows)
φείδομαι	to spare, refrain, hold back
χήρα, -ας, ἡ	widow
ὦ	O!, oh!

▷ List 8 — 10×

ἀπορ(ρ)ίπτω	to throw away, discard, reject
ἀπώλεια, -ας, ἡ	destruction, ruin, loss
ἀρχιμάγειρος, -ου, ὁ	chief of the royal guard, chief cook
ἐνιαυτός, -οῦ, ὁ	year
ἐξολεθρεύω	to utterly destroy, eradicate
εὐφραίνω	to make happy, cheer; (*pas*) to rejoice
θησαυρός, -οῦ, ὁ	treasure, treasury, storehouse
καταλύω	to lodge, bring down, destroy
κλαυθμός, -ου, ὁ	weeping, crying
κλίνω	to incline, lean, turn over, bend
μεθύσκω	to make drunk; (*pas*) to be drunk
τάσσω	to position, appoint; (*mid*) to indicate
χαλκοῦς, -ῆ, -οῦν	(made of) bronze
ἀσθενέω	*to be weak, become less functional*
οὐαί	*woe!, ah!*

▷ LIST 9 — 10 TO 9×

ἀγγεῖον, -ον, τό	vessel, container
ἄδικος, -ος, -ον	unjust, unrighteous; (*subst*) wrongdoing
ἀθετέω	to refuse, reject, breach
ἅμα	at once, together
βδέλυγμα, -ατος, τό	abomination, detestable object
βουλή, -ῆς, ἡ	plan, advice, council
δρυμός, -οῦ, ὁ	forest, thicket
εἰσάγω	to bring in, lead in, introduce
ἐκτείνω	to stretch out, reach out, extend
ἐπιβαίνω	to get on, walk over, fall upon
ἐφίστημι	to cast over, place on
θλίβω	to press, oppress, afflict
χρυσίον, -ου, τό	gold
ψεῦδος, -ους, τό	lie, falsehood
ἄνεμος, -ου, ὁ	*wind*

▷ LIST 10 — 9×

ἰάομαι	to heal, cure, restore
κυκλόθεν	all around, from all sides
μαχητής, -οῦ, ὁ	fighter, warrior
νήπιος, -α/ος, -ον	infant, child
νομή, -ῆς, ἡ	pasture, feeding area
οἰκέω	to inhabit, live
ὄλλυμι	to destroy, kill
οὐθείς, οὐθέν	no one, none, nothing
πένθος, -ους, τό	grief, mourning
πετεινός, -ή, -όν	winged; (*subst*) bird
πίμπλημι	to fill, satisfy
πληγή, -ῆς, ἡ	blow, wound, misfortune, plague
πρόσταγμα, -ατος, τό	ordinance, command
τραυματίας, -ου, ὁ	wounded person, casualty
ποτήριον, -ου, τό	*cup*

▷ List 11 — 9 to 8×

ἀδικέω	to do wrong, harm
ἀθῷος, -ος, -ον	guiltless, innocent
ἀκοή, -ῆς, ἡ	report, news
ἁλίσκομαι	to be captured, be caught
ἀνταποδίδωμι	to give back, repay
ἅρμα, -ατος, τό	chariot
ἀτιμία, -ας, ἡ	shame, dishonor
βοάω	to cry out, shout
βουνός, -οῦ, ὁ	hill
δάκρυον, -ου, τό	tear, drop
εἰσπορεύομαι	to go in, enter
ἐξαίρω	to raise up, remove, pack up camp and go
φυτεύω	to plant
χώρα, -ας, ἡ	country, land, region
ψευδοπροφήτης, -ου, ὁ	false prophet

▷ List 12 — 8×

ἐρημόω	to make desolate, dry up
κατάγω	to bring down, reduce
λῆμμα, -ατος, τό	profit, gain; (prophetic) statement
λογισμός, -οῦ, ὁ	thought, (line of) reasoning
μάταιος, -α/ος, -ον	vain, pointless, worthless
ὀσφύς, -ύος, ἡ	loins, waist
παιδεία, -ας, ἡ	training, discipline, instruction
πενθέω	to grieve, mourn
πλατύς, -εῖα, -ύ	wide, broad; [*fem subst* πλατεῖα] street, square
ποίμνιον, -ου, τό	flock
πόνος, -ου, ὁ	toil, distress, pain
ποταμός, -οῦ, ὁ	river, stream
στρέφω	to change, turn; (*mid*) to rotate, flip
σῦκον, -ου, τό	fig
τρίβος, -ου, ἡ/ὁ	path, route

▹ List 13 — 8 to 7×

αἰνέω	to praise
αἰσχύνη, -ης, ἡ	shame, disgrace
ἀνασῴζω	to deliver, rescue, preserve
ἀνομία, -ας, ἡ	lawlessness, wrongful conduct
ἀπατάω	to deceive, trick
ἀποδοκιμάζω	to reject as unworthy
ἀριθμός, -οῦ, ὁ	number, total
βρῶσις, -εως, ἡ	food, consuming
γέ	(*emphatic particle*) indeed, really
γένος, -ους, τό	kind, people group, family (lineage)
δοκιμάζω	to prove, put to the test
ἐκφέρω	to bring out, produce
ὑποκάτω	(+*gen*) under, below
χρηματίζω	to declare (by oracle); to be occupied
ὠφελέω	to profit, benefit, be useful

▹ List 14 — 7×

ἐμπί(μ)πλημι	to fill up, satisfy; [ἐ. τὰς χεῖρας] to consecrate as priest
ἐνοικέω	to inhabit, dwell in
ἔξοδος, -ου, ἡ	departure, way out
ἑορτή, -ῆς, ἡ	feast, festival
ἐπάνω	over, more than; (+*gen*) above, higher than
ἐπιβλέπω	to look at (attentively), observe, anticipate
κινέω	to move, disturb
κτῆσις, -εως, ἡ	acquisition, property
μεγαλύνω	to enlarge, increase, magnify
μιαίνω	to make unclean, defile, pollute
μόσχος, -ου, ὁ	calf, young bull
νεότης, -ητος, ἡ	youth
περιάργυρος, -ος, -ον	overlaid with silver
περίζωμα, -ατος, τό	apron, skirt
περίχρυσος, -ος, -ον	overlaid with gold, gilded

▷ List 15 — 7 to 6×

ἁγιάζω	to make holy, consecrate, sanctify
πέτρα, -ας, ἡ	rock, stone, cave
ποιμαίνω	to shepherd, tend
ποτίζω	to give drink to, water
πρότερος, -α, -ον	former, earlier, before
σάλπιγξ, -ιγγος, ἡ	trumpet, horn
σπένδω	to pour out (as an offering)
σπονδή, -ῆς, ἡ	drink offering
στῦλος, -ου, ὁ	pillar, column
σφαγή, -ῆς, ἡ	slaughter, destruction
ταλαιπωρία, -ας, ἡ	misery, hardship, distress
τέταρτος, -η, -ον	fourth
ὕβρις, -εως, ἡ	arrogance, insult, insolence
χρηστός, -ή, -όν	kind, fine (quality), pleasant
χρυσοῦς, -ῆ, -οῦν / χρύσεος, -α, -ον	golden; (*subst*) golden coin

▷ List 16 — 6×

ἄμπελος, -ου, ἡ	vine, vineyard
ἀμπελών, -ῶνος, ὁ	vineyard
ἀναλαμβάνω	to take up, carry, assume
ἀνατολή, -ῆς, ἡ	sprouting, rising; morning; (*pl*) east
ἀνθίστημι	to resist, oppose
ἀνοικοδομέω	to rebuild, restore
ἀποικισμός, -οῦ, ὁ	captivity, exile
ἀποκαθίστημι	to restore, put back, pay
ἀργυροῦς, -ᾶ, -οῦν	(made of) silver
ἀσεβέω	to act wickedly, be ungodly
βασίλισσα, -ης, ἡ	queen
βραχίων, -ονος, ὁ	arm, (strength)
βωμός, -οῦ, ὁ	altar (typically pagan)
δέησις, -εως, ἡ	supplication, request
δέκατος, -η, -ον	tenth; (*subst*) tithe

▹ List 17 — 6×

διαλείπω	to wait (for a period), stop (temporarily)
διαρ(ρ)ήγνυμι *or* διαρ(ρ)ήσσω	to tear, divide, break through
δικαίωμα, -ατος, τό	ordinance, decree, rightful claim
ἐκκλίνω	to bend, turn away; (*intr*) to avoid, deviate
ἐκκόπτω	to cut off, do away with
ἐκλύω	to loosen; (*mid*) to grow weak, tire out
ἐντείνω	to stretch tight, bend
ἐνύπνιον, -ου, τό	dream
ἐρήμωσις, -εως, ἡ	desolation
θάπτω	to bury
θηρεύω	to hunt, chase, catch
θρῆνος, -ου, ὁ	lamentation, wailing
καθά	as, just as
καταδιώκω	to seek eagerly, chase down
κατακρύπτω	to hide, conceal

▹ List 18 — 6×

καταλαμβάνω	to take hold of, overtake, capture
κατασκάπτω	to destroy, burn to the ground
κενός, -ή, -όν	empty, worthless, pointless
κοιλία, -ας, ἡ	belly, stomach, womb
κολλάω	to join together, adhere to
κριός, -οῦ, ὁ	ram
μακρόθεν	from a distance, from far off
μανθάνω	to learn, find out
μεγιστάν, -ᾶνος, ὁ	noble, magistrate, influential person
μερίς, -ίδος, ἡ	share, part, portion
μοιχάομαι	to commit adultery, be sexually unfaithful
νεφέλη, -ης, ἡ	cloud
νοέω	to understand, perceive
νύμφη, -ης, ἡ	bride, daughter-in-law
ὁλοκαύτωμα, -ατος, τό	whole burnt offering

▷ LIST 19 — 6×

ὅπλον, -ου, τό	weapon; (*pl*) arms, armor
ὄρθρος, -ου, ὁ	early morning, dawn
ὀρφανός, -ή, -όν	orphaned (person)
ὀχυρός, -ά, -όν	secure, fortified, firm
ὀχύρωμα, -ατος, τό	stronghold, fortress
παιδεύω	to instruct, discipline
παραπικραίνω	to provoke, infuriate
παροργίζω	to anger, provoke
πέραν	beyond; (+*gen*) on the other side
πλάσσω	to form, mold
σάκκος, -ου, ὁ	sackcloth
σοφός, -ή, -όν	wise, skilled, learned
συνετός, -ή, -όν	sensible, clever, intelligent
συντριβή, -ῆς, ἡ	breaking, damage
συρίζω	to hiss, whistle

▷ LIST 20 — 6 TO 5×

ἁγίασμα, -ατος, τό	sanctuary, sacred offering
ἀναπαύω	to stop, refresh, rest; to give rest
ἀποκαλύπτω	to uncover, reveal, disclose
ἀσεβής, -ής, -ές	ungodly, wicked, sacrilegious
ἀφαιρέω	to separate, remove; (*mid*) to deprive, seize, take away
ἄφεσις, -εως, ἡ	forgiveness, release (from debt), outlet (of water)
βιβρώσκω	to consume, eat
βοήθεια, -ας, ἡ	help, support
γλυπτός, -ή, -όν	carved, graven; [τὸ γλύπτον] graven image
διασῴζω	to preserve, keep safe; (*pas*) to be spared, escape
διατίθημι	to treat; (*mid*) to grant, arrange
ταλαιπωρέω	to endure hardship, suffer distress
ὕστερος, -α, -ον	later, afterward
φίλος, -η, -ον	friendly; (*subst*) friend, associate
ὡσεί	as (if), like, approximately

▷ List 21 5×

ἐκζητέω	to search for, seek out, demand
ἐμβάλλω	to throw in, put inside
ἐμπυρίζω	to set on fire, burn
ἔναντι	(+*gen*) opposite, before, in the presence of
ἔνατος, -η, -ον	ninth
ἐνδύω	to dress, clothe
ἕνεκα *or* ἕνεκεν/εἵνεκεν	(+*gen*) on account of, because of
ἐξεγείρω	to awake, rouse, raise
ἐξίστημι	to amaze, overwhelm, confuse
ἐπέρχομαι	to come upon, happen upon, attack
ἐπικατάρατος, -ος, -ον	cursed
ἐπιλαμβάνω	to catch, grab, obtain
ἐπίσταμαι	to know, be acquainted with
εὐλαβέομαι	to be concerned, be afraid, show respect
ἐγγύς	(+gen) *near, close to*

▷ List 22 5×

θηλάζω	to nurse, suckle
ἵλεως, -ως, -ων	gracious, merciful
κακόω	to do wrong, mistreat
κατάρα, -ας, ἡ	curse
κυριεύω	to rule over, dominate, control
λυπέω	to vex, displease; (*mid/pas*) to be distressed, grieve
λυτρόω	(*mid*) to redeem, ransom
νεφρός, -οῦ, ὁ	kidney, heart (as seat of emotions)
νῆσος, -ου, ἡ	island
ξυράω	to shave
παγίς, -ίδος, ἡ	trap, snare
παιδίσκη, -ης, ἡ	young woman, female servant
καυχάομαι	*to boast (about)*
μάρτυς, -υρος, ὁ	*witness*
παραλαμβάνω	*to receive, take along*

▷ List 23 5×

παραπορεύομαι	to pass by, travel along, overlook
πάροικος, -ος, -ον	strange, alien; (*subst*) foreigner
περιζώννυμι *or* περιζωννύω	to wrap around, put on
περιτίθημι	to put on, put around
πηγή, -ῆς, ἡ	spring, fountain
πῆχυς, -εως, ὁ	cubit, (length of the) forearm
πολεμιστής, -οῦ, ὁ	combatant, warrior
πονηρεύομαι	to act wickedly, behave evilly
πότε	when?, how long?
πρεσβύτης, -ου, ὁ	old man, elder
προνομή, -ῆς, ἡ	spoils (of war), plunder
σκιά, -ᾶς, ἡ	shadow
σός, σή, σόν	your, yours
σπήλαιον, -ου, τό	cave
σύνεσις, -εως, ἡ	understanding, intelligence

▷ List 24 5×

συνίημι	to understand, notice, ponder
ταράσσω	to trouble, disturb
ὑετός, -οῦ, ὁ	rain
ὑπακούω	to obey, comply (with)
ὑπομένω	to remain, endure, wait for
ὕψος, -ους, τό	height, summit
ὑψόω	to lift up, raise high, exalt
φάραγξ, -αγγος, ἡ	ravine, valley
ὠδίν, -ῖνος, ἡ	pains of childbirth, birth pangs
ὡσαύτως	in the same way, similarly

EZEKIEL

▹ List 1 — 96 to 33×

ἀδικία, -ας, ἡ	unrighteousness, wrongdoing, injustice
ἀνατολή, -ῆς, ἡ	sprouting, rising; morning; (*pl*) east
ἀνομία, -ας, ἡ	lawlessness, wrongful conduct
αὐλή, -ῆς, ἡ	court, courtyard
βορέας, -ου, ἡ / βορρᾶς, -ᾶ, ἡ	north
εἴκοσι	twenty
ἔνθεν	from here; on one side . . . on the other side
εὖρος, -ους, τό	breadth, width
κύκλῳ	(*dat of* κύκλος) (all) around, surrounding
μάχαιρα, -ας, ἡ	sword, dagger
μῆκος, -ους, τό	length, end-to-end measurement
ὅρασις, -εως, ἡ	seeing, appearance, (prophetic) vision
πῆχυς, -εως, ὁ	cubit, (length of the) forearm
προφητεύω	to prophesy
ῥομφαία, -ας, ἡ	sword

▹ List 2 — 32 to 24×

αιλαμ, τό (*translit*)	porch
βεβηλόω	to profane, desecrate
διαμετρέω	to measure (out)
εἰσάγω	to bring in, lead in, introduce
ἐκχέω	to pour out, spill
ἐξαίρω	to raise up, remove, pack up camp and go
κυκλόθεν	all around, from all sides
μέτρον, -ου, τό	measurement, dimension, rule
μιαίνω	to make unclean, defile, pollute
νότος, -ου, ὁ	south (wind)
πεδίον, -ου, τό	plain, field, level area
ποταμός, -οῦ, ὁ	river, stream
τραυματίας, -ου, ὁ	wounded person, casualty
τροχός, -οῦ, ὁ	wheel
χερουβ, τό (*translit*)	cherub

▷ LIST 3	23 TO 19×
ἀδελφή, -ῆς, ἡ	sister, beloved woman
ἀπαρχή, -ῆς, ἡ	first portion, firstfruits
ἀφηγέομαι	to be leader
εἰσπορεύομαι	to go in, enter
ἐξέδρα, -ας, ἡ	hall, arcade
ἐσώτερος, -α, -ον	inner, inside
ἥκω	to have come, reach, be present
κρίμα, -ατος, τό	decision, judgment, punishment
παραπικραίνω	to provoke, infuriate
πορνεία, -ας, ἡ	sexual immorality, prostitution, fornication
πτέρυξ, -υγος, ἡ	wing
συντελέω	to finish, complete, accomplish
τοῖχος, -ου, ὁ	wall
τρόπος, -ου, ὁ	manner, way, conduct
χώρα, -ας, ἡ	country, land, region

▷ LIST 4	19 TO 17×
αἰχμαλωσία, -ας, ἡ	captivity, (group of) captives
ἄνομος, -ος, -ον	lawless, wicked
ἀσέβεια, -ας, ἡ	ungodliness, wickedness
ἐκδίκησις, -εως, ἡ	vengeance, punishment
ἐκτείνω	to stretch out, reach out, extend
ἐνθύμημα, -ατος, τό	argument, reasoning; invention
ἐξάγω	to lead out, take out, bring out
ἐξώτερος, -α, -ον	outermost
κάλαμος, -ου, ὁ	reed
κατάσχεσις, -εως, ἡ	possession
ὁλοκαύτωμα, -ατος, τό	whole burnt offering
πλάτος, -ους, τό	breadth, width
πληθύνω	to increase, multiply
πρόσταγμα, -ατος, τό	ordinance, command
συντρίβω	to break, crush, wreck

▷ List 5 — 17 to 15×

ἁγιάζω	to make holy, consecrate, sanctify
αιλαμμω, τό (*translit*)	(its) porch
ἀφανίζω	to cause to vanish, destroy
βδέλυγμα, -ατος, τό	abomination, detestable object
διασπείρω	to scatter, spread around
δικαίωμα, -ατος, τό	ordinance, decree, rightful claim
ἑκατόν	one hundred
ἐκπορνεύω	to commit sexual immorality
ἔλαιον, -ου, τό	(olive) oil
ἐπάγω	to bring (up)on
ἐρημόω	to make desolate, dry up
λειτουργέω	to serve (as priest), minister
πεντακόσιοι, -αι, -α	five hundred
πεντήκοντα	fifty
ποιμήν, -ένος, ὁ	shepherd

▷ List 6 — 15 to 13×

διασκορπίζω	to scatter, disperse
ἐμπί(μ)πλημι	to fill up, satisfy; [ἐ. τὰς χεῖρας] to consecrate as priest
ἐνδύω	to dress, clothe
θύρωμα, -ατος, τό	doorway, panel
κατέναντι	(+*gen*) in front of, opposite, against
κληρονομία, -ας, ἡ	inheritance, possession(s)
κριός, -οῦ, ὁ	ram
κτῆνος, -ους, τό	(domesticated) animal; (*pl*) herd, cattle
μόσχος, -ου, ὁ	calf, young bull
νεφέλη, -ης, ἡ	cloud
ὁμοίωμα, -ατος, τό	similarity, likeness, representation
ὀστοῦν, -οῦ, τό	bone
πίμπλημι	to fill, satisfy
ῥάβδος, -ου, ἡ	rod, staff, scepter
ὑψηλός, -ή, -όν	elevated, proud; (*subst*) high place

▷ List 7 — 13 to 12×

ἄμωμος, -ος, -ον	unblemished, spotless
ἀναλαμβάνω	to take up, carry, assume
ἀπερίτμητος, -ος, -ον	uncircumcised
ἀπωθέω	to thrust away, drive back, reject
εἴδωλον, -ου, τό	image (of a god), idol
ἔμπορος, -ου, ὁ	trader, merchant
ἕξ	six
ἐξαποστέλλω	to dispatch, dismiss, permit to leave
ἐπιτήδευμα, -ατος, τό	intentional pursuit, consistent practice
ζῷον, -ου, τό	living thing, creature
θεε (*translit*)	niche, alcove
κοιμάω	(*mid*) to lie (down), sleep; [κ. +μετά] to have sexual intercourse
λιμός, -οῦ, ὁ	hunger, famine
μιμνῄσκομαι	to remember, recall
ὀσφύς, -ύος, ἡ	loins, waist

▷ List 8 — 12 to 11×

ἀκαθαρσία, -ας, ἡ	uncleanness, impurity
ἀπώλεια, -ας, ἡ	destruction, ruin, loss
βόσκω	to feed, graze
διαστέλλω	to distinguish, separate, state precisely; (*mid*) to command
ἔσωθεν	(from) within, inside
θυρίς, -ίδος, ἡ	window
ἵππος, -ου, ὁ	horse
ἴσος, -η, -ον	equal, same
κάλλος, -ους, τό	beauty
καταβάλλω	to throw down, overthrow, ruin
νῶτος/ον, -ου, ὁ/τό	back, rear surface
πέμμα, -ατος, τό	cake, baked good
πρόθυρον, -ου, τό	doorway
ὑψόω	to lift up, raise high, exalt
φοῖνιξ, -ικος, ὁ	palm tree *or* leaf

▷ **List 9**	**11 to 10×**
ἀνάγω	to lead up, bring up, raise up
ἀποκαλύπτω	to uncover, reveal, disclose
ἀπόλοιπον, -ου, τό	remaining (space)
ἅρπαγμα, -ατος, τό	prey, spoils
βραχίων, -ονος, ὁ	arm, (strength)
διάστημα, -ατος, τό	space, (architectural) opening
ἐκδικέω	to avenge, punish
ἐκζητέω	to search for, seek out, demand
ἐξολεθρεύω	to utterly destroy, eradicate
ἔξωθεν	outside; (+*gen*) from outside
ἑορτή, -ῆς, ἡ	feast, festival
ἡγέομαι	to go before, guide, act as leader, think, consider
θρῆνος, -ου, ὁ	lamentation, wailing
τάσσω	to position, appoint; (*mid*) to indicate
ὑποκάτω	(+*gen*) under, below

▷ **List 10**	**10 to 9×**
ἀφανισμός, -οῦ, ὁ	disappearance, annihilation
βόθρος, -ου, ὁ	ditch, pit
ἐξιλάσκομαι	to propitiate, make atonement
καλύπτω	to cover, conceal
κατάλοιπος, -ος, -ον	left over; (*subst*) rest, remainder
λέων, -οντος, ὁ	lion
μάταιος, -α/ος, -ον	vain, pointless, worthless
νόμιμος, -η/ος, -ον	lawful; (*subst*) ordinance, statute
παράπτωμα, -ατος, τό	mistake, error
περικύκλῳ	in a circle, on all sides, all around
πετεινός, -ή, -όν	winged; (*subst*) bird
πλευρόν, -οῦ, τό	side
προνομή, -ῆς, ἡ	spoils (of war), plunder
στηρίζω	to support, strengthen, establish
φείδομαι	to spare, refrain, hold back

▷ List 11 — 9 to 8×

αἴθριος, -ος, -ον	in the open air; (*subst*) main hall
ἀμνός, -οῦ, ὁ	lamb
ἀνασῴζω	to deliver, rescue, preserve
ἁρπάζω	to snatch, carry off
ἀφίστημι	to keep away, remove; (*mid*) to depart, withdraw
δέκατος, -η, -ον	tenth; (*subst*) tithe
πλήρης, -ης, -ες	full, complete
σύμμικτος, -ος, -ον	intermingled, variegated, mixed
σφάζω	to slaughter, slay
τέταρτος, -η, -ον	fourth
τράπεζα, -ης, ἡ	table
ὑετός, -οῦ, ὁ	rain
ὕψος, -ους, τό	height, summit
φάραγξ, -αγγος, ἡ	ravine, valley
χρυσίον, -ου, τό	gold

▷ List 12 — 8 to 7×

αἰσχύνη, -ης, ἡ	shame, disgrace
ἀλείφω	to anoint, smear, apply
ἄμπελος, -ου, ἡ	vine, vineyard
εἴσοδος, -ου, ἡ	entering, entryway, area of entrance
κατεσθίω	to eat up, devour
κόπτω	to cut, strike; (*mid*) to mourn
μαναα, τό (*translit*)	gift, offering
νῆσος, -ου, ἡ	island
πέμπτος, -η, -ον	fifth
πέρας, -ατος, τό	limit, end
περιβάλλω	to put around, cover, clothe
πλησίον	(+*gen*) near, close; (*subst*) neighbor
σκυλεύω	to plunder, spoil, strip (of goods)
τεῖχος, -ους, τό	(city) wall
ψευδής, -ής, -ές	lying, false; (*subst*) liar

▹ List 13 7×

ἀναμιμνῄσκω	to remind; (*pas*) to remember
ἀπέναντι *or* ἀπεναντίον	(+*gen*) opposite, contrary to, against
ἀσεβής, -ής, -ές	ungodly, wicked, sacrilegious
βάθος, -ους, τό	depth, bottom
βάσανος, -ου, ἡ	torment, (instrument of) torture
βουνός, -οῦ, ὁ	hill
διορίζω	to distinguish, separate, divide
ἐκλεκτός, -ή, -όν	chosen, select, elite
ἐμπορία, -ας, ἡ	business, merchandise
ἕνεκα *or* ἕνεκεν/εἵνεκεν	(+*gen*) on account of, because of
ἐπίλεκτος, -ος, -ον	chosen
ἰχθύς, -ύος, ὁ	fish
κατάβρωμα, -ατος, τό	food, that which is eaten
καταδυναστεύω	to oppress, prevail against
κατοικίζω	to settle (a group), establish (residency)

▹ List 14 7×

κρέας, κρέως, τό	meat
μαντεύομαι	to practice divination, prophesy
μέγεθος, -ους, τό	greatness, size, significance
μίσθωμα, -ατος, τό	price (of hire), payment
ὀκτώ	eight
ὄψις, -εως, ἡ	appearance, face, perception
περίστυλον, -ου, τό	colonnade
πλατύς, -εῖα, -ύ	wide, broad; [*fem subst* πλατεῖα] street, square
προνομεύω	to plunder, despoil
πρωί	in the morning; (*subst*) morning
πτῶσις, -εως, ἡ	fall, downfall, calamity
ῥύομαι	to rescue, save
στολή, -ῆς, ἡ	robe, cloak
τεσσαράκοντα	forty
ὑποκάτωθεν	from beneath; (+*gen*) under

▷ List 15 — 7 to 6×

ἀλλότριος, -α, -ον	foreign, strange, unfamiliar
ἀναπαύω	to stop, refresh, rest; to give rest
ἀναστρέφω	to return, change course; (*mid*) to conduct oneself, live
ἀπορ(ρ)ίπτω	to throw away, discard, reject
ἀριθμός, -οῦ, ὁ	number, total
ἀτιμία, -ας, ἡ	shame, dishonor
ἀφαιρέω	to separate, remove; (*mid*) to deprive, seize, take away
γίγας, -αντος, ὁ	giant, mighty person
γυμνός, -ή, -όν	naked
διαστρέφω	to turn, divert, mislead, pervert
δρυμός, -οῦ, ὁ	forest, thicket
ἐγκαταλείπω	to abandon, leave behind
φέγγος, -ους, τό	light, splendor
ὦμος, -ου, ὁ	shoulder
ἄνεμος, -ου, ὁ	*wind*

▷ List 16 — 6×

εἰσακούω	to hear, listen to, obey
εἰσδέχομαι	to receive, welcome
ἐκλείπω	to abandon, neglect; (*intr*) to fail, run out, cease
ἐξίστημι	to amaze, overwhelm, confuse
ἐπάνω	over, more than; (+*gen*) above, higher than
ἐραστής, -οῦ, ὁ	admirer, lover
ζῆλος, -ου, ὁ	jealousy, zeal
θρηνέω	to lament, mourn, wail
ιν (*translit*)	hin (liquid measure)
ἱππεύς, -έως, ὁ	rider, cavalryman
κατευθύνω	to direct, guide; (*pas*) to prosper
καύχησις, -εως, ἡ	(reason for) boasting, pride
κλάδος, -ου, ὁ	branch (of a plant)
κλείω	to shut, close
κλιμακτήρ, -ῆρος, ὁ	step (of a stairway)

▷ List 17 — 6×

κόλασις, -εως, ἡ	punishment, vengeance
κωπηλάτης, -ου, ὁ	rower, oarsman
λοιμός, -οῦ, ὁ	pestilence, (public) nuisance
μέλι, -ιτος, τό	honey
νομή, -ῆς, ἡ	pasture, feeding area
ξηραίνω	to dry up, make dry
παραβαίνω	to deviate, turn away
παράπαν	absolutely, entirely
πλευρά, -ᾶς, ἡ	side; rib
προσήλυτος, -ου, ὁ	immigrant, foreign guest
πυλών, -ῶνος, ὁ	gate, porch
ῥίζα, -ης, ἡ	root
σκῦλον, -ου, τό	plunder, spoils
σωτήριον, -ου, τό	salvation, (offering for) deliverance
τετρακισχίλιοι, -αι, -α	four thousand

▷ List 18 — 6 to 5×

ἁγίασμα, -ατος, τό	sanctuary, sacred offering
ἄνθραξ, -ακος, ὁ	coal, precious dark red stone
ἅρμα, -ατος, τό	chariot
ἀφορίζω	to separate, mark out; (*mid*) to split
βοῦς, βοός, ὁ/ἡ	ox, cow
διαπορεύομαι	to go through, pass by, walk about
δόμα, -ατος, τό	gift
ἕβδομος, -η, -ον	seventh
ἕκτος, -η, -ον	sixth
ἐκφέρω	to bring out, produce
ἐξαιρέω	to take out, remove; (*mid*) to set free
ἐπιβλέπω	to look at (attentively), observe, anticipate
ἐπιστήμη, -ης, ἡ	skill, competence, understanding
τρυφή, -ῆς, ἡ	delight, luxury
δικαιόω	*to justify, vindicate, pronounce righteous*

▷ List 19 — 5×

ἑσπέρα, -ας, ἡ	evening
κακία, -ας, ἡ	evil, harm, misfortune
κατακαίω	to burn up, consume
κατακληρονομέω	to give as inheritance, become owner, dispossess
καταλύω	to lodge, bring down, destroy
κατοικία, -ας, ἡ	dwelling place, settlement
κέρας, κέρατος, τό	horn, flank (of an army)
κλίτος, -ους, τό	side
λέβης, -ητος, ὁ	cauldron, kettle
μισθός, -οῦ, ὁ	payment, wages, reward
νεανίσκος, -ου, ὁ	young man
νεότης, -ητος, ἡ	youth
ξηρός, -ά, -όν	dry, withered, arid
ὀνειδισμός, -οῦ, ὁ	disgrace, insult
καινός, -ή, -όν	*new*

▷ List 20 — 5×

πόρνη, -ης, ἡ	prostitute, harlot
σάλπιγξ, -ιγγος, ἡ	trumpet, horn
στερέωμα, -ατος, τό	firmness, strength; firmament
συντέλεια, -ας, ἡ	end, conclusion, perfection; annihilation
ταράσσω	to trouble, disturb
τελευτάω	to die
ὕβρις, -εως, ἡ	arrogance, insult, insolence
χαλκός, -οῦ, ὁ	bronze, brass, copper
χεῖλος, -ους, τό	lip, language, edge
ὦ	O!, oh!
οὐαί	*woe!, ah!*

DANIEL (OG & Θ, INCL. ADDITIONS)

▷ List 1	37 to 19×
ἀναγγέλλω	to report, announce, publicize
γνωρίζω	to make known, publicize
διανοέομαι	to plan (an action), intend (to do), ponder
ἐνύπνιον, -ου, τό	dream
κάμινος, -ου, ἡ	oven, furnace
κέρας, κέρατος, τό	horn, flank (of an army)
λάκκος, -ου, ὁ	pit, cistern, cavity
ὅραμα, -ατος, τό	vision, (object of) sight
ὅρασις, -εως, ἡ	seeing, appearance, (prophetic) vision
σύγκρισις, -εως, ἡ	interpretation, assessment, decision
συνίημι	to understand, notice, ponder
συντέλεια, -ας, ἡ	end, conclusion, perfection, annihilation
ὑμνέω	to sing praise to, sing a hymn
ὑπερυψόω	to raise to the highest, exceedingly exalt
χώρα, -ας, ἡ	country, land, region

▷ List 2	19 to 13×
ἀλλοιόω	to change, alter
ἀφίστημι	to keep away, remove; (*mid*) to depart, withdraw
δηλόω	to disclose, make (oneself) clear, show
εἰκών, -όνος, ἡ	image, (idol)
ἐμβάλλω	to throw in, put inside
ἰσχυρός, -ά, -όν	strong, powerful
καθίστημι	to place, appoint, establish; (*mid*) to stand against
κατισχύω	to strengthen, overpower; (*intr*) to be encouraged, become powerful
λέων, -οντος, ὁ	lion
μεγαλύνω	to enlarge, increase, magnify
πρόσταγμα, -ατος, τό	ordinance, command
σοφός, -ή, -όν	wise, skilled, learned
ὕψιστος, -η, -ον	highest, most high (God)
χρυσοῦς, -ῆ, -οῦν / χρύσεος, -α, -ον	golden; (*subst*) golden coin
ὡσεί	as (if), like, approximately

▷ List 3 — 12 to 10×

ἀποκαλύπτω	to uncover, reveal, disclose
βορέας, -ου, ὁ / βορρᾶς, -ᾶ, ὁ	north
διαφθείρω	to utterly destroy, ruin
δόγμα, -ατος, τό	decree
ἐξαιρέω	to take out, remove; (*mid*) to set free
καίω	to light (a flame), burn
κυριεύω	to rule over, dominate, control
νότος, -ου, ὁ	south (wind)
παράδεισος, -ου, ὁ	orchard, enclosed garden
ῥίπτω	to throw (away), defeat, reject
σιδηροῦς, -ᾶ, -οῦν	(made of) iron
σύνεσις, -εως, ἡ	understanding, intelligence
συντρίβω	to break, crush, wreck
ὑποδείκνυμι *or* ὑποδεικνύω	to demonstrate, inform, point out
ἐπιθυμία, -ας, ἡ	*desire, lust*

▷ List 4 — 10 to 8×

αἰνέω	to praise
ἅμα	at once, together
ἀξιόω	to deem worthy, place a request upon, entreat
δέομαι	to ask (for), pray (for)
ἐπέρχομαι	to come upon, happen upon, attack
κριός, -οῦ, ὁ	ram
λατρεύω	to serve, perform cultic duties (for)
λεπτύνω	to pulverize, crush, grind to dust
μυστήριον, -ου, τό	mystery, secret, rite
πέρας, -ατος, τό	limit, end
προστάσσω	to command, order
σίδηρος, -ου, ὁ	iron (tool)
σύγκριμα, -ατος, τό	decree; interpretation; (musical) concert
ὑψόω	to lift up, raise high, exalt
φθάνω	to come before; to overtake, reach

▷ **List 5**	**8×**
βασίλειον, -ου, τό	royal palace, kingdom
βραχίων, -ονος, ὁ	arm, (strength)
δένδρον, -ου, τό	tree
δεσπότης, -ου, ὁ	master, absolute ruler
δρόσος, -ου, ἡ	dew
ἑβδομάς, -άδος, ἡ	period of seven days *or* years; seven-member grouping
εἰσάγω	to bring in, lead in, introduce
εἰσπορεύομαι	to go in, enter
ἐξομολογέω	to acknowledge, admit, confess
ἥκω	to have come, reach, be present
ἰσχύω	to be strong, be capable; (*trans*) to intensify
κατέναντι	(+*gen*) in front of, opposite, against
μάγος, -ου, ὁ	priestly sage, astrologer, enchanter
μεγιστάν, -ᾶνος, ὁ	noble, magistrate, influential person
νεανίσκος, -ου, ὁ	young man

▷ **List 6**	**8 to 7×**
αἰχμαλωσία, -ας, ἡ	captivity, (group of) captives
ἀναιρέω	to get rid of, destroy; (*mid*) to take up
ἀρχιευνοῦχος, -ου, ὁ	chief eunuch
βασιλικός, -ή, -όν	royal, belonging to the king
βοάω	to cry out, shout
εἴδωλον, -ου, τό	image (of a god), idol
εἰσακούω	to hear, listen to, obey
ὁρισμός, -οῦ, ὁ	oath, decree, obligation
πρᾶγμα, -ατος, τό	thing, matter, affair, deed
πρωΐ	in the morning; (*subst*) morning
σοφιστής, -οῦ, ὁ	wise man, diviner, expert
σφραγίζω	to seal, authenticate (with a seal)
τέταρτος, -η, -ον	fourth
τράπεζα, -ης, ἡ	table
χαλκοῦς, -ῆ, -οῦν	(made of) bronze

▷ List 7 — 7 to 6×

ἄγνοια, -ας, ἡ	ignorance; sin of ignorance
ἀληθινός, -ή, -όν	true, genuine
ἀναβοάω	to cry out
ἐξάγω	to lead out, take out, bring out
ἐπαοιδός, -οῦ, ὁ	enchanter
ἐρήμωσις, -εως, ἡ	desolation
εὐοδόω	to lead safely, ensure success, grant; (*pas*) to prosper
ἡγέομαι	to go before, guide, act as leader, think, consider
νέος, -α, -ον	new, young; (*subst*) child
ποταμός, -οῦ, ὁ	river, stream
πρεσβύτης, -ου, ὁ	old man, elder
ῥύομαι	to rescue, save
σατράπης, -ου, ὁ	governor, satrap
σέβομαι	to worship, revere
παραλαμβάνω	*to receive, take along*

▷ List 8 — 6×

διαλογισμός, -οῦ, ὁ	deliberation, thought, discussion
δυνάστης, -ου, ὁ	ruler, master, official
ἔνδοξος, -ος, -ον	reputable, honored, distinguished
ἐνδύω	to dress, clothe
ἐπάγω	to bring (up)on
ἐπάνω	over, more than; (+*gen*) above, higher than
ἐπιτάσσω	to command, provide instruction
εὐλογητός, -ή, -όν	praised, blessed
καθάπερ	just as
κατευθύνω	to direct, guide; (*pas*) to prosper
κοίτη, -ης, ἡ	bed; sexual intercourse, ejaculation
κρίμα, -ατος, τό	decision, judgment, punishment
κυριεία, -ας, ἡ	power, authority, dominion
οἰκτιρμός, -οῦ, ὁ	compassion, pity
ἀσθενέω	*to be weak, become less functional*

▹ List 9 6×

ὀπτασία, -ας, ἡ	vision, appearance
ὄστρακον, -ου, τό	piece of pottery
παιδάριον, -ου, τό	child, little boy, servant
παρέρχομαι	to go past, pass by, move on
ῥίζα, -ης, ἡ	root
συμπατέω	to trample (on)
συντελέω	to finish, complete, accomplish
τράγος, -ου, ὁ	(male) goat
τριάκοντα	thirty
τρίς	three times
ὕπνος, -ου, ὁ	sleep
ὑποκάτω	(+*gen*) under, below
φθείρω	to corrupt, ruin
φλόξ, φλογός, ἡ	flame
τιμή, -ῆς, ἡ	*honor, value, price*

▹ List 10 5×

ἄγριος, -α, -ον	wild, fierce
αἰσχύνη, -ης, ἡ	shame, disgrace
ἀνομέω	to act lawlessly, be wicked
ἀπώλεια, -ας, ἡ	destruction, ruin, loss
ἀργυροῦς, -ᾶ, -οῦν	(made of) silver
γαζαρηνός, -οῦ, ὁ	soothsayer, astrologer
γένος, -ους, τό	kind, people group, family (lineage)
δέησις, -εως, ἡ	supplication, request
δόλος, -ου, ὁ	deceit, dishonesty, craftiness
δράκων, -οντος, ὁ	dragon, large serpent
ἑβδομήκοντα	seventy
ἐνιαυτός, -οῦ, ὁ	year
ἐνισχύω	to strengthen, grow strong(er), prevail (over)
ἀναγινώσκω	*to read (aloud)*
ἄνεμος, -ου, ὁ	*wind*

▷ List 11 — 5×

ἐξαίρω	to raise up, remove, pack up camp and go
εὔχομαι	to pray, vow
κατεσθίω	to eat up, devour
κατοικία, -ας, ἡ	dwelling place, settlement
μεγαλωσύνη, -ης, ἡ	majesty, greatness
μεθίστημι	to remove, deprive of, change
μορφή, -ῆς, ἡ	shape, appearance
οἰκέω	to inhabit, live
ὀνειδισμός, -οῦ, ὁ	disgrace, insult
περισσός, -ή, -όν	more, remaining, excessive
πληθύνω	to increase, multiply
προσάγω	to bring to, approach
σπουδή, -ῆς, ἡ	haste, hurry, exertion
στρατηγός, -οῦ, ὁ	commander, captain
συνταράσσω	to throw into confusion, send into panic

▷ List 12 — 5 to 4×

ἀδικία, -ας, ἡ	unrighteousness, wrongdoing, injustice
ἀμφότεροι, -αι, -α	both
ἀνατολή, -ῆς, ἡ	sprouting, rising; morning; (*pl*) east
ἀνθίστημι	to resist, oppose
ἀνομία, -ας, ἡ	lawlessness, wrongful conduct
ἄνομος, -ος, -ον	lawless, wicked
ἀποκλείω	to shut, lock up, exclude
ἀποφέρω	to carry off
ταπεινόω	to bring down, humiliate, humble
ταράσσω	to trouble, disturb
φίλος, -η, -ον	friendly; (*subst*) friend, associate
χαλκός, -οῦ, ὁ	bronze, brass, copper
χίλιοι, -αι, -α	one thousand
χόρτος, -ου, ὁ	grass, hay
χρυσίον, -ου, τό	gold

▷ List 13 4×

ἀρέσκω	to please, gain favor
βοηθέω	to help, aid
βουλεύω	to consider, resolve, counsel
βοῦς, βοός, ὁ/ἡ	ox, cow
δακτύλιος, -ου, ὁ	ring
δεῦρο	come!, go!
δῆμος, -ου, ὁ	crowd, populace, district
διαιρέω	to divide, split, dispense
ἐγκαταλείπω	to abandon, leave behind
ἐκκόπτω	to cut off, do away with
ἑξήκοντα	sixty
ἐπακούω	to hear, listen to, comply
θρίξ, τριχός, ἡ	hair
καθότι	as, insofar as, since
θαυμάζω	*to be astonished, marvel at*

▷ List 14 4×

καταλαμβάνω	to take hold of, overtake, capture
καταλείπω	to leave (behind), abandon; (*pas*) to remain
κινέω	to move, disturb
κλάδος, -ου, ὁ	branch (of a plant)
κριτής, -οῦ, ὁ	judge
κρύπτω	to hide, conceal
λυπέω	to vex, displease; (*mid/pas*) to be distressed, grieve
νεφέλη, -ης, ἡ	cloud
οἰκουμένη, -ης, ἡ	(inhabited) world, realm
ὄρνεον, -ου, τό	bird
οὐθείς, οὐθέν	no one, none, nothing
παρατίθημι	to set before, present; (*mid*) to entrust
πορφύρα, -ας, ἡ	(cloth of) purple (color)
πρότερος, -α, -ον	former, earlier, before
πράσσω	*to act, do, accomplish*

▷ List 15 — 4 to 3×

αἴξ, αἰγός, ὁ	goat
ἀλλάσσω	to alter, substitute, (take in) exchange
σάλπιγξ, -ιγγος, ἡ	trumpet, horn
στάσις, -εως, ἡ	standing, position; rebellion
συντηρέω	to preserve, defend, treasure up
τάσσω	to position, appoint; (*mid*) to indicate
τρόπος, -ου, ὁ	manner, way, conduct
ὑπολείπω	to leave remaining; (*mid*) to remain
ὑψηλός, -ή, -όν	elevated, proud; (*subst*) high place
ὕψος, -ους, τό	height, summit
φοβερός, -ά, -όν	intimidating, fearful, terrible
φρόνησις, -εως, ἡ	insight, understanding
χεῖλος, -ους, τό	lip, language, edge
ψευδής, -ής, -ές	lying, false; (*subst*) liar
φαίνω	*to shine;* (mid) *to appear, seem*

▷ List 16 — 3×

ἀναπαύω	to stop, refresh, rest; to give rest
ἀναστρέφω	to return, change course; (*mid*) to conduct oneself, live
ἄνευ	(+*gen*) without, far from
ἀνυψόω	to lift up, raise, exalt
ἀποτρέχω	to run away, depart
ἀριθμέω	to number, count
ἄστρον, -ου, τό	star
ἀφαιρέω	to separate, remove; (*mid*) to deprive, seize, take away
ἀφανίζω	to cause to vanish, destroy
βδέλυγμα, -ατος, τό	abomination, detestable object
βίβλος, -ου, ἡ	scroll, book, record
βουλή, -ῆς, ἡ	plan, advice, council
γόνυ, γόνατος, τό	knee
δάκτυλος, -ου, ὁ	finger
διάνοια, -ας, ἡ	mind, thought, understanding

▹ List 17 3×

δόμα, -ατος, τό	gift
δουλεύω	to serve (as a slave)
δυναστεία, -ας, ἡ	power, dominance
δυσμή, -ῆς, ἡ	(*always pl*) setting (of the sun), west
ἐάω	to permit, pass over, allow
εἴκοσι	twenty
εἰσφέρω	to lead in, bring in
ἐκκαίω	to inflame, kindle, burn
ἐκκλίνω	to bend, turn away; (*intr*) to avoid, deviate
ἔλαιον, -ου, τό	(olive) oil
ἐμπίπτω	to fall into, fall on, attack
ἕνεκα *or* ἕνεκεν/εἵνεκεν	(+*gen*) on account of, because of
ἕξ	six
ἐξεγείρω	to awake, rouse, raise
ἐπιπίπτω	to fall upon, embrace, attack

▹ List 18 3×

ἐπιστήμη, -ης, ἡ	skill, competence, understanding
ἐπισυνάγω	to bring together, gather up
ἐρημόω	to make desolate, dry up
ἑσπέρα, -ας, ἡ	evening
εὐφραίνω	to make happy, cheer; (*pas*) to rejoice
εὐχή, -ῆς, ἡ	prayer, vow
ἥμισυς, -εια, -υ	half
ἡνίκα	when
θαυμάσιος, -α, -ον	remarkable, amazing
θυμόω	to anger; (*pas*) to be(come) angry
ἴχνος, -ους, τό	footprint, track, sole (of the foot)
καταισχύνω	to put to shame, disappoint
καταπατέω	to walk all over, deal harshly with, oppress
καταστρέφω	to turn over, overthrow, ruin
κραταιός, -ά, -όν	powerful, forceful, severe

▷ List 19 3×

κύκλῳ	(*dat of* κύκλος) (all) around, surrounding
λυτρόω	(*mid*) to redeem, ransom
μιαίνω	to make unclean, defile, pollute
μιμνῄσκομαι	to remember, recall
μυριάς, -άδος, ἡ	ten thousand, countless number
ὀδούς, -όντος, ὁ	tooth
ὀργίζω	to make angry; (*pas*) to be angry
παλλακή, -ῆς, ἡ	concubine, mistress
περιτίθημι	to put on, put around
πετεινός, -ή, -όν	winged; (*subst*) bird
πῆχυς, -εως, ὁ	cubit, (length of the) forearm
πλήρης, -ης, -ες	full, complete
πότος, -ου, ὁ	drinking party
ὅμοιος, -α, -ον	*like, similar to*
πειρά(ζ)ω	*to tempt, test, try*

▷ List 20 3×

ῥομφαία, -ας, ἡ	sword
σπεύδω	to hasten, hurry
συλλαμβάνω	to capture, catch; to become pregnant
τράχηλος, -ου, ὁ	neck, throat
τρέχω	to run, advance
τύραννος, -ου, ὁ	sovereign ruler
ὑπολαμβάνω	to say in response, take up, consider
χράω	to use, employ; (*mid*) to treat (in a certain way)
χρῆμα, -ατος, τό	wealth, property
ψεύδομαι	to lie, speak deceitfully

TWELVE PROPHETS

▹ List 1 — 110 to 18×

ἀδικία, -ας, ἡ	unrighteousness, wrongdoing, injustice
ἀσέβεια, -ας, ἡ	ungodliness, wickedness
ἐκδικέω	to avenge, punish
ἐξαίρω	to raise up, remove, pack up camp and go
ἐξαποστέλλω	to dispatch, dismiss, permit to leave
ἐξολεθρεύω	to utterly destroy, eradicate
ἐπιβλέπω	to look at (attentively), observe, anticipate
ἥκω	to have come, reach, be present
ἵππος, -ου, ὁ	horse
κατάλοιπος, -ος, -ον	left over; (*subst*) rest, remainder
κατεσθίω	to eat up, devour
κρίμα, -ατος, τό	decision, judgment, punishment
παντοκράτωρ, -ορος, ὁ	ruler of all, almighty
ῥομφαία, -ας, ἡ	sword
τρόπος, -ου, ὁ	manner, way, conduct

▹ List 2 — 17 to 14×

αἰχμαλωσία, -ας, ἡ	captivity, (group of) captives
ἅρμα, -ατος, τό	chariot
ἀφανίζω	to cause to vanish, destroy
ἀφανισμός, -οῦ, ὁ	disappearance, annihilation
βουνός, -οῦ, ὁ	hill
εἰσακούω	to hear, listen to, obey
ἐκλείπω	to abandon, neglect; (*intr*) to fail, run out, cease
ἕνεκα *or* ἕνεκεν/εἵνεκεν	(+*gen*) on account of, because of
ἐξεγείρω	to awake, rouse, raise
κακία, -ας, ἡ	evil, harm, misfortune
λέων, -οντος, ὁ	lion
πλησίον	(+*gen*) near, close; (*subst*) neighbor
ποταμός, -οῦ, ὁ	river, stream
ὑπολείπω	to leave remaining; (*mid*) to remain
οὐαί	*woe!, ah!*

▷ **List 3**	**13 to 11×**
ἄμπελος, -ου, ἡ	vine, vineyard
ἐκζητέω	to search for, seek out, demand
ἐκχέω	to pour out, spill
ἑορτή, -ῆς, ἡ	feast, festival
εὐφραίνω	to make happy, cheer; (*pas*) to rejoice
ξηραίνω	to dry up, make dry
πεδίον, -ου, τό	plain, field, level area
πληθύνω	to increase, multiply
ποιμήν, -ένος, ὁ	shepherd
πορνεία, -ας, ἡ	sexual immorality, prostitution, fornication
σῖτος, -ου, ὁ	grain
τάσσω	to position, appoint; (*mid*) to indicate
χρυσίον, -ου, τό	gold
ψευδής, -ής, -ές	lying, false; (*subst*) liar
ἀσθενέω	*to be weak, become less functional*

▷ **List 4**	**11 to 10×**
ἀλλότριος, -α, -ον	foreign, strange, unfamiliar
ἀνταποδίδωμι	to give back, repay
ἀπορ(ρ)ίπτω	to throw away, discard, reject
ἀπωθέω	to thrust away, drive back, reject
ἔλαιον, -ου, τό	(olive) oil
θεμέλιον/ος, -ου, τό	foundation
καταισχύνω	to put to shame, disappoint
κτῆνος, -ους, τό	(domesticated) animal; (*pl*) herd, cattle
μάταιος, -α/ος, -ον	vain, pointless, worthless
μεγαλύνω	to enlarge, increase, magnify
μιμνῄσκομαι	to remember, recall
ὄμνυμι *or* ὀμνύω	to swear, take an oath
ὅρασις, -εως, ἡ	seeing, appearance, (prophetic) vision
ποίμνιον, -ου, τό	flock
προφητεύω	to prophesy

▷ **List 5**	**10 to 9×**
ἐγκαταλείπω	to abandon, leave behind
ἐλαία, -ας, ἡ	olive, olive tree
ἐμπί(μ)πλημι	to fill up, satisfy; [ἐ. τὰς χεῖρας] to consecrate as priest
ἐπέρχομαι	to come upon, happen upon, attack
ἐπιβαίνω	to get on, walk over, fall upon
ἐπιτήδευμα, -ατος, τό	intentional pursuit, consistent practice
θύω	to sacrifice, slaughter
κατασκηνόω	to dwell, settle
κατισχύω	to strengthen, overpower; (*intr*) to be encouraged, become powerful
συκῆ, -ῆς, ἡ	fig tree
συντέλεια, -ας, ἡ	end, conclusion, perfection, annihilation
συντρίβω	to break, crush, wreck
τεῖχος, -ους, τό	(city) wall
ὕβρις, -εως, ἡ	arrogance, insult, insolence
φεύγω	to flee, escape, vanish

▷ **List 6**	**9 to 8×**
ἀνάγω	to lead up, bring up, raise up
ἄνομος, -ος, -ον	lawless, wicked
βορέας, -ου, ἡ / βορρᾶς, -ᾶ, ἡ	north
διαρπάζω	to seize property, plunder
εἰσδέχομαι	to receive, welcome
εἰσπορεύομαι	to go in, enter
κέρας, κέρατος, τό	horn, flank (of an army)
κληρονομία, -ας, ἡ	inheritance, possession(s)
μαχητής, -οῦ, ὁ	fighter, warrior
νηστεία, -ας, ἡ	fast (from eating)
ποιμαίνω	to shepherd, tend
προσάγω	to bring to, approach
σείω	to shake, sway, stir up
τίκτω	to give birth to, bear, produce
ὑποκάτω	(+*gen*) under, below

▷ **List 7**	**8×**
ἐκκλίνω	to bend, turn away; (*intr*) to avoid, deviate
ἡγέομαι	to go before, guide, act as leader, think, consider
θρηνέω	to lament, mourn, wail
ἰσχυρός, -ά, -όν	strong, powerful
καταδυναστεύω	to oppress, prevail against
κατακληρονομέω	to give as inheritance, become owner, dispossess
κλῆρος, -ου, ὁ	lot, share, portion
κοπετός, -οῦ, ὁ	mourning, lamentation
κόπτω	to cut, strike; (*mid*) to mourn
μερίς, -ίδος, ἡ	share, part, portion
πίμπλημι	to fill, satisfy
ῥάβδος, -ου, ἡ	rod, staff, scepter
ταλαιπωρία, -ας, ἡ	misery, hardship, distress
ἐμαυτοῦ, -ῆς, -οῦ	*myself*
μετανοέω	*to repent, reconsider*

▷ **List 8**	**8 to 7×**
ἁγιάζω	to make holy, consecrate, sanctify
ἀκρίς, -ίδος, ἡ	locust, swarm of locusts
ἀνατολή, -ῆς, ἡ	sprouting, rising; morning; (*pl*) east
ἀνθίστημι	to resist, oppose
ἀνοικοδομέω	to rebuild, restore
ἁρπάζω	to snatch, carry off
διασῴζω	to preserve, keep safe; (*pas*) to be spared, escape
δουλεύω	to serve (as a slave)
εἴδωλον, -ου, τό	image (of a god), idol
ἐκπορνεύω	to commit sexual immorality
ἐκσπάω	to draw (a sword), pull out
ἐκτείνω	to stretch out, reach out, extend
τόξον, -ου, τό	bow (to shoot arrows)
ὦ	O!, oh!
ἐγγύς	(+gen) *near, close to*

▷ List 9 — 7×

ἐξαιρέω	to take out, remove; (*mid*) to set free
ἥμισυς, -εια, -υ	half
καλάμη, -ης, ἡ	straw, stalk (of grain or grass)
καλύπτω	to cover, conceal
καταλαμβάνω	to take hold of, overtake, capture
καταστρέφω	to turn over, overthrow, ruin
κοιλάς, -άδος, ἡ	valley
κοιλία, -ας, ἡ	belly, stomach, womb
κυκλόθεν	all around, from all sides
λῆμμα, -ατος, τό	profit, gain; (prophetic) statement
μέτρον, -ου, τό	measurement, dimension, rule
μιαίνω	to make unclean, defile, pollute
μισθός, -οῦ, ὁ	payment, wages, reward
ὀχύρωμα, -ατος, τό	stronghold, fortress
παρατάσσω	to form a battle line, battle

▷ List 10 — 7 to 6×

αἱρετίζω	to choose
αἰχμαλωτεύω	to take prisoner, deport
ἅλων, -ωνος, ὁ	threshing (floor)
πενθέω	to grieve, mourn
πρωί	in the morning; (*subst*) morning
σαλεύω	to shake, rock, disrupt
σάλπιγξ, -ιγγος, ἡ	trumpet, horn
σκύμνος, -ου, ὁ	cub, whelp (of a lion)
συντελέω	to finish, complete, accomplish
ταλαιπωρέω	to endure hardship, suffer distress
τετράς, -άδος, ἡ	fourth, fourth day
ὕψος, -ους, τό	height, summit
φείδομαι	to spare, refrain, hold back
χώρα, -ας, ἡ	country, land, region
ψεῦδος, -ους, τό	lie, falsehood

▷ LIST 11	6×
ἀνασῴζω	to deliver, rescue, preserve
ἀνατέλλω	to spring up, rise, appear
ἀποκαλύπτω	to uncover, reveal, disclose
βαρύνω	to make heavy, burden
βροῦχος, -ου, ὁ	locust
βρῶμα, -ατος, τό	food, provisions
διανοίγω	to open up, spread apart
διατίθημι	to treat; (*mid*) to grant, arrange
διαφθείρω	to utterly destroy, ruin
δρόσος, -ου, ἡ	dew
δρυμός, -οῦ, ὁ	forest, thicket
εἰκάς, -άδος, ἡ	twentieth day of the month
ἐξίστημι	to amaze, overwhelm, confuse
ἐπάγω	to bring (up)on
ἐπακούω	to hear, listen to, comply

▷ LIST 12	6×
ἐπιλανθάνω	(*mid*) to forget, overlook, ignore
ἐπισκέπτομαι	to visit, examine, account for
ἐπιφανής, -ής, -ές	glorious, distinguished
εὐλαβέομαι	to be concerned, be afraid, show respect
θαρσέω	to be courageous
θήρα, -ας, ἡ	hunting; prey, game; snare
ἰάομαι	to heal, cure, restore
ἱππεύς, -έως, ὁ	rider, cavalryman
καθότι	as, insofar as, since
κατάγω	to bring down, reduce
καταπατέω	to walk all over, deal harshly with, oppress
κόπος, -ου, ὁ	difficulty, trouble, toil
κραυγή, -ῆς, ἡ	outcry, shouting
κυκλόω	to encircle, surround
λυτρόω	(*mid*) to redeem, ransom

▷ List 13	6×
μόσχος, -ου, ὁ	calf, young bull
νέμω	to pasture, tend (livestock)
νεφέλη, -ης, ἡ	cloud
νομή, -ῆς, ἡ	pasture, feeding area
ὀδύνη, -ης, ἡ	pain, grief
ὀστοῦν, -οῦ, τό	bone
πέρας, -ατος, τό	limit, end
πόνος, -ου, ὁ	toil, distress, pain
πορεία, -ας, ἡ	journey, course, way
πορνεύω	to commit sexual immorality, act unfaithfully
προσδέχομαι	to accept, receive favorably, anticipate
σάκκος, -ου, ὁ	sackcloth
συγχέω	to confuse, mix up
ὑπομένω	to remain, endure, wait for
ὑφίστημι	to set up, stand (in place), resist

▷ List 14	6 to 5×
ᾅδης, -ου, ὁ	Hades, the underworld
αἰσχύνη, -ης, ἡ	shame, disgrace
ἀμπελών, -ῶνος, ὁ	vineyard
ἀνάπτω	to light up, set on fire
ἀσεβέω	to act wickedly, be ungodly
ἀτιμία, -ας, ἡ	shame, dishonor
ἀφαιρέω	to separate, remove; (*mid*) to deprive, seize, take away
βαδίζω	to go, proceed, walk
βεβηλόω	to profane, desecrate
βοάω	to cry out, shout
βουλή, -ῆς, ἡ	plan, advice, council
βρέχω	to rain, drench
γλυπτός, -ή, -όν	carved, graven; [τὸ γλύπτον] graven image
ὑψόω	to lift up, raise high, exalt
φέγγος, -ους, τό	light, splendor

▷ List 15	5×
δεσμός, -οῦ, ὁ	chain, restraints
διασκεδάζω	to break, thwart, scatter
δίκη, -ης, ἡ	penalty, punishment, justice
δρέπανον, -ου, τό	sickle, pruning knife
δύω	to cause to sink, sink; (*mid*) to enter
εἰσφέρω	to lead in, bring in
ἐκδέχομαι	to welcome, take in, accept
ἐκλεκτός, -ή, -όν	chosen, select, elite
ἐκφέρω	to bring out, produce
ἐνδύω	to dress, clothe
ἐξερημόω	to make desolate, lay waste to
ἐξουδ(θ)ενό(έ)ω	to disdain, reject
ἐραστής, -οῦ, ὁ	admirer, lover
ἔσθω	to eat
εὐλογία, -ας, ἡ	praise, blessing

▷ List 16	5×
εὐφροσύνη, -ης, ἡ	joy, gladness
ἐφίστημι	to cast over, place on
ἐφοράω	to scrutinize, survey, oversee
θεμελιόω	to establish, build a foundation
κατακόπτω	to beat down, cut off
κατέναντι	(+*gen*) in front of, opposite, against
κλέπτης, -ου, ὁ	thief
κολόκυνθα, -ης, ἡ	round gourd
κορυφή, -ῆς, ἡ	top, highest point
κριτής, -οῦ, ὁ	judge
κτίζω	to establish, build, create
λυπέω	to vex, displease; (*mid/pas*) to be distressed, grieve
μαρτύριον, -ου, τό	proof, testimony, witness
μεταστρέφω	to turn (back), change, alter
ἱκανός, -ή, -όν	*sufficient, adequate, capable*

▷ List 17 5×

νεανίσκος, -ου, ὁ	young man
νόμιμος, -η/ος, -ον	lawful; (*subst*) ordinance, statute
νύμφη, -ης, ἡ	bride, daughter-in-law
ξηρός, -ά, -όν	dry, withered, arid
ὀδούς, -όντος, ὁ	tooth
οἴμμοι	oh!, woe!, alas!
ὅπλον, -ου, τό	weapon; (*pl*) arms, armor
πένης, -ητος, ὁ	poor person, day laborer
πένθος, -ους, τό	grief, mourning
περιβάλλω	to put around, cover, clothe
περιοδεύω	to travel around
πετεινός, -ή, -όν	winged; (*subst*) bird
πλατύς, -εῖα, -ύ	wide, broad; [*fem subst* πλατεῖα] street, square
προσέχω	to pay attention to, be concerned about
προστάσσω	to command, order

▷ List 18 5 to 4×

ἀετός, -οῦ, ὁ	eagle, vulture
αἰχμάλωτος, -ος, -ον	captive, prisoner
πτερνίζω	to trip up, defraud
πτέρυξ, -υγος, ἡ	wing
πτοέω	to startle, alarm, terrify
πτῶσις, -εως, ἡ	fall, downfall, calamity
σκήνωμα, -ατος, τό	tent, temporary dwelling
συσκοτάζω	to darken
σχοινίον, -ου, τό	cord, rope, (measuring) line
ταπεινόω	to bring down, humiliate, humble
ταράσσω	to trouble, disturb
τήκω	to melt; to waste away
τρύγητος, -ου, ὁ	fruit harvest, vintage
ὑετός, -οῦ, ὁ	rain
φλόξ, φλογός, ἡ	flame

▷ List 19 4×

ἀκοή, -ῆς, ἡ	report, news
ἀλλογενής, -ής, -ές	foreign born
ἀναβάτης, -ου, ὁ	horse rider, charioteer
ἀναβοάω	to cry out
ἀναλαμβάνω	to take up, carry, assume
ἀνομία, -ας, ἡ	lawlessness, wrongful conduct
ἀνταπόδομα, -ατος, τό	repayment, recompense, reward
ἀπέχω	to be far away, be unavailable, withdraw, receive payment; (*mid*) to stay away
ἀποκαθίστημι	to restore, put back, pay
ἀσεβής, -ής, -ές	ungodly, wicked, sacrilegious
ἄστρον, -ου, τό	star
βάθος, -ους, τό	depth, bottom
βδελύσσω	to make detestable; (*mid*) to detest
βραχίων, -ονος, ὁ	arm, (strength)
γένημα, -ατος, τό	fruit, yield, produce, (offspring)

▷ List 20 4×

γυμνός, -ή, -όν	naked
δάκνω	to bite
δάμαλις, -εως, ἡ	young cow, heifer
διαρ(ρ)ήγνυμι *or* διαρ(ρ)ήσσω	to tear, divide, break through
διασκορπίζω	to scatter, disperse
διαστέλλω	to distinguish, separate, state precisely; (*mid*) to command
εἰρηνικός, -ή, -όν	peaceful, peaceable
ἐλέγχω	to question, rebuke, reprove
ἐμβάλλω	to throw in, put inside
ἐμπαίζω	to mock, make sport of, abuse
ἐμφράσσω	to stop up, block up
ἐναντίος, -α, -ον	against, opposed, opposite
ἐνισχύω	to strengthen, grow strong(er), prevail (over)
ἐντείνω	to stretch tight, bend
ἐξάλλομαι	to leap forth, leap up

▷ List 21 — 4×

ἐξερευνάω	to search out, investigate
ἐξιλάσκομαι	to propitiate, make atonement
ἐξωθέω	to drive out, thrust out, expel
ἑορτάζω	to celebrate a holiday, keep festival
ἐπαίρω	to lift up, raise, magnify
ἐπάνω	over, more than; (+*gen*) above, higher than
ἐπεγείρω	to raise up, incite
ἐπιλαμβάνω	to catch, grab, obtain
ἐπισυνάγω	to bring together, gather up
ἐπιχαίρω	to rejoice maliciously, be glad at someone's expense
ἑρπετόν, -οῦ, τό	reptile, creeping thing
ζῆλος, -ου, ὁ	jealousy, zeal
ζηλόω	to be jealous of *or* for, envy, strive for
ζυγός/ζυγόν, -οῦ, ὁ/τό	yoke; balance scale
θησαυρός, -οῦ, ὁ	treasure, treasury, storehouse

▷ List 22 — 4×

θρῆνος, -ου, ὁ	lamentation, wailing
καθαρός, -ά, -όν	pure, clean
κακόω	to do wrong, mistreat
καταδιώκω	to seek eagerly, chase down
κατακρατέω	to prevail, seize, overcome, strengthen
καταλαλέω	to slander, speak negatively (about)
καταναλίσκω	to consume, use up
κατάρχω	to rule over, govern; (*mid*) to begin
κατασκάπτω	to destroy, burn to the ground
κατοικία, -ας, ἡ	dwelling place, settlement
κέδρος, -ου, ἡ	cedar
κῆτος, -ους, τό	huge fish, large sea creature
κληρονομέω	to inherit, become heir to, give as inheritance
κλίβανος, -ου, ὁ	oven, furnace
καλῶς	*well*

▷ LIST 23 4×

κοπάζω	to stop, (cause to) cease, rest
κρέας, κρέως, τό	meat
κριθή, -ῆς, ἡ	barley
κυλίω	to roll (down), toss
λέβης, -ητος, ὁ	cauldron, kettle
λειτουργέω	to serve (as priest), minister
ληνός, -οῦ, ἡ	winepress, trough
μακράν	far away, distant
μεγιστάν, -ᾶνος, ὁ	noble, magistrate, influential person
μίσθωμα, -ατος, τό	price (of hire), payment
οἰκτιρμός, -οῦ, ὁ	compassion, pity
ὀλιγοστός, -ή, -όν	few in number
ὀλιγόω	to diminish, make few
ὀλολύζω	to wail, howl
ὁμοιόω	to be similar, make like, compare

▷ LIST 24 4×

ὀνειδισμός, -οῦ, ὁ	disgrace, insult
ὀργίζω	to make angry; (*pas*) to be angry
ὄρθρος, -ου, ὁ	early morning, dawn
ὀρφανός, -ή, -όν	orphaned (person)
παιδεία, -ας, ἡ	training, discipline, instruction
παιδεύω	to instruct, discipline
παρασιωπάω	to keep quiet, refrain from comment
παροξύνω	to sharpen; to provoke, defy
περιαιρέω	to take away, remove
περιστερά, -ᾶς, ἡ	dove, pigeon
πηλός, -οῦ, ὁ	mud, clay
πλάσσω	to form, mold
πληγή, -ῆς, ἡ	blow, wound, misfortune, plague
πόρνη, -ης, ἡ	prostitute, harlot
παρίστημι	*to place near, present;* (intr) *to stand near, be present to serve*

▷ List 25 4×

πρόϊμος	early (rain)
ῥίζα, -ης, ἡ	root
σαλπίζω	to blow (a trumpet), trumpet (a sound)
σελήνη, -ης, ἡ	moon
συγκλείω	to close off, shut in, encase, prevent
συλλαμβάνω	to capture, catch; to become pregnant
συνίημι	to understand, notice, ponder
σχοίνισμα, -ατος, τό	allotment, surveyed portion of land
ταπεινός, -ή, -όν	humble, abject, oppressed
ὑπεράνω	(+*gen*) well above, far beyond
ὑποκάτωθεν	from beneath; (+*gen*) under
ὑπόλειμμα, -ατος, τό	residue, remainder, remnant
φαντασία, -ας, ἡ	appearance, imagination, vision
χεῖλος, -ους, τό	lip, language, edge
χείμαρρος/ους, -ου, ὁ	stream, (seasonal) brook

▷ List 26 4×

χοῦς, χοός, ὁ	dust, dry soil
χρυσοῦς, -ῆ, -οῦν / χρύσεος, -α, -ον	golden; (*subst*) golden coin
ᾠδή, -ῆς, ἡ	song, ode
ὠδίν, -ῖνος, ἡ	pains of childbirth, birth pangs

JUDITH

▹ List 1	18 to 7×
ἅβρα, -ας, ἡ	companion, faithful servant
ἀναγγέλλω	to report, announce, publicize
ἀπέναντι *or* ἀπεναντίον	(+*gen*) opposite, contrary to, against
βοάω	to cry out, shout
γένος, -ους, τό	kind, people group, family (lineage)
δούλη, -ης, ἡ	female slave
ἐξολεθρεύω	to utterly destroy, eradicate
θεράπων, -οντος, ὁ	servant, aide
καθά	as, just as
κράτος, -ους, τό	might, strength, power
ὀρεινός, -ή, -όν	mountainous; (*subst*) hill country
πεδίον, -ου, τό	plain, field, level area
πεζός, -ή, -όν	by foot; (*subst*) infantry
πῆχυς, -εως, ὁ	cubit, (length of the) forearm
πλησίον	(+*gen*) near, close; (*subst*) neighbor

▹ List 2	7 to 6×
ἀνάβασις, -εως, ἡ	ascent, going up
ἀναλαμβάνω	to take up, carry, assume
ἀρχιστράτηγος, -ου, ὁ	chief captain, army leader
δεσπότης, -ου, ὁ	master, absolute ruler
ἑκατόν	one hundred
ἐκδικέω	to avenge, punish
ἐπιπίπτω	to fall upon, embrace, attack
ἐφίστημι	to cast over, place on
ἵππος, -ου, ὁ	horse
κάλλος, -ους, τό	beauty
κλίνη, -ης, ἡ	bed, couch
κορυφή, -ῆς, ἡ	top, highest point
νεανίσκος, -ου, ὁ	young man
ῥομφαία, -ας, ἡ	sword
σάκκος, -ου, ὁ	sackcloth

▷ List 3 — 6 to 5×

ἀνθίστημι	to resist, oppose
αὐλών, -ῶνος, ὁ	valley
βουλεύω	to consider, resolve, counsel
ἐκλείπω	to abandon, neglect; (*intr*) to fail, run out, cease
ἐπισκέπτομαι	to visit, examine, account for
ἡγέομαι	to go before, guide, act as leader, think, consider
ἱππεύς, -έως, ὁ	rider, cavalryman
καλύπτω	to cover, conceal
ὁμοθυμαδόν	with one accord, together
παραλία, -ας, ἡ	coast, shore
παρεμβάλλω	to set up, pitch (a tent), encamp
πηγή, -ῆς, ἡ	spring, fountain
ὑψηλός, -ή, -όν	elevated, proud; (*subst*) high place
θαυμάζω	*to be astonished, marvel at*
παρίστημι	*to place near, present;* (intr) *to stand near, be present to serve*

▷ List 4 — 5×

κληρονομία, -ας, ἡ	inheritance, possession(s)
κτῆνος, -ους, τό	(domesticated) animal; (*pl*) herd, cattle
κυκλόω	to encircle, surround
νήπιος, -α/ος, -ον	infant, child
παιδίσκη, -ης, ἡ	young woman, female servant
παντοκράτωρ, -ορος, ὁ	ruler of all, almighty
παράταξις, -εως, ἡ	battle, line of battle
προκαταλαμβάνω	to capture first, seize swiftly
προνομεύω	to plunder, despoil
σκήνωμα, -ατος, τό	tent, temporary dwelling
στρατηγός, -οῦ, ὁ	commander, captain
στρατιά, -ᾶς, ἡ	army, large company (of people)
συντάσσω	to command, prescribe, set in order
ταράσσω	to trouble, disturb
τεῖχος, -ους, τό	(city) wall

▷ List 5 — 5 to 4×

ἁγιάζω	to make holy, consecrate, sanctify
αἰχμαλωσία, -ας, ἡ	captivity, (group of) captives
ἁμάρτημα, -ατος, τό	sin (offering)
ἀναβοάω	to cry out
ἀναζεύγνυμι	to pack up camp, relocate, move on
ἀναστρέφω	to return, change course; (*mid*) to conduct oneself, live
ἀπάτη, -ης, ἡ	deceit, deceitfulness
ἀπώλεια, -ας, ἡ	destruction, ruin, loss
ἅρμα, -ατος, τό	chariot
βοήθεια, -ας, ἡ	help, support
διαρπαγή, -ῆς, ἡ	spoils, (act of) plundering
δουλεύω	to serve (as a slave)
δυσμή, -ῆς, ἡ	(*always pl*) setting (of the sun), west
ὕψος, -ους, τό	height, summit
φάραγξ, -αγγος, ἡ	ravine, valley

▷ List 6 — 4×

εἰσακούω	to hear, listen to, obey
ἐκδίδωμι	to hand over, pay out; (*mid/pas*) to give in marriage
ἐξίστημι	to amaze, overwhelm, confuse
καθότι	as, insofar as, since
καταστρώννυμι *or* καταστρωννύω	to set (a table), extend, spread out, lay out flat
κοιτών, -ῶνος, ὁ	bedroom
κύκλῳ	(*dat of* κύκλος) (all) around, surrounding
κωνώπιον, -ου, τό	couch *or* bed with a canopy
παρέρχομαι	to go past, pass by, move on
πλάτος, -ους, τό	breadth, width
πολεμιστής, -οῦ, ὁ	combatant, warrior
προνομή, -ῆς, ἡ	spoils (of war), plunder
πύργος, -ου, ὁ	tower
συλλαμβάνω	to capture, catch; to become pregnant
συντελέω	to finish, complete, accomplish

▷ List 7	4 to 3×
ἀδικία, -ας, ἡ	unrighteousness, wrongdoing, injustice
αἰνέω	to praise
αἰσχύνη, -ης, ἡ	shame, disgrace
ἄκρος, -α, -ον	(far) end, tip, top
ἀναιρέω	to get rid of, destroy; (*mid*) to take up
ἀπαρτία, -ας, ἡ	baggage, household goods
ἀπατάω	to deceive, trick
ἀποδιδράσκω	to run away, escape
ἀρέσκω	to please, gain favor
ἀρεστός, -ή, -όν	pleasing, acceptable
ἀριθμός, -οῦ, ὁ	number, total
συντρέχω	to draw down, subdue, humiliate
χείμαρρος/ους, -ου, ὁ	stream, (seasonal) brook
χήρευσις, -εως, ἡ	widowhood
χρυσίον, -ου, τό	gold

▷ List 8	3×
ἀφαιρέω	to separate, remove; (*mid*) to deprive, seize, take away
ἀφανισμός, -οῦ, ὁ	disappearance, annihilation
ἀφίστημι	to keep away, remove; (*mid*) to depart, withdraw
βεβήλωσις, -εως, ἡ	desecration, profanation
βοηθός, -οῦ, ὁ	help, helper
βουλή, -ῆς, ἡ	plan, advice, council
γερουσία, -ας, ἡ	council, senate
δῆμος, -ου, ὁ	crowd, populace, district
διαφυλάσσω	to watch over, guard, keep
δίψα, -ης, ἡ	thirst
δυνάστης, -ου, ὁ	ruler, master, official
ἑβδομήκοντα	seventy
ἐμπίπρημι	to set on fire
ἐνδύω	to dress, clothe
ἐπανίστημι	to oppose, attack, rise up against

▷ List 9	3×
ἐπιτήδευμα, -ατος, τό	intentional pursuit, consistent practice
εὖ	well, good
εὐφροσύνη, -ης, ἡ	joy, gladness
ἡνίκα	when
θαρσέω	to be courageous
θῆλυς, -εια, -υ	female
κατευθύνω	to direct, guide; (*pas*) to prosper
κυριεύω	to rule over, dominate, control
μίασμα, -ατος, τό	pollution, defilement
μισθωτός, -ή, -όν	hired; (*subst*) hired worker, mercenary
νότος, -ου, ὁ	south (wind)
ὄνειδος, -ους, τό	disgrace, loss of esteem
ὀσφύς, -ύος, ἡ	loins, waist
παροικέω	to dwell as a foreigner
παύω	to stop, prevent; (*mid*) to cease, come to an end

▷ List 10	3×
πήρα, -ας, ἡ	leather pouch, (travel) bag
πλατύς, -εῖα, -ύ	wide, broad; [*fem subst* πλατεῖα] street, square
πότος, -ου, ὁ	drinking party
πρᾶγμα, -ατος, τό	thing, matter, affair, deed
προστάσσω	to command, order
πρότερος, -α, -ον	former, earlier, before
προφυλακή, -ῆς, ἡ	outpost, advance guard
σκάνδαλον, -ου, τό	obstacle, cause of offense, enticement to sin
σκυλεύω	to plunder, spoil, strip (of goods)
στολή, -ῆς, ἡ	robe, cloak
συγκαλέω	to call together, invite, summon
συνεδρία, -ας, ἡ	council, conference
ταπείνωσις, -εως, ἡ	low status, humiliation, humility
ὑπερασπίζω	to shield (from harm), defend
πειρά(ζ)ω	*to tempt, test, try*

TOBIT (GI & GII)

▷ LIST 1	25 TO 8×
ἀδελφή, -ῆς, ἡ	sister, beloved woman
βαδίζω	to go, proceed, walk
γάμος, -ου, ὁ	marriage, wedding (feast)
ἐλεημοσύνη, -ης, ἡ	kind act, charitable giving, mercy
ἐξομολογέω	to acknowledge, admit, confess
εὐλογητός, -ή, -όν	praised, blessed
εὐοδόω	to lead safely, ensure success, grant; (*pas*) to prosper
θάπτω	to bury
ἰχθύς, -ύος, ὁ	fish
λυπέω	to vex, displease; (*mid/pas*) to be distressed, grieve
μιμνῄσκομαι	to remember, recall
μισθός, -οῦ, ὁ	payment, wages, reward
συντελέω	to finish, complete, accomplish
ὑγιαίνω	to be in good health, be well
ὑποδείκνυμι *or* ὑποδεικνύω	to demonstrate, inform, point out

▷ LIST 2	8 TO 6×
ἀδικία, -ας, ἡ	unrighteousness, wrongdoing, injustice
ἀμφότεροι, -αι, -α	both
ἀπάγω	to lead away, divert
αὐλίζομαι	to lodge overnight, stay
γένος, -ους, τό	kind, people group, family (lineage)
ἥμισυς, -εια, -υ	half
ἧπαρ, -ατος, τό	liver
θαρσέω	to be courageous
κοινῶς	together, jointly
λεύκωμα, -ατος, τό	whiteness, white spot (on the eye)
ὀνειδισμός, -οῦ, ὁ	disgrace, insult
παιδάριον, -ου, τό	child, little boy, servant
παιδίσκη, -ης, ἡ	young woman, female servant
παρατίθημι	to set before, present; (*mid*) to entrust
χολή, -ῆς, ἡ	gall, gallbladder

▷ **List 3**	**6 to 5×**
αἰχμαλωσία, -ας, ἡ	captivity, (group of) captives
αἰχμαλωτίζω	to take into captivity, capture
αὐλή, -ῆς, ἡ	court, courtyard
δέομαι	to ask (for), pray (for)
εἰσπορεύομαι	to go in, enter
ἐξαποστέλλω	to dispatch, dismiss, permit to leave
ἐπίσταμαι	to know, be acquainted with
εὐλογία, -ας, ἡ	praise, blessing
κληρονομέω	to inherit, become heir to, give as inheritance
κρύπτω	to hide, conceal
μαστιγόω	to flog, whip, torment
μέχρι(ς)	(+*gen*) until, as far as; (*conj*) until
μήποτε	lest, in order that . . . not
συμπορεύομαι	to go with, travel together
ὑψόω	to lift up, raise high, exalt

▷ **List 4**	**5 to 4×**
ἀναπηδάω	to jump up, spring up, leap
βίβλος, -ου, ἡ	scroll, book, record
δέκατος, -η, -ον	tenth; (*subst*) tithe
δῶρον, -ου, τό	gift, offering
εἰσάγω	to bring in, lead in, introduce
ἐνδόξως	honorably, illustriously, gloriously
ἐντίμως	honorably, respectably
ἐπιτάσσω	to command, provide instruction
νεανίσκος, -ου, ὁ	young man
οἴχομαι	to go, depart
πρίν	before
τάφος, -ου, ὁ	grave, tomb
φάρμακον, -ου, τό	medicine, poison, (magical) potion
φεύγω	to flee, escape, vanish
ἐγγύς	(+gen) *near, close to*

▷ List 5 4 to 3×

ᾅδης, -ου, ὁ	Hades, the underworld
ἀναβλέπω	to look up
ἀνακαλύπτω	to uncover, disclose
ἀξιόω	to deem worthy, place a request upon, entreat
ἀπάγχω	to hang (to death), strangle
εὐφραίνω	to make happy, cheer; (*pas*) to rejoice
λύπη, -ης, ἡ	sorrow, pain
μεγαλωσύνη, -ης, ἡ	majesty, greatness
νύμφη, -ης, ἡ	bride, daughter-in-law
οἰκέτης, -ου, ὁ	household servant
πενθερός, -οῦ, ὁ	father-in-law
πόσος, -η, -ον	how much?, how many?
ταμιεῖον, -ου, τό	storeroom, private chamber
χειρόγραφον, -ου, τό	handwritten document
θεραπεύω	*to serve, care for, heal*

▷ List 6 3×

ἀποτρέχω	to run away, depart
ἀρεστός, -ή, -όν	pleasing, acceptable
ἄριστον, -ου, τό	midday meal, dinner
γένημα, -ατος, τό	fruit, yield, produce, (offspring)
γηράσκω	to grow old
διασκορπίζω	to scatter, disperse
δύω	to cause to sink, sink; (*mid*) to enter
ἐντεῦθεν	from here; on this side . . . on that side
ἑορτή, -ῆς, ἡ	feast, festival
εὐφροσύνη, -ης, ἡ	joy, gladness
ἥκω	to have come, reach, be present
θεάομαι	to see, observe
ἰάομαι	to heal, cure, restore
καθαρός, -ά, -όν	pure, clean
δικαιόω	*to justify, vindicate, pronounce righteous*

▷ List 7 3×

καθήκω	to belong to, be proper, be due to
κάμηλος, -ου, ὁ/ἡ	camel
καπνίζω	to (emit) smoke
κατάγω	to bring down, reduce
καταλείπω	to leave (behind), abandon; (*pas*) to remain
κοιμάω	(*mid*) to lie (down), sleep; [κ. +μετά] to have sexual intercourse
κομίζω	to bring, carry; (*mid*) to receive
κοράσιον, -ου, τό	girl, young female servant
λίαν	very much, exceedingly
λούω	to wash; (*mid*) to bathe
μηκέτι	no longer, no more
μνημονεύω	to remember, keep in mind
μονογενής, -ής, -ές	only, unique
ὀδύνη, -ης, ἡ	pain, grief
οἰκέω	to inhabit, live

▷ List 8 3×

ὀκτώ	eight
ὀρύσσω	to dig (out)
πατριά, -ᾶς, ἡ	paternal lineage, family line
πεντήκοντα	fifty
πόθεν	from where?
πολλάκις	many times, often
ῥύομαι	to rescue, save
σιγάω	to be silent, become quiet
σκορπίζω	to scatter, disperse
συμβαίνω	to happen, come about, befall
τεῖχος, -ους, τό	(city) wall
τράχηλος, -ου, ὁ	neck, throat
ὅμοιος, -α, -ον	*like, similar to*
ποῖος, -α, -ον	*what (kind of)?, which?*
συνέρχομαι	*to assemble, meet, join together*

1 MACCABEES

▹ List 1	55 to 18×
ἄκρα, -ας, ἡ	hilltop, citadel
ἀπαίρω	to remove, take away
ἑκατοστός, -ή, -όν	hundredth
ἐπιστολή, -ῆς, ἡ	letter, epistle
ἵππος, -ου, ὁ	horse
καταλαμβάνω	to take hold of, overtake, capture
ὀχύρωμα, -ατος, τό	stronghold, fortress
παρεμβάλλω	to set up, pitch (a tent), encamp
πολεμέω	to wage war, fight
πρότερος, -α, -ον	former, earlier, before
σκῦλον, -ου, τό	plunder, spoils
συντρίβω	to break, crush, wreck
φεύγω	to flee, escape, vanish
φίλος, -η, -ον	friendly; (*subst*) friend, associate
χώρα, -ας, ἡ	country, land, region

▹ List 2	17 to 14×
ἁγίασμα, -ατος, τό	sanctuary, sacred offering
βουλεύω	to consider, resolve, counsel
ἐμπυρίζω	to set on fire, burn
ἐξαίρω	to raise up, remove, pack up camp and go
ἐπισυνάγω	to bring together, gather up
καθαιρέω	to take down, overpower, destroy
καθίστημι	to place, appoint, establish; (*mid*) to stand against
κατακρατέω	to prevail, seize, overcome, strengthen
καταλείπω	to leave (behind), abandon; (*pas*) to remain
κύκλῳ	(*dat of* κύκλος) (all) around, surrounding
ὅπλον, -ου, τό	weapon; (*pl*) arms, armor
πεδίον, -ου, τό	plain, field, level area
συλλαμβάνω	to capture, catch; to become pregnant
τεῖχος, -ους, τό	(city) wall
φιλία, -ας, ἡ	friendship, love

▷ List 3 — 14 to 10×

ἀντίγραφον, -ου, τό	copy (of a document)
ἀπαντάω	to receive (someone), encounter, befall
δῆμος, -ου, ὁ	crowd, populace, district
ἐνιαυτός, -οῦ, ὁ	year
ἐπιδέχομαι	to receive (gladly), welcome (cheerfully)
ἐπιλέγω	to pick out, select
ἡγέομαι	to go before, guide, act as leader, think, consider
ἰσχυρός, -ά, -όν	strong, powerful
μηχανή, -ῆς, ἡ	device, mechanism
ὀχυρόω	to fortify, secure
ῥομφαία, -ας, ἡ	sword
συνάντησις, -εως, ἡ	meeting
συνάπτω	to join together, engage, border on
χρυσίον, -ου, τό	gold
χρυσοῦς, -ῆ, -οῦν / χρύσεος, -α, -ον	golden; (*subst*) golden coin

▷ List 4 — 10 to 9×

ἄνομος, -ος, -ον	lawless, wicked
βεβηλόω	to profane, desecrate
δόλος, -ου, ὁ	deceit, dishonesty, craftiness
δόμα, -ατος, τό	gift
ἕτοιμος, -η/ος, -ον	ready, prepared
εὐφροσύνη, -ης, ἡ	joy, gladness
κυκλόθεν	all around, from all sides
μιμνῄσκομαι	to remember, recall
ὀχυρός, -ά, -όν	secure, fortified, firm
πληγή, -ῆς, ἡ	blow, wound, misfortune, plague
πύργος, -ου, ὁ	tower
σάλπιγξ, -ιγγος, ἡ	trumpet, horn
συμμαχία, -ας, ἡ	alliance
σύμμαχος, -ος, -ον	allied with (militarily); (*subst*) ally
φόρος, -ου, ὁ	levy, tax, tribute

▷ **List 5**	**9 to 8×**
βοήθεια, -ας, ἡ	help, support
βοηθέω	to help, aid
βωμός, -οῦ, ὁ	altar (typically pagan)
διάδημα, -ατος, τό	diadem, crown
εἰρηνικός, -ή, -όν	peaceful, peaceable
ἐκτείνω	to stretch out, reach out, extend
εὐδοκέω	to consent, accept, be pleased
κυκλόω	to encircle, surround
πορφύρα, -ας, ἡ	(cloth of) purple (color)
σαλπίζω	to blow (a trumpet), trumpet (a sound)
συναντάω	to meet (with), fall upon, happen
τρισχίλιοι, -αι, -α	three thousand
τροπόω	to cause to turn away, put to flight
ὑψόω	to lift up, raise high, exalt
χάριν	(+*gen*) for the sake of

▷ **List 6**	**8 to 7×**
ἀθροίζω	to gather, assemble
ἀλλότριος, -α, -ον	foreign, strange, unfamiliar
ἀνανεόω	to renew, restore
ἀσεβής, -ής, -ές	ungodly, wicked, sacrilegious
βοάω	to cry out, shout
βουλή, -ῆς, ἡ	plan, advice, council
διαπεράω	to go over, pass through
ἐκζητέω	to search for, seek out, demand
ἐκκλίνω	to bend, turn away; (*intr*) to avoid, deviate
ἐλέφας, -αντος, ὁ	elephant
ἑορτή, -ῆς, ἡ	feast, festival
ἐπίλοιπος, -ος, -ον	remaining; (*subst*) remnant
κυριεύω	to rule over, dominate, control
χείμαρρος/ους, -ου, ὁ	stream, (seasonal) brook
χρεία, -ας, ἡ	*necessity, need*

▷ List 7 — 7 to 6×

ἅμα	at once, together
ἀφαιρέω	to separate, remove; (*mid*) to deprive, seize, take away
νόμιμος, -η/ος, -ον	lawful; (*subst*) ordinance, statute
ὅμηρα, -ων, τά	hostage, group of hostages
ὀργίζω	to make angry; (*pas*) to be angry
παιδάριον, -ου, τό	child, little boy, servant
πενθέω	to grieve, mourn
πέραν	beyond; (+*gen*) on the other side
ποταμός, -οῦ, ὁ	river, stream
πρᾶγμα, -ατος, τό	thing, matter, affair, deed
προκαταλαμβάνω	to capture first, seize swiftly
στέφανος, -ου, ὁ	crown, (victor's) garland
στρατηγός, -οῦ, ὁ	commander, captain
συγκλείω	to close off, shut in, encase, prevent
φρουρά, -ᾶς, ἡ	garrison, guard

▷ List 8 — 6×

βασιλικός, -ή, -όν	royal, belonging to the king
διαρ(ρ)ήγνυμι *or* διαρ(ρ)ήσσω	to tear, divide, break through
ἑβδομηκοστός, -ή, -όν	seventieth
ἕβδομος, -η, -ον	seventh
εἰσπορεύομαι	to go in, enter
ἑκατόν	one hundred
ἐκδίκησις, -εως, ἡ	vengeance, punishment
ἐναντίος, -α, -ον	against, opposed, opposite
ἐπιτάσσω	to command, provide instruction
εὐφραίνω	to make happy, cheer; (*pas*) to rejoice
ζηλόω	to be jealous of *or* for, envy, strive for
ἡσυχάζω	to be quiet, rest
θανατόω	to kill, put to death
ἱππεύς, -έως, ὁ	rider, cavalryman
κτῆνος, -ους, τό	(domesticated) animal; (*pl*) herd, cattle

▷ List 9 — 6 to 5×

ἀθετέω	to refuse, reject, breach
αἰχμαλωτίζω	to take into captivity, capture
ὄμνυμι *or* ὀμνύω	to swear, take an oath
πένθος, -ους, τό	grief, mourning
περιβάλλω	to put around, cover, clothe
πρόσταγμα, -ατος, τό	ordinance, command
πρωί	in the morning; (*subst*) morning
συμμαχέω	to be a military ally, fight together
συνίστημι	to appoint, put together, collect; (*mid*) to join up, organize, bring about
συντηρέω	to preserve, defend, treasure up
τάλαντον, -ου, τό	talent (*monetary unit*)
τεσσαρακοστός, -ή, -όν	fortieth
τραυματίας, -ου, ὁ	wounded person, casualty
χαλκοῦς, -ῆ, -οῦν	(made of) bronze
χίλιοι, -αι, -α	one thousand

▷ List 10 — 5×

ἀνδραγαθία, -ας, ἡ	bravery, heroic virtue
ἀνήκω	to belong to, be appropriate, fit
ἀνθίστημι	to resist, oppose
ἀρέσκω	to please, gain favor
ἀρχιερωσύνη, -ης, ἡ	high priesthood
ἀφίστημι	to keep away, remove; (*mid*) to depart, withdraw
βρῶμα, -ατος, τό	food, provisions
διαβαίνω	to go through, cross (over)
δισχίλιοι, -αι, -α	two thousand
εἴκοσι	twenty
ἐκδικέω	to avenge, punish
ἐκτρίβω	to rub firmly, destroy completely
ἐλεύθερος, -α, -ον	free, noble
ἔνδοξος, -ος, -ον	reputable, honored, distinguished
ἐνδόξως	honorably, illustriously, gloriously

▷ List 11 5×

ἐνδύω	to dress, clothe
ἔνεδρον, -ου, τό	ambush, trap
ἐντυγχάνω	to petition, urge, supplicate
ἑξηκοστός, -ή, -όν	sixtieth
ἐρημόω	to make desolate, dry up
ἐχθραίνω	to be at enmity with, oppose
θάπτω	to bury
θλίβω	to press, oppress, afflict
θυσιάζω	to sacrifice
θύω	to sacrifice, slaughter
κακία, -ας, ἡ	evil, harm, misfortune
κατασκευάζω	to put together, construct, make ready
κέρας, κέρατος, τό	horn, flank (of an army)
μήποτε	lest, in order that . . . not
ἱκανός, -ή, -όν	*sufficient, adequate, capable*

▷ List 12 5 to 4×

ἀνταποδίδωμι	to give back, repay
ἀξιόω	to deem worthy, place a request upon, entreat
ἀποκλείω	to shut, lock up, exclude
ἀποσκευή, -ῆς, ἡ	household member, belongings
μιαίνω	to make unclean, defile, pollute
μνημόσυνον, -ου, τό	memory, memorial, reminder
νῆσος, -ου, ἡ	island
οἰκέω	to inhabit, live
πέμπτος, -η, -ον	fifth
περικάθημαι	to besiege, encamp around
περιτίθημι	to put on, put around
πρεσβευτής, -οῦ, ὁ	ambassador, envoy
ὑφίστημι	to set up, stand (in place), resist
ὑψηλός, -ή, -όν	elevated, proud; (*subst*) high place
φάλαγξ, -αγγος, ἡ	battle formation, phalanx

▷ List 13 4×

ἀποτάσσω	to set apart; (*mid*) to renounce, give up
ἀσπίς, -ίδος, ἡ	shield
αὐλή, -ῆς, ἡ	court, courtyard
γένημα, -ατος, τό	fruit, yield, produce, (offspring)
δαπάνη, -ης, ἡ	cost, expense
δέλτος, -ου, ἡ	writing tablet
διαπορεύομαι	to go through, pass by, walk about
διηγέομαι	to describe in detail, relate fully
δικαίωμα, -ατος, τό	ordinance, decree, rightful claim
ἐγκαινίζω	to renew, dedicate, restore
ἐγκαταλείπω	to abandon, leave behind
εἰκάς, -άδος, ἡ	twentieth day of the month
ἐκλείπω	to abandon, neglect; (*intr*) to fail, run out, cease
ἐμβατεύω	to take possession, set foot upon, enter into
ἔνθεν	from here; on one side . . . on the other side

▷ List 14 4×

ἐπαίρω	to lift up, raise, magnify
ἐπάνω	over, more than; (+*gen*) above, higher than
ἐπεί	when, after, since, inasmuch as
ἐπιπίπτω	to fall upon, embrace, attack
ἐπιτήδειος, -α, -ον	useful, necessary, suitable
εὐοδόω	to lead safely, ensure success, grant; (*pas*) to prosper
ἔχθρα, -ας, ἡ	hatred, hostility
καταδιώκω	to seek eagerly, chase down
καταφθείρω	to destroy
κατοικίζω	to settle (a group), establish (residency)
κληρονομία, -ας, ἡ	inheritance, possession(s)
κοπετός, -οῦ, ὁ	mourning, lamentation
κόπτω	to cut, strike; (*mid*) to mourn
κρύφος, -ου, ὁ	hiding place
λύπη, -ης, ἡ	sorrow, pain

▷ List 15 4×

νέος, -α, -ον	new, young; (*subst*) child
νομός, -οῦ, ὁ	district, province
ὀκτακισχίλιοι, -αι, -α	eight thousand
ὁλοκαύτωμα, -ατος, τό	whole burnt offering
ὄπισθε(ν)	from behind; (+*gen*) behind, after
ὅρμημα, -ατος, τό	vigorous outburst, sudden attack
παράνομος, -ος, -ον	unlawful, lawless
παράταξις, -εως, ἡ	battle, line of battle
πεντακόσιοι, -αι, -α	five hundred
πεντηκοστός, -ή, -όν	fiftieth; Pentecost
πληθύνω	to increase, multiply
πλησίον	(+*gen*) near, close; (*subst*) neighbor
πρέσβυς, -εως, ὁ	elder, ambassador
προσάγω	to bring to, approach
παραλαμβάνω	*to receive, take along*

▷ List 16 4×

ῥίπτω	to throw (away), defeat, reject
ῥύομαι	to rescue, save
σαλεύω	to shake, rock, disrupt
σκορπίζω	to scatter, disperse
στηρίζω	to support, strengthen, establish
συντελέω	to finish, complete, accomplish
τάφος, -ου, ὁ	grave, tomb
ὑπεναντίος, -α, -ον	against, opposite; (*subst*) enemy
ὑπερηφανία, -ας, ἡ	arrogance, pride

2 MACCABEES

▷ List 1 — 22 to 10×

ἀξιόω	to deem worthy, place a request upon, entreat
γένος, -ους, τό	kind, people group, family (lineage)
καθίστημι	to place, appoint, establish; (*mid*) to stand against
κελεύω	to command, order
παντοκράτωρ, -ορος, ὁ	ruler of all, almighty
πολέμιος, -α, -ον	hostile; (*subst*) enemy (force)
πρᾶγμα, -ατος, τό	thing, matter, affair, deed
προσάγω	to bring to, approach
στρατηγός, -οῦ, ὁ	commander, captain
συμβαίνω	to happen, come about, befall
τεῖχος, -ους, τό	(city) wall
τρόπος, -ου, ὁ	manner, way, conduct
τυγχάνω	to happen, obtain, meet
ἄξιος, -α, -ον	*deserving, appropriate*
φαίνω	*to shine;* (mid) *to appear, seem*

▷ List 2 — 10 to 8×

γενναίως	nobly, bravely
δυνάστης, -ου, ὁ	ruler, master, official
ἱππεύς, -έως, ὁ	rider, cavalryman
καταλείπω	to leave (behind), abandon; (*pas*) to remain
κατασφάζω	to slay, slaughter
μεταλλάσσω	to change, alter; to cease (life)
μυριάς, -άδος, ἡ	ten thousand, countless number
ὅπλον, -ου, τό	weapon; (*pl*) arms, armor
πάτριος, -α, -ον	ancestral, of one's father
πατρίς, -ίδος, ἡ	homeland, native country
πολίτης, -ου, ὁ	citizen
προστάσσω	to command, order
συνοράω	to perceive, notice, recognize
ταχέως	quickly, hastily, soon(er)
χρῆμα, -ατος, τό	wealth, property

▷ LIST 3 — 8 TO 7×

ἀναγκάζω	to force, compel
ἀναδείκνυμι	to disclose, display, appoint
βασιλικός, -ή, -όν	royal, belonging to the king
βίος, -ου, ὁ	life, existence
βοήθεια, -ας, ἡ	help, support
διασαφέω	to explain, describe clearly
ἑκατοστός, -ή, -όν	hundredth
ἔνδον	inside, within, internal to
ἐπιβάλλω	to lay upon, throw upon
ἐπιφανής, -ής, -ές	glorious, distinguished
εὔνοια, -ας, ἡ	(token of) goodwill, affection
ἥκω	to have come, reach, be present
κοινός, -ή, -όν	common, impure
μεταλαμβάνω	to share in, receive (notice), exchange
εὐθέως	*immediately, at once*

▷ LIST 4 — 7×

ἡλικία, -ας, ἡ	stage (of life), (social) stature
καθάπερ	just as
καταλαμβάνω	to take hold of, overtake, capture
κεῖμαι	to lie down; to be valid for
νέος, -α, -ον	new, young; (*subst*) child
ὅθεν	from where, consequently
ὀχύρωμα, -ατος, τό	stronghold, fortress
παρακομίζω	to carry, transport
πάρειμι	to be near, be present, have arrived
προσπίπτω	to fling oneself; to befall, happen
πρότερος, -α, -ον	former, earlier, before
συνίστημι	to appoint, put together, collect; (*mid*) to join up, organize, bring about
τάλαντον, -ου, τό	talent (*monetary unit*)
τάσσω	to position, appoint; (*mid*) to indicate
χρεία, -ας, ἡ	*necessity, need*

▷ List 5 6×

αἰτία, -ας, ἡ	cause, reason
ἀναφέρω	to bring up, offer, bear
ἀρχιερωσύνη, -ης, ἡ	high priesthood
γαζοφυλάκιον, -ου, τό	treasury
διαφυλάσσω	to watch over, guard, keep
δισμύριοι, -αι, -α	twenty thousand
ἐάω	to permit, pass over, allow
ἐπιστολή, -ῆς, ἡ	letter, epistle
ἐπιτελέω	to complete, perform, finish
ἐπιφάνεια, -ας, ἡ	appearing, manifestation
ἔφοδος, -ου, ἡ	plan, approach, attack
ἡγέομαι	to go before, guide, act as leader, think, consider
ἥσσων (ττ), -ων, -ον	worse, less, inferior
ἱερός, -ά, -όν	holy, sacred; (*subst*) temple, sanctuary
ἅπας, ἅπασα, ἅπαν	*all, every*

▷ List 6 6×

ἵππος, -ου, ὁ	horse
καθήκω	to belong to, be proper, be due to
κακία, -ας, ἡ	evil, harm, misfortune
νεανίας, -ου, ὁ	young man
ὁρμάω	to get started, rush (upon)
παραχρῆμα	immediately
προλέγω	to foretell, say previously
προτείνω	to stretch forth, hold up
πύργος, -ου, ὁ	tower
στάδιον, -ου, ὁ	stade (unit of measure), arena
συγγενής, -ής, -ές	related, kin; (*subst*) relative
συντελέω	to finish, complete, accomplish
φίλος, -η, -ον	friendly; (*subst*) friend, associate
χίλιοι, -αι, -α	one thousand
ἱκανός, -ή, -όν	*sufficient, adequate, capable*

▹ List 7 — 6 to 5×

ἀγών, -ῶνος, ὁ	struggle, fight, contest
αἰκίζομαι	to torture, torment
ἀλγηδών, -όνος, ἡ	suffering, grief
ἀναιρέω	to get rid of, destroy; (*mid*) to take up
ἀναλαμβάνω	to take up, carry, assume
ἀσφάλεια, -ας, ἡ	security, stability, safety
δέος, -ους, τό	awe, fear, trembling
δεσπότης, -ου, ὁ	master, absolute ruler
δηλόω	to disclose, make (oneself) clear, show
διασῴζω	to preserve, keep safe; (*pas*) to be spared, escape
διόπερ	therefore
δισχίλιοι, -αι, -α	two thousand
ἑκάτερος, -α, -ον	each (of a set), both
χώρα, -ας, ἡ	country, land, region
ἄρτι	*(just) now, at this moment*

▹ List 8 — 5×

ἐλάσσων (ττ), -ων, -ον	smaller, less, fewer
ἐπισυνάγω	to bring together, gather up
εὖ	well, good
ἐφοράω	to scrutinize, survey, oversee
καθαρισμός, -οῦ, ὁ	cleansing, purification
κομίζω	to bring, carry; (*mid*) to receive
κράτος, -ους, τό	might, strength, power
μαστιγόω	to flog, whip, torment
μεγάλως	greatly, intensely
μιαρός, -ά, -όν	polluted, vile, abominable
οἴομαι	to suppose, think, reckon
ὁμοεθνής, -ής, -ές	of the same people (group) *or* nation
ὁμοῦ	together, at once
ὀχυρός, -ά, -όν	secure, fortified, firm
παντελῶς	entirely, quite, without qualification

▷ List 9 — 5×

παράνομος, -ος, -ον	unlawful, lawless
πεντακισχίλιοι, -αι, -α	five thousand
πεντακόσιοι, -αι, -α	five hundred
προηγέομαι	to lead, precede
προσβάλλω	to attack, strike violently
προσδοκάω	to await, anticipate, expect
πρόσταγμα, -ατος, τό	ordinance, command
σποδός, -οῦ, ἡ	ashes
σύμπας, -πασα, -παν	everything, the whole
συμφορά, -ᾶς, ἡ	misfortune, calamity
συνθήκη, -ης, ἡ	agreement, pact
συντηρέω	to preserve, defend, treasure up
τάξις, -εως, ἡ	order, class, rank
ταραχή, -ῆς, ἡ	trouble, upheaval, vexation
τοσοῦτος, -αύτη, -οῦτον	so much, so great

▷ List 10 — 5 to 4×

ἀδιαλείπτως	without ceasing, continually
ἅμα	at once, together
ἀναζεύγνυμι	to pack up camp, relocate, move on
ἀναλύω	to go away, depart
ἄνοια, -ας, ἡ	folly, madness
ἀποδέχομαι	to receive, accept, acknowledge
τρέπω	to turn, shift
τριακόσιοι, -αι, -α	three hundred
ὑπερηφανία, -ας, ἡ	arrogance, pride
φανερός, -ά, -όν	obvious, known, manifest
φεύγω	to flee, escape, vanish
χαρίζομαι	to give freely, grant
χράω	to use, employ; (*mid*) to treat (in a certain way)
χρυσοῦς, -ῆ, -οῦν / χρύσεος, -α, -ον	golden; (*subst*) golden coin
ὑποτάσσω	*to subdue;* (mid/pas) *to (be) subject, submit*

▷ List 11 4×

ἀποκαθίστημι	to restore, put back, pay
ἀρετή, -ῆς, ἡ	virtue, excellence
αὐτόθι	there, at that place
βάρβαρος, -ος, -ον	uncultured, foreign, barbaric
βασανίζω	to torment, torture
γνώμη, -ης, ἡ	intent, will, decree, decision
διαγινώσκω	to discern, investigate, consider
δυσσεβής, -ής, -ές	ungodly, wicked, impious
δυσχερής, -ής, -ές	annoying, difficult to bear
ἑβδομάς, -άδος, ἡ	period of seven days *or* years; seven-member grouping
ἐγκρατής, -ής, -ές	self-controlled, having control over
ἐλεήμων, -ων, -ον	merciful, showing pity
ἐμπίπρημι	to set on fire
ἐμπίπτω	to fall into, fall on, attack
ἕνεκα *or* ἕνεκεν/εἵνεκεν	(+*gen*) on account of, because of

▷ List 12 4×

ἐνίστημι	to arrive, be present, be current
ἐνσείω	to drive toward, assail, throw to the ground
ἐνταῦθα	here; on one side . . . on the other side
ἐντυγχάνω	to petition, urge, supplicate
ἑορτή, -ῆς, ἡ	feast, festival
ἐπαγγέλλομαι	to promise, pledge, profess
ἐπίβουλος, -ος, -ον	plotting (against), treacherous
ἐπιδέχομαι	to receive (gladly), welcome (cheerfully)
ἐπίκαιρος, -ος, -ον	opportune, advantageous
ἐπιχειρέω	to undertake, attempt; to attack
ἕτοιμος, -η/ος, -ον	ready, prepared
εὐημερία, -ας, ἡ	prosperity, wealth
εὔχομαι	to pray, vow
ἱκετεία, -ας, ἡ	supplication, entreaty
ἵλεως, -ως, -ων	gracious, merciful

▷ List 13 4×

ἱστορία, -ας, ἡ	account, history, story
καταβάλλω	to throw down, overthrow, ruin
καταντάω	to come to, attain
καταστρώννυμι *or* καταστρωννύω	to set (a table), extend, spread out, lay out flat
κρέας, κρέως, τό	meat
λήγω	to stop, cease
μάλα	quite, certainly, especially
νίκη, -ης, ἡ	victory
νομίζω	to think, suppose
ὀγδοήκοντα	eighty
ὄγδοος, -η, -ον	eighth
ὀκτώ	eight
ὅρκος, -ου, ὁ	oath
καλῶς	*well*
μέλος, -ους, τό	*body part*

▷ List 14 4×

πανοπλία, -ας, ἡ	(full set of) armor
πάνυ	very, entirely
πατρῷος, -α, -ον	paternal, of one's forefather
πεζός, -ή, -όν	by foot; (*subst*) infantry
πέμπτος, -η, -ον	fifth
περιέχω	to surround, encircle, contain
περιπίπτω	to encounter (unintentionally), happen upon
πιπράσκω	to sell
πληγή, -ῆς, ἡ	blow, wound, misfortune, plague
πορεία, -ας, ἡ	journey, course, way
προάγω	to go before, impel, promote
προβαίνω	to move on, advance
παραγγέλλω	*to give orders, command, proclaim*
πάσχω	*to suffer, undergo*
πράσσω	*to act, do, accomplish*

▷ List 15 4×

προπίπτω	to fall flat, bow down
προσαγγέλλω	to announce, inform, report
προσαγορεύω	to call (by the name of), address
προσκαλέω	to call upon, summon, invite
πρόσοδος, -ου, ἡ	right of access, coming in (of revenue)
πυρόω	to burn (red hot), purify (in fire)
ῥώννυμι	(*pas*) to be in good condition, fare well
στράτευμα, -ατος, τό	army, troops; campaign
συγχωρέω	to permit, grant, concede
τελευτάω	to die
τεσσαρακοστός, -ή, -όν	fortieth
ὑγιαίνω	to be in good health, be well
ὕμνος, -ου, ὁ	hymn, song of praise
ὑπεροχή, -ῆς, ἡ	prominence, superiority
φροντίζω	to be concerned (about), be intent on

▷ List 16 4 to 3×

ἀγωγή, -ῆς, ἡ	manner of life, custom, policy
ἀγωνία, -ας, ἡ	agony, conflict
ἀγωνίζομαι	to strive, fight, contend
ἄδικος, -ος, -ον	unjust, unrighteous; (*subst*) wrongdoing
ἀθέμιτος, -ος, -ον	unlawful, godless
ἀκμή, -ῆς, ἡ	highest point, prime, culmination
ἀκρόπολις, -εως, ἡ	acropolis, citadel
ἀλιτήριος, -ον	wretched, sinful; (*subst*) sinner
ἁμάρτημα, -ατος, τό	sin (offering)
ἀναλίσκω	to use up, exhaust, consume
ἀνάπτω	to light up, set on fire
ἀντίλημψις, -εως, ἡ	help, aid
φυγαδεύω	to make *or* become a fugitive
ψήφισμα, -ατος, τό	decree, decision (by casting lots)
ὡσαύτως	in the same way, similarly

▹ List 17 3×

ἀπάντησις, -εως, ἡ	meeting
ἀπολαμβάνω	to receive, get back, take aside
ἀπολείπω	to leave (behind), abandon; to cease
ἀσεβέω	to act wickedly, be ungodly
ἀσεβής, -ής, -ές	ungodly, wicked, sacrilegious
ἀφίστημι	to keep away, remove; (*mid*) to depart, withdraw
βλασφημία, -ας, ἡ	abusive speech, blasphemy
βλάσφημος, -ος, -ον	blasphemous; (*subst*) blasphemer
βραχέως	for a short while, temporarily
βωμός, -οῦ, ὁ	altar (typically pagan)
γενναῖος, -α, -ον	noble, exemplary
γερουσία, -ας, ἡ	council, senate
γῆρας, -ως, τό	old age
δαπανάω	to spend, use up
διακόσιοι, -αι, -α	two hundred

▹ List 18 3×

διάνοια, -ας, ἡ	mind, thought, understanding
διατάσσω	to appoint, arrange, direct
διαφέρω	to carry over, transport, differ (from)
διάφορος, -ος, -ον	various, different
δικαίως	justly, rightly
δραχμή, -ῆς, ἡ	drachma (weight *or* coin)
δυσμένεια, -ας, ἡ	enmity, hostility
εἰκάς, -άδος, ἡ	twentieth day of the month
εἰσφέρω	to lead in, bring in
ἑκατόν	one hundred
ἔκθυμος, -ος, -ον	angry, incensed
ἐκρίπτω	to drive away, chase off
ἐκφεύγω	to escape, flee
ἐλέφας, -αντος, ὁ	elephant
ἑξακόσιοι, -αι, -α	six hundred

▹ List 19 3×

ἐξαποστέλλω	to dispatch, dismiss, permit to leave
ἐπέρχομαι	to come upon, happen upon, attack
ἐπιβοηθέω	to come to the aid of
ἐπίθεσις, -εως, ἡ	attempt, attack
ἐπινεύω	to consent, grant
ἐπίσκεψις, -εως, ἡ	numbering, investigation, inspection
ἐπίτροπος, -ου, ὁ	guardian, steward, manager
ἐπιφαίνω	to appear, show forth, display
εὐημερέω	to be successful
εὐρώστως	strongly, mightily
ἡγεμών, -όνος, ὁ	leader
ἡδέως	gladly, with pleasure, cheerfully
ἡμέτερος, -α, -ον	our
θεῖος, -α, -ον	divine
θνῄσκω	to die

▹ List 20 3×

καθαγιάζω	to consecrate as holy, sanctify
καρτερός, -ά, -όν	strong, intense, violent
καταλλάσσω	to reconcile (with), change orientation toward
καταπλήσσω	to terrify; (*pas*) to be astonished
κατάρχω	to rule over, govern; (*mid*) to begin
κατηγορέω	to accuse, reproach
κτίστης, -ου, ὁ	creator
κώμη, -ης, ἡ	village, small town
λαλιά, -ᾶς, ἡ	chat, (manner *or* subject of) speech
λιμήν, -ένος, ὁ	harbor, haven
μάστιξ, -ιγος, ἡ	whip, suffering
μεταβαίνω	to move to, depart from, change (state)
μετέχω	to partake of, share in
μέχρι(ς)	(+*gen*) until, as far as; (*conj*) until
μηδαμῶς	by no means, certainly not

▷ **List 21**	3×
μηνύω	to make known, inform
μιμνῄσκομαι	to remember, recall
μύριοι, -αι, -α	ten thousand, innumerable
νήπιος, -α/ος, -ον	infant, child
ξένος, -η, -ον	foreign, strange
οἰκέω	to inhabit, live
ὅμως	yet, nevertheless, likewise
ὀρφανός, -ή, -όν	orphaned (person)
ὀσμή, -ῆς, ἡ	fragrance, scent, smell
οὐδαμῶς	by no means, certainly not
ὄψις, -εως, ἡ	appearance, face, perception
παράκειμαι	to be present, be available, be nearby
παρατάσσω	to form a battle line, battle
πεντήκοντα	fifty
παραλαμβάνω	*to receive, take along*

▷ **List 22**	3×
πολεμοτροφέω	to maintain war with
πολιτεία, -ας, ἡ	citizenship, civic life, polity
ποτέ	at some time, once, formerly
προδότης, -ου, ὁ	traitor
προσδέχομαι	to accept, receive favorably, anticipate
προχειρίζω	(*mid*) to choose, appoint
πυλών, -ῶνος, ὁ	gate, porch
πυρά, -ᾶς, ἡ	conflagration, pyre
σεμνός, -ή, -όν	solemn, reverent, worthy of respect
σκῦλον, -ου, τό	plunder, spoils
σπεῖρα, -ας, ἡ	tactical unit, division of soldiers
σπεύδω	to hasten, hurry
σπλαγχνισμός, -οῦ, ὁ	eating the entrails of a sacrifice
στρατιά, -ᾶς, ἡ	army, large company (of people)
συγκλείω	to close off, shut in, encase, prevent

▷ List 23 3×

συγχέω	to confuse, mix up
συλλαμβάνω	to capture, catch; to become pregnant
σύμμαχος, -ος, -ον	allied with (militarily); (*subst*) ally
συμμ(ε)ίγνυμι	to mix with, associate with, come near
συμφεύγω	to take refuge, flee together
συνεγγίζω	to draw near
συνελαύνω	to force away
συννοέω	to understand, perceive, realize
σύνταξις, -εως, ἡ	tax; arrangement, formation
σφαγή, -ῆς, ἡ	slaughter, destruction
σῶος, -ος, -ον	safe, undamaged, whole
ταχύς, -εῖα, -ύ	quickly, soon
τέμενος, -ους, τό	sacred area, shrine
τιμάω	to honor; (*mid*) to value (at a price)
τιμή, -ῆς, ἡ	*honor, value, price*

▷ List 24 3×

τραυματίας, -ου, ὁ	wounded person, casualty
τροπόω	to cause to turn away, put to flight
τύραννος, -ου, ὁ	sovereign ruler
ὑπεναντίος, -α, -ον	against, opposite; (*subst*) enemy
ὑπερβάλλω	to surpass; (*mid*) to postpone
ὑπισχνέομαι	to promise to do, undertake
ὑπογράφω	to write below, indicate
ὑποκρίνομαι	to pretend, feign, be a hypocrite
ὑπονοθεύω	to obtain by underhanded means
ὑποφέρω	to endure, bear
ὑποχείριος, -ος, -ον	controlled, under authority, subordinate
ὑφάπτω	to set on fire
φρονέω	to gain understanding, form an opinion
φρούριον, -ου, τό	fort, fortress
χαλεπός, -ή, -όν	grievous, harsh, difficult

▹ List 25 3×

χήρα, -ας, ἡ	widow
χορηγέω	to supply, provide
χωρέω	to have room for, contain, give way to
χωρίζω	to separate, remove; (*pas*) to depart, exclude
χωρίον, -ου, τό	place, field, large area of land

3–4 MACCABEES

▷ **List 1**	**74 to 17×**
ἀρετή, -ῆς, ἡ	virtue, excellence
βασανίζω	to torment, torture
βάσανος, -ου, ἡ	torment, (instrument of) torture
βίος, -ου, ὁ	life, existence
εὐσέβεια, -ας, ἡ	godliness, piety
θεῖος, -α, -ον	divine
καθίστημι	to place, appoint, establish; (*mid*) to stand against
λογισμός, -οῦ, ὁ	thought, (line of) reasoning
μέχρι(ς)	(+*gen*) until, as far as; (*conj*) until
πάθος, -ους, τό	misfortune, trouble, emotion
πόνος, -ου, ὁ	toil, distress, pain
πρᾶγμα, -ατος, τό	thing, matter, affair, deed
τρόπος, -ου, ὁ	manner, way, conduct
τύραννος, -ου, ὁ	sovereign ruler
ὦ	O!, oh!

▷ **List 2**	**16 to 11×**
ἀνάγκη, -ης, ἡ	constraint, distress
ἀπειλή, -ῆς, ἡ	threat, anger
γέ	(*emphatic particle*) indeed, really
γέρων, -οντος, ὁ	old man
δίκη, -ης, ἡ	penalty, punishment, justice
ἐπεί	when, after, since, inasmuch as
ἐπικρατέω	to rule over, prevail, hold power
ἡδονή, -ῆς, ἡ	enjoyment, (experience of) pleasure
ἱερός, -ά, -όν	holy, sacred; (*subst*) temple, sanctuary
καταλύω	to lodge, bring down, destroy
νικάω	to prevail, triumph
ὑπομένω	to remain, endure, wait for
φίλος, -η, -ον	friendly; (*subst*) friend, associate
ἅπας, ἅπασα, ἅπαν	*all, every*
ἐπιθυμία, -ας, ἡ	*desire, lust*

▷ List 3 — 11 to 10×

ἀλγηδών, -όνος, ἡ	suffering, grief
γένος, -ους, τό	kind, people group, family (lineage)
δορυφόρος, -ου, ὁ	spear-bearer, bodyguard
εὐσεβής, -ής, -ές	pious, devout, religious
ἡλικία, -ας, ἡ	stage (of life), (social) stature
καθάπερ	just as
καίπερ	though, even though
νοῦς, νοός, ὁ	mind, thought
πάρειμι	to be near, be present, have arrived
πικρός, -ά, -όν	bitter
πολέμιος, -α, -ον	hostile; (*subst*) enemy (force)
προστάσσω	to command, order
συνίστημι	to appoint, put together, collect; (*mid*) to join up, organize, bring about
τοίνυν	accordingly, so
ὑπομονή, -ῆς, ἡ	*endurance, perseverance, staying*

▷ List 4 — 10 to 8×

βαρύς, -εῖα, -ύ	heavy, difficult
βοηθέω	to help, aid
γενναῖος, -α, -ον	noble, exemplary
γῆρας, -ως, τό	old age
ἡμέτερος, -α, -ον	our
θνῄσκω	to die
μιαροφαγέω	to eat ceremonially unclean food
νομίζω	to think, suppose
ὅθεν	from where, consequently
πάτριος, -α, -ον	ancestral, of one's father
τοσοῦτος, -αύτη, -οῦτον	so much, so great
τροχός, -οῦ, ὁ	wheel
φύσις, -εως, ἡ	nature, natural disposition
θαυμάζω	*to be astonished, marvel at*
φαίνω	*to shine;* (mid) *to appear, seem*

▹ List 5 — 8 to 7×

ἀναγκάζω	to force, compel
γεραιός, -ά, -όν	aged; (*subst*) old man
δάκρυον, -ου, τό	tear, drop
δεσπότης, -ου, ὁ	master, absolute ruler
διάνοια, -ας, ἡ	mind, thought, understanding
θράσος, -ους, τό	audacity, cockiness, confidence
κελεύω	to command, order
ὁμοῦ	together, at once
πλησίον	(+*gen*) near, close; (*subst*) neighbor
ῥύομαι	to rescue, save
στρέβλη, -ης, ἡ	instrument of torture
σώφρων, -ων, -ον	self-controlled, temperate, prudent
τοι	surely, truly
λύω	*to loosen, release*
μήτε	*and not, neither . . . nor*

▹ List 6 — 7 to 6×

ἁγιάζω	to make holy, consecrate, sanctify
ἀγών, -ῶνος, ὁ	struggle, fight, contest
αἰτία, -ας, ἡ	cause, reason
ἀκυρόω	to cancel (out), set to naught, invalidate
ἀναιρέω	to get rid of, destroy; (*mid*) to take up
ἀναλύω	to go away, depart
ἀνδρεῖος, -α, -ον	courageous, virtuous
βία, -ας, ἡ	violence, force
γονεύς, -έως, ὁ	parent
δέομαι	to ask (for), pray (for)
ἐλέφας, -αντος, ὁ	elephant
ἔξειμι	[ἔξεστι(ν)] to be possible
συμπάθεια, -ας, ἡ	sympathy, compassion
τιμωρία, -ας, ἡ	punishment
τρέπω	to turn, shift

▷ **List 7**	**6×**
ἐπαινέω	to praise
ἐπιδείκνυμι	to demonstrate, point out
εὐγενής, -ής, -ές	of high *or* noble birth
εὐφροσύνη, -ης, ἡ	joy, gladness
εὐωχία, -ας, ἡ	celebratory feasting
ἰσχύω	to be strong, be capable; (*trans*) to intensify
καθοπλίζω	to arm *or* equip fully
καρτερία, -ας, ἡ	endurance, perseverance, obstinacy
καταικίζω	to disfigure, torture
κοινός, -ή, -όν	common, impure
κολάζω	to penalize, punish
κράτος, -ους, τό	might, strength, power
κωλύω	to hinder, prevent, withhold
νεανίας, -ου, ὁ	young man
μέλος, -ους, τό	*body part, musical part*

▷ **List 8**	**6×**
νεανίσκος, -ου, ὁ	young man
ὄργανον, -ου, τό	part (of the body), (musical) instrument, contraption
παντοκράτωρ, -ορος, ὁ	ruler of all, almighty
παραβαίνω	to deviate, turn away
πατρίς, -ίδος, ἡ	homeland, native country
πρίν	before
πρόγονος, -ον	(*subst*) forefather, ancestor
ῥώννυμι	(*pas*) to be in good condition, fare well
σός, σή, σόν	your, yours
σπλάγχνον, -ου, τό	entrails, guts, (seat of emotion)
στρατηγός, -οῦ, ὁ	commander, captain
συμβαίνω	to happen, come about, befall
σύνολος, -ος, -ον	in every instance
σωφροσύνη, -ης, ἡ	self-control, prudence, sound judgment
χράω	to use, employ; (*mid*) to treat (in a certain way)

▷ List 9 — 6 to 5×

ἀδελφότης, -ητος, ἡ	brotherhood
ἄλλως	otherwise, besides, contrarily
ἀνδρεία, -ας, ἡ	courage, virtue
ἀνίκητος, -ος, -ον	invincible, unconquerable
ἀπογεύομαι	to taste, partake of
αὐτοκράτωρ, -ορος, ὁ	sovereign master
βασανιστήριον, -ου, τό	instrument of torture
δεσπόζω	to be master, rule over
διάθεσις, -εως, ἡ	inclination, disposition, condition
διακομίζω	to carry across; (*pas*) to cross
δόγμα, -ατος, τό	decree
ἕλκω	to draw, pull, drag
ἐνθυμέομαι	to reflect, ponder
χρῆμα, -ατος, τό	wealth, property
ἄξιος, -α, -ον	*deserving, appropriate*

▷ List 10 — 5×

ἐπιστολή, -ῆς, ἡ	letter, epistle
ἐπιφαίνω	to appear, show forth, display
εὐγενῶς	nobly, bravely
εὔνοια, -ας, ἡ	(token of) goodwill, affection
ἦθος, -ους, τό	disposition, manner, custom
κακοήθεια, -ας, ἡ	evil disposition, malignity, meanness
καλοκἀγαθία, -ας, ἡ	nobility of character
καρτερέω	to endure, be patient, persevere
καταπέλτης, -ου, ὁ	catapult
καταφρονέω	to scorn, disdain, show contempt
μάλιστα	most of all, exceedingly
μιαρός, -ά, -όν	polluted, vile, abominable
μόρος, -ου, ὁ	fate, doom
νέος, -α, -ον	new, young; (*subst*) child
νόμιμος, -η/ος, -ον	lawful; (*subst*) ordinance, statute

▷ List 11 5×

ὀξύς, -εῖα, -ύ	swift, sharp, severe
πάντοθεν	on all sides, from every direction
περικρατέω	to exercise control (over)
ποικίλος, -η, -ον	multicolored, various
πολιτεία, -ας, ἡ	citizenship, civic life, polity
πολιτεύομαι	to live (as a citizen)
προλέγω	to foretell, say previously
πρόνοια, -ας, ἡ	foreknowledge, attention, providence
πυκνός, -ή, -όν	frequent, incessant, rapid
πυνθάνομαι	to inquire, question
σιδηροῦς, -ᾶ, -οῦν	(made of) iron
στερέω	to deprive (of), prevent
στρεβλόω	to twist, pervert, torture
ταχέως	quickly, hastily, soon(er)
τελευτάω	to die

▷ List 12 5 to 4×

ἁγνός, -ή, -όν	(morally) pure
ᾅδης, -ου, ὁ	Hades, the underworld
αἰκισμός, -οῦ, ὁ	torture, torment
αἰνέω	to praise
ἀλόγιστος, -ος, -ον	senseless, unreasoning, irrational
ἄνομος, -ος, -ον	lawless, wicked
ἀπειθέω	to be disobedient, refuse
ἀπογραφή, -ῆς, ἡ	registration, record, enrollment
ἀπογράφω	to register, record (in writing)
ὑπερήφανος, -ος, -ον	arrogant, haughty, lofty
φιλοσοφία, -ας, ἡ	philosophy, philosophical exposition
φιλοτεκνία, -ας, ἡ	parental love for children
χαρίζομαι	to give freely, grant
χορός, -οῦ, ὁ	dance; group of dancers, choir
χώρα, -ας, ἡ	country, land, region

▹ List 13 4×

ἀπώλεια, -ας, ἡ	destruction, ruin, loss
ἀσέβεια, -ας, ἡ	ungodliness, wickedness
βδελύσσω	to make detestable; (*mid*) to detest
βέβηλος, -ος, -ον	common, profane
βίαιος, -α, -ον	strong, forceful, violent
βοή, -ῆς, ἡ	cry, shout
γαστήρ, γαστρός, ἡ	belly, womb
γόος, -ου, ὁ	weeping, wailing
γοῦν	and so, certainly then
δέησις, -εως, ἡ	supplication, request
δεινός, -ή, -όν	awful, terrible, dreadful
δεσμός, -οῦ, ὁ	chain, restraints
δυνάστης, -ου, ὁ	ruler, master, official
ἐκκόπτω	to cut off, do away with
ἄρτι	*(just) now, at this moment*

▹ List 14 4×

ἐναντιόομαι	to oppose, withstand
ἐξόμνυμι	(*mid*) to renounce publicly
ἐπειδή	when, since
ἐπιβουλή, -ῆς, ἡ	plot (against), plan
ἐπικράτεια, -ας, ἡ	mastery, control (over)
ἐπισπάω	to drag (upon), persuade, obtain
ἐπιστήμη, -ης, ἡ	skill, competence, understanding
εὐλογιστία, -ας, ἡ	circumspection, caution
εὐνομία, -ας, ἡ	observance of the law
εὐπείθεια, -ας, ἡ	meticulous obedience
εὐσεβέω	to act piously, show reverence
ἡδύς, -εῖα, -ύ	pleasant, enjoyable
θρῆνος, -ου, ὁ	lamentation, wailing
ἱκετεύω	to entreat, supplicate
ἵλεως, -ως, -ων	gracious, merciful

▷ List 15 4×

καίτοι	yet, and yet, and further
κακῶς	badly, harmfully, wickedly
κάμινος, -ου, ἡ	oven, furnace
καταπλήσσω	to terrify, astonish
κομίζω	to bring, carry; (*mid*) to receive
λέων, -οντος, ὁ	lion
λήθη, -ης, ἡ	forgetfulness, forgetting
μανθάνω	to learn, find out
μεθίστημι	to remove, deprive of, change
μεταβάλλω	to turn, change, alter
μεταλαμβάνω	to share in, receive (notice), exchange
μετατρέπω	to turn around, change (the mind)
μηχανάομαι	to contrive, plot
μιαροφαγία, -ας, ἡ	eating of defiled food
οἰκτίρω	to show mercy (to), have compassion (on)

▷ List 16 4×

ὁμοθυμαδόν	with one accord, together
οὐδαμῶς	by no means, certainly not
οὐράνιος, -ος, -ον	heavenly
παράγω	to pass by, influence, introduce
παρανομέω	to violate the law
παρανομία, -ας, ἡ	wrongdoing, legal violation, iniquity
παρέχω	to bring about, contribute (to)
παροράω	to overlook, ignore, disregard
πατρῷος, -α, -ον	paternal, of one's forefather
περιπλέκω	to embrace, wrap up, bind
πρέπω	to be fitting, be proper, be appropriate
πρόθεσις, -εως, ἡ	purpose, intention
ὀφείλω	*to owe, be obligated*
παρίστημι	*to place near, present;* (intr) *to stand near, be present to serve*
πάσχω	*to suffer, undergo*

▷ List 17 — 4×

προσκαλέω	to call upon, summon, invite
προφέρω	to bring out, urge
ῥίπτω	to throw (away), defeat, reject
σβέννυμι	to extinguish, smother
στοργή, -ῆς, ἡ	love, intimate affection
στρατιώτης, -ου, ὁ	soldier
συμβουλεύω	to advise; (*mid*) to consult, take counsel
συμποσία, -ας, ἡ	banquet
συνήθεια, -ας, ἡ	close companionship, intimacy
σωτήριος, -ος, -ον	bringing salvation, saving
τάχος, -ους, τό	swiftness, quickness
τιμωρέω	to punish, take vengeance on
τοιγαροῦν	therefore, for that reason
τροφή, -ῆς, ἡ	food, provisions
τιμή, -ῆς, ἡ	*honor, value, price*

▷ List 18 — 4 to 3×

ἀγνοέω	to be ignorant, be unaware
ἄγριος, -α, -ον	wild, fierce
ἄγχω	to constrict, strangle
ἀεί	always, constantly
ἀθάνατος, -ος, -ον	immortal
ἀθλητής, -οῦ, ὁ	athlete, champion
τυγχάνω	to happen, obtain, meet
τυραννίς, -ίδος, ἡ	tyranny, despotic rule
ὕβρις, -εως, ἡ	arrogance, insult, insolence
ὑπερασπίζω	to shield (from harm), defend
ὑπεροράω	to disregard, ignore
ὑποδείκνυμι *or* ὑποδεικνύω	to demonstrate, inform, point out
ὑπολαμβάνω	to say in response, take up, consider
ὕστερος, -α, -ον	later, afterward
φιλοσοφέω	to be a philosopher; to seek knowledge

▷ List 19 — 3×

αἰδέομαι	to respect, show regard; (+*inf*) to be ashamed
αἰκίζομαι	to torture, torment
αἰσχρός, -ά, -όν	ugly, revolting, shameful
ἄκρα, -ας, ἡ	hilltop, citadel
ἀλαζονεία, -ας, ἡ	arrogance, pretentiousness
ἀλάστωρ, -ορος, ὁ	one whose deeds deserve vengeance
ἀληθῶς	truly, actually
ἄλογος, -ος, -ον	ineloquent, unreasoning, discounted
ἀμέτρητος, -ος, -ον	boundless, immeasurable
ἀναβοάω	to cry out
ἀνάγω	to lead up, bring up, raise up
ἀναλαμβάνω	to take up, carry, assume
ἄνανδρος, -ος, -ον	unmanly, cowardly
ἀναρίθμητος, -ος, -ον	innumerable, countless
ἄνευ	(+*gen*) without, far from

▷ List 20 — 3×

ἀνέχω	to withhold, keep in check; (*mid*) to tolerate, endure
ἀνθίστημι	to resist, oppose
ἀνθρώπινος, -η, -ον	human
ἀνόητος, -ος, -ον	lacking understanding, unintelligent
ἀνόσιος, -ος, -ον	unholy, profane, ungodly
ἀντιλέγω	to speak against, oppose, contradict
ἀντίλημψις, -εως, ἡ	help, aid
ἀπείθεια, -ας, ἡ	disobedience
ἀποδείκνυμι	to appoint, assign; to demonstrate
ἀποδέχομαι	to receive, accept, acknowledge
ἀπολαύω	to enjoy, take delight in
ἀπροσδόκητος, -ος, -ον	unexpected
ἀπωθέω	to thrust away, drive back, reject
αὐλή, -ῆς, ἡ	court, courtyard
αὐτοδέσποτος, -ου, ὁ	sovereign master

▹ List 21 3×

ἀφοράω	to pay close attention to
βαθύς, -εῖα, -ύ	deep, profound
βασιλικός, -ή, -όν	royal, belonging to the king
βέβαιος, -α, -ον	solid, firm, certain
βιάζομαι	to urge, pressure, (use) force
βουλή, -ῆς, ἡ	plan, advice, council
γελοῖος, -α, -ον	ridiculous, ludicrous, laughable
γνωρίζω	to make known, publicize
γόνυ, γόνατος, τό	knee
δακρύω	to weep, shed tears
δάκτυλος, -ου, ὁ	finger
διάγω	to put through, bring through, spend time
διασῴζω	to preserve, keep safe; (*pas*) to be spared, escape
διατάσσω	to appoint, arrange, direct
δέω	*to bind, constrain*

▹ List 22 3×

διηνεκῶς	continually, persistently
δίψα, -ης, ἡ	thirst
δόρυ, δόρατος, τό	spear
δυσμενής, -ής, -ές	hostile
δυσσεβής, -ής, -ές	ungodly, wicked, impious
ἑβδομάς, -άδος, ἡ	period of seven days *or* years; seven-member grouping
ἔδαφος, -ους, τό	ground, bottom
ἐκμελίζω	to dismember
ἐκτέμνω	to cut out, cut off
ἐλεύθερος, -α, -ον	free, noble
ἐμπί(μ)πλημι	to fill up, satisfy; [ἐ. τὰς χεῖρας] to consecrate as priest
ἐνέργεια, -ας, ἡ	activity, operation, action
ἐνίστημι	to arrive, be present, be current
ἔνοπλος, -ος, -ον	armed
ἐμαυτοῦ, -ῆς, -οῦ	*myself*

▷ List 23 3×

ἔντιμος, -ος, -ον	precious, valuable
ἐξορμάω	to rush out
ἐπίβουλος, -ος, -ον	plotting (against), treacherous
ἐπιθυμέω	to desire, yearn for
ἐπιτείνω	to increase intensity, exert, stretch out
ἐπιτρέπω	to entrust to, permit, allow
ἐπιφάνεια, -ας, ἡ	appearing, manifestation
ἐπιχειρέω	to undertake, attempt; to attack
ἕτοιμος, -η/ος, -ον	ready, prepared
ἐφοράω	to scrutinize, survey, oversee
ζῷον, -ου, τό	living thing, creature
ἡγεμών, -όνος, ὁ	leader
ἡγέομαι	to go before, guide, act as leader, think, consider
ἥκω	to have come, reach, be present
θανατηφόρος, -ος, -ον	deadly, fatal

▷ List 24 3×

θαρραλέως	bravely, courageously
θεοσέβεια, -ας, ἡ	godliness, fear of God, religious piety
θήρ, θηρός, ὁ	feral animal, wild beast
ἱππόδρομος, -ου, ὁ	hippodrome, chariot road
ἴσως	perhaps
κακία, -ας, ἡ	evil, harm, misfortune
καρτερός, -ά, -όν	strong, intense, violent
κατάγω	to bring down, reduce
καταξιόω	to consider worthy, bestow attention
καταπατέω	to walk all over, deal harshly with, oppress
κατασκευάζω	to put together, construct, make ready
καταφλέγω	to burn, consume
κεῖμαι	to lie down; to be valid for
κίνδυνος, -ου, ὁ	danger
κόλασις, -εως, ἡ	punishment, vengeance

▷ List 25 3×

κοσμέω	to set in order, adorn, decorate
κραυγή, -ῆς, ἡ	outcry, shouting
κτίσις, -εως, ἡ	creation, creature
κωλυτικός, -ή, -όν	hindering
λέβης, -ητος, ὁ	cauldron, kettle
λιμήν, -ένος, ὁ	harbor, haven
μακαρίζω	to bless, call happy
μάστιξ, -ιγος, ἡ	whip, suffering
μεγάλως	greatly, intensely
μειράκιον, -ου, τό	boy, lad, young man
μετέρχομαι	to pursue, go over to
μηδέποτε	never
μιαίνω	to make unclean, defile, pollute
νήπιος, -α/ος, -ον	infant, child
οἰκτιρμός, -οῦ, ὁ	compassion, pity

▷ List 26 3×

οἶκτος, -ου, ὁ	sympathy, pity, grief
οἷος, οἵα, οἷον	such (that), of the kind that
ὄλεθρος, -ου, ὁ	destruction, ruin
ὀλοφύρομαι	to lament over
ὄμμα, -ατος, τό	eye
ὁμολογέω	to confess, admit; to praise
ὁμολογουμένως	confessedly, undeniably
ὅπλον, -ου, τό	weapon; (*pl*) arms, armor
ὁρμή, -ῆς, ἡ	zeal, impulse, onrush, assault
ὀστοῦν, -οῦ, τό	bone
παιδεία, -ας, ἡ	training, discipline, instruction
πάνσοφος, -ος, -ον	all wise, most wise
παντοῖος, -α, -ον	of every kind
παράνομος, -ος, -ον	unlawful, lawless
παρρησία, -ας, ἡ	*boldness, freedom of action*

▷ List 27 — 3×

πέμπτος, -η, -ον	fifth
περιέχω	to surround, encircle, contain
περιφρονέω	to disregard, ascribe little value to
πηγή, -ῆς, ἡ	spring, fountain
πόθεν	from where?
πολιά, -ᾶς, ἡ	gray hair
πολυτρόπος, -ος, -ον	manifold, various, varied
πόμα, -ατος, τό	drink
ποτέ	at some time, once, formerly
πότος, -ου, ὁ	drinking party
πρηνής, -ής, -ές	levelled, prostrate
προαιρέω	to pick out, prefer
προασπίζω	to defend, protect
πρόκειμαι	to set before, present, appoint
πειρά(ζ)ω	*to tempt, test, try*

▷ List 28 — 3×

πρόσκαιρος, -ος, -ον	temporary, short-lived
προσπίπτω	to fling oneself; to befall, happen
προτρέπω	to encourage, urge on
πυρόω	to burn (red hot), purify (in fire)
σέβομαι	to worship, revere
σεμνός, -ή, -όν	solemn, reverent, worthy of respect
σκυλμός, -οῦ, ὁ	cruel treatment
σπεύδω	to hasten, hurry
σπουδή, -ῆς, ἡ	haste, hurry, exertion
στρατιά, -ᾶς, ἡ	army, large company (of people)
στρατός, -οῦ, ὁ	army
συγγενής, -ής, -ές	related, kin; (*subst*) relative
συλλαμβάνω	to capture, catch; to become pregnant
σύμβουλος, -ου, ὁ	adviser, counselor
συμπαθής, -ής, -ές	sympathetic

WISDOM OF SOLOMON AND PSALMS OF SOLOMON

▷ List 1 — 29 to 11×

ἄδικος, -ος, -ον	unjust, unrighteous; (*subst*) wrongdoing
ἀπώλεια, -ας, ἡ	destruction, ruin, loss
ἀσεβής, -ής, -ές	ungodly, wicked, sacrilegious
βίος, -ου, ὁ	life, existence
γένεσις, -εως, ἡ	beginning, birth, family origin
ζῷον, -ου, τό	living thing, creature
κολάζω	to penalize, punish
κρίμα, -ατος, τό	decision, judgment, punishment
ὅσιος, -α, -ον	holy, pious, devout
παιδεία, -ας, ἡ	training, discipline, instruction
παράνομος, -ος, -ον	unlawful, lawless
ῥύομαι	to rescue, save
σός, σή, σόν	your, yours
ἄξιος, -α, -ον	*deserving, appropriate*
ἐπιθυμία, -ας, ἡ	*desire, lust*

▷ List 2 — 11 to 8×

ᾅδης, -ου, ὁ	Hades, the underworld
ἀδικία, -ας, ἡ	unrighteousness, wrongdoing, injustice
ἀνομία, -ας, ἡ	lawlessness, wrongful conduct
ἀτιμία, -ας, ἡ	shame, dishonor
ἄφρων, -ων, -ον	foolish, senseless; (*subst*) fool
ἐλέγχω	to question, rebuke, reprove
ἐπισκοπή, -ῆς, ἡ	inspection, consideration, visitation
εὐφροσύνη, -ης, ἡ	joy, gladness
κακία, -ας, ἡ	evil, harm, misfortune
ὄψις, -εως, ἡ	appearance, face, perception
παιδεύω	to instruct, discipline
πόνος, -ου, ὁ	toil, distress, pain
φείδομαι	to spare, refrain, hold back
φρόνησις, -εως, ἡ	insight, understanding
ψαλμός, -οῦ, ὁ	psalm, song of praise

▷ List 3 — 8 to 7×

ἀγνοέω	to be ignorant, be unaware
ἀήρ, ἀέρος, ὁ	air, sky
ἁμάρτημα, -ατος, τό	sin (offering)
ἀνθίστημι	to resist, oppose
ἀφίστημι	to keep away, remove; (*mid*) to depart, withdraw
βία, -ας, ἡ	violence, force
γνῶσις, -εως, ἡ	knowledge, understanding
δεινός, -ή, -όν	awful, terrible, dreadful
εἰκών, -όνος, ἡ	image, (idol)
ἰσχύω	to be strong, be capable; (*trans*) to intensify
κάλλος, -ους, τό	beauty
κληρονομία, -ας, ἡ	inheritance, possession(s)
πάρειμι	to be near, be present, have arrived
ὑπερηφανία, -ας, ἡ	arrogance, pride
δικαιόω	*to justify, vindicate, pronounce righteous*

▷ List 4 — 7 to 6×

ἀλλότριος, -α, -ον	foreign, strange, unfamiliar
ἄστρον, -ου, τό	star
βουλή, -ῆς, ἡ	plan, advice, council
δεσπότης, -ου, ὁ	master, absolute ruler
εἴδωλον, -ου, τό	image (of a god), idol
ἔλεγχος, -ου, ὁ	reproof, conviction, refutation
κτίζω	to establish, build, create
λογισμός, -οῦ, ὁ	thought, (line of) reasoning
μερίς, -ίδος, ἡ	share, part, portion
οὐθείς, οὐθέν	no one, none, nothing
πλοῦτος, -ου, ὁ	wealth, riches
φεύγω	to flee, escape, vanish
χρηστός, -ή, -όν	kind, fine (quality), pleasant
χρηστότης, -ητος, ἡ	kindness, goodness, generosity
πειρά(ζ)ω	*to tempt, test, try*

▷ List 5 6×

ἐξαίρω	to raise up, remove, pack up camp and go
ἐπέρχομαι	to come upon, happen upon, attack
ἡγέομαι	to go before, guide, act as leader, think, consider
θλίβω	to press, oppress, afflict
κατασκευάζω	to put together, construct, make ready
κατευθύνω	to direct, guide; (*pas*) to prosper
μακράν	far away, distant
μιμνῄσκομαι	to remember, recall
μνήμη, -ης, ἡ	memory, remembrance
πέρας, -ατος, τό	limit, end
πλάσσω	to form, mold
πονηρία, -ας, ἡ	evil, vice
ταράσσω	to trouble, disturb
τρίβος, -ου, ἡ/ὁ	path, route
ὅμοιος, -α, -ον	*like, similar to*

▷ List 6 6 to 5×

ἄγνοια, -ας, ἡ	ignorance; sin of ignorance
ἀθανασία, -ας, ἡ	immortality
ἀκαθαρσία, -ας, ἡ	uncleanness, impurity
ἀληθής, -ής, -ές	true, genuine
ἄνομος, -ος, -ον	lawless, wicked
ἀπότομος, -ος, -ον	relentless, severe
ἄτιμος, -ος, -ον	dishonored, not respectable, disreputable
ἄχρηστος, -ος, -ον	useless, unprofitable
γένος, -ους, τό	kind, people group, family (lineage)
γῆρας, -ως, τό	old age
ὕπνος, -ου, ὁ	sleep
φλόξ, φλογός, ἡ	flame
χεῖλος, -ους, τό	lip, language, edge
ἄνεμος, -ου, ὁ	*wind*
ἅπας, ἅπασα, ἅπαν	*all, every*

▷ List 7 5×

δέομαι	to ask (for), pray (for)
δίκη, -ης, ἡ	penalty, punishment, justice
δόλος, -ου, ὁ	deceit, dishonesty, craftiness
εἴσοδος, -ου, ἡ	entering, entryway, area of entrance
ἐπίσταμαι	to know, be acquainted with
ἐρημόω	to make desolate, dry up
κριτής, -οῦ, ὁ	judge
κτίσις, -εως, ἡ	creation, creature
μιαίνω	to make unclean, defile, pollute
ξένος, -η, -ον	foreign, strange
ὅρκος, -ου, ὁ	oath
παράπτωμα, -ατος, τό	mistake, error
παροδεύω	to pass by, disregard, overlook
ποθέω	to desire, yearn for
πάσχω	*to suffer, undergo*

▷ List 8 5 to 4×

ἁγιάζω	to make holy, consecrate, sanctify
ἀδίκως	wrongfully, unjustly, falsely
αἰνέω	to praise
ποτέ	at some time, once, formerly
σκορπίζω	to scatter, disperse
σοφός, -ή, -όν	wise, skilled, learned
σωτήρ, -ῆρος, ὁ	savior, deliverer
ταχέως	quickly, hastily, soon(er)
τήκω	to melt; to waste away
τιμάω	to honor; (*mid*) to value (at a price)
τροφή, -ῆς, ἡ	food, provisions
τύραννος, -ου, ὁ	sovereign ruler
ὑπομένω	to remain, endure, wait for
φροντίς, -ίδος, ἡ	care, attention, thought
ψευδής, -ής, -ές	lying, false; (*subst*) liar

▷ List 9 4×

ἄκακος, -ος, -ον	innocent, ingenuous
ἄνευ	(+*gen*) without, far from
ἀνθρωπάρεσκος, -ου, ὁ	people pleaser
ἅπαξ	once
ἄπειμι	to be absent, be away from
ἀπιστέω	to disbelieve, refuse to trust
ἀφαιρέω	to separate, remove; (*mid*) to deprive, seize, take away
βαρύνω	to make heavy, burden
βασανίζω	to torment, torture
βάσανος, -ου, ἡ	torment, (instrument of) torture
βασίλειον, -ου, τό	royal palace, kingdom
βέβηλος, -ος, -ον	common, profane
βραχίων, -ονος, ὁ	arm, (strength)
γογγυσμός, -οῦ, ὁ	grumbling, muttering, complaint
διαφέρω	to carry over, transport, differ (from)

▷ List 10 4×

διαφυλάσσω	to watch over, guard, keep
διοδεύω	to pass through, travel throughout
διοικέω	to manage, administer
δοκιμάζω	to prove, put to the test
ἐλάχιστος, -η, -ον	smallest, least, fewest
ἐμπί(μ)πλημι	to fill up, satisfy; [ἐ. τὰς χεῖρας] to consecrate as priest
ἐμφανίζω	to make visible, make known
ἐνέργεια, -ας, ἡ	activity, operation, action
ἐνθυμέομαι	to reflect, ponder
ἐξομολογέω	to acknowledge, admit, confess
ἐπακούω	to hear, listen to, comply
ἐπίνοια, -ας, ἡ	purpose, design, invention
ἐπισκέπτομαι	to visit, examine, account for
ἐπιταγή, -ῆς, ἡ	commandment, directive
εὐεργετέω	to show kindness (to), confer benefit

▷ List 11 4×

εὐλογία, -ας, ἡ	praise, blessing
εὐτελής, -ής, -ές	worthless, poor in quality
εὐφραίνω	to make happy, cheer; (*pas*) to rejoice
ἐφίστημι	to cast over, place on
ἴσος, -η, -ον	equal, same
ἰσχυρός, -ά, -όν	strong, powerful
καθαρός, -ά, -όν	pure, clean
καταδικάζω	to pronounce guilty, judge against
καταδυναστεύω	to oppress, prevail against
κατισχύω	to strengthen, overpower; (*intr*) to be encouraged, become powerful
κόλασις, -εως, ἡ	punishment, vengeance
κραταιός, -ά, -όν	powerful, forceful, severe
κράτος, -ους, τό	might, strength, power
κῦμα, -ατος, τό	wave, billow
θαυμάζω	*to be astonished, marvel at*

▷ List 12 4×

μανθάνω	to learn, find out
μνημονεύω	to remember, keep in mind
μυστήριον, -ου, τό	mystery, secret, rite
νέος, -α, -ον	new, young; (*subst*) child
νήπιος, -α/ος, -ον	infant, child
νικάω	to prevail, triumph
νουθετέω	to warn, admonish
ὀλεθρεύω	to destroy (totally)
ὄλεθρος, -ου, ὁ	destruction, ruin
ὄμνυμι *or* ὀμνύω	to swear, take an oath
ὄρεξις, -εως, ἡ	appetite, passion, yearning
ὁσιότης, ὁσιότητος, ἡ	piety, holiness
ὀστοῦν, -οῦ, τό	bone
παρανομία, -ας, ἡ	wrongdoing, legal violation, iniquity
ὁμοίως	*likewise*

▷ List 13 4×

παρέρχομαι	to go past, pass by, move on
πενία, -ας, ἡ	need, shortfall, lack, poverty
πηλός, -οῦ, ὁ	mud, clay
πίμπλημι	to fill, satisfy
πλήρης, -ης, -ες	full, complete
ποταμός, -οῦ, ὁ	river, stream
προσδέχομαι	to accept, receive favorably, anticipate
ῥίζα, -ης, ἡ	root
σαλεύω	to shake, rock, disrupt
σύνεσις, -εως, ἡ	understanding, intelligence
συνέχω	to constrain, enclose, afflict
τελευτή, -ῆς, ἡ	end, death
τέρας, -ατος, τό	wonder, omen, remarkable sight
τέχνη, -ης, ἡ	craft, trade, skill
τίμιος, -α, -ον	reputable, valuable, expensive

▷ List 14 4 to 3×

ἀγαθότης, ἀγαθότητος, ἡ	goodness, moral integrity
ἁγίασμα, -ατος, τό	sanctuary, sacred offering
ἀδύνατος, -ος, -ον	powerless, incapacitated
αἰνετός, -ή, -όν	praiseworthy
αἰτία, -ας, ἡ	cause, reason
ἄλογος, -ος, -ον	ineloquent, unreasoning, discounted
ἄμεμπτος, -ος, -ον	blameless
ἀμίαντος, -ος, -ον	undefiled
τρέφω	to feed, nourish; (*mid*) to grow up
ὕβρις, -εως, ἡ	arrogance, insult, insolence
ὑετός, -οῦ, ὁ	rain
ὕμνος, -ου, ὁ	hymn, song of praise
ὑπηρετέω	to render service, help
ὕψιστος, -η, -ον	highest, most high (God)
ψίθυρος, -ος, -ον	slanderous, whispering

▷ List 15 3×

ἀνάγκη, -ης, ἡ	constraint, distress
ἀνακαλύπτω	to uncover, disclose
ἀναλύω	to set free; to go away, depart
ἀναστρέφω	to return, change course; (*mid*) to conduct oneself, live
ἀνατολή, -ῆς, ἡ	sprouting, rising; morning; (*pl*) east
ἀνόμημα, -ατος, τό	lawlessness, wrongful conduct
ἀντιλαμβάνομαι	to aid, assist
ἀπέχω	to be far away, be unavailable, withdraw, receive payment; (*mid*) to stay away
ἀποκρύπτω	to conceal, hide
ἀπολείπω	to leave (behind), abandon; to cease
ἀπορία, -ας, ἡ	discomfort, distress, perplexity
ἀπορ(ρ)ίπτω	to throw away, discard, reject
ἀπωθέω	to thrust away, drive back, reject
ἀρεστός, -ή, -όν	pleasing, acceptable
ἀρετή, -ῆς, ἡ	virtue, excellence

▷ List 16 3×

ἀρχαῖος, -α, -ον	former, old, ancient
ἀσθενής, -ής, -ές	weak, helpless
ἀσφαλής, -ής, -ές	safe, steadfast, secure
ἀσφαλίζω	to secure, make safe
ἀφθαρσία, -ας, ἡ	incorruptibility, immortality
βαρύς, -εῖα, -ύ	heavy, difficult
βοήθεια, -ας, ἡ	help, support
βραχύς, -εῖα, -ύ	short, small
γάμος, -ου, ὁ	marriage, wedding (feast)
γεῦσις, -εως, ἡ	taste, (act of) tasting
δειλός, -ή, -όν	cowardly, afraid, miserable
δεσπόζω	to be master, rule over
διαφθείρω	to utterly destroy, ruin
ἀρνέομαι	*to deny, disown, forsake*
ἀσθενέω	*to be weak, become less functional*

▷ **List 17**	3×
δικαίως	justly, rightly
δόμα, -ατος, τό	gift
εἰκάζω	to conjecture, make an inference
εἶτα	then, further
ἔκβασις, -εως, ἡ	end (of life), result, event
ἐκλείπω	to abandon, neglect; (*intr*) to fail, run out, cease
ἐκλεκτός, -ή, -όν	chosen, select, elite
ἐκταράσσω	to throw into confusion, agitate
ἐκχέω	to pour out, spill
ἐλεήμων, -ων, -ον	merciful, showing pity
ἐμπαιγμός, -οῦ, ὁ	mockery, mocking
ἐμφανής, -ής, -ές	visible, manifest, out in the open
ἔντιμος, -ος, -ον	precious, valuable
ἔξοδος, -ου, ἡ	departure, way out
ἐμαυτοῦ, -ῆς, -οῦ	*myself*

▷ **List 18**	3×
ἐξουδ(θ)ενό(έ)ω	to disdain, reject
ἐπαγγέλλομαι	to promise, pledge, profess
ἐπιθυμέω	to desire, yearn for
ἐπιλανθάνω	(*mid*) to forget, overlook, ignore
ἐπιστήμη, -ης, ἡ	skill, competence, understanding
ἐπιστροφή, -ῆς, ἡ	return, turning, conversion
ἐργασία, -ας, ἡ	work, occupation, product
εὐδοκία, -ας, ἡ	goodwill, approval; satisfaction
εὐπρέπεια, -ας, ἡ	attractiveness, dignity, loveliness
εὐστάθεια, -ας, ἡ	stability, tranquility
ζῆλος, -ου, ὁ	jealousy, zeal
ἥκω	to have come, reach, be present
ἦχος, -ου/ους, ὁ/τό	noise, sound
θνητός, -ή, -όν	mortal
ἱκανός, -ή, -όν	*sufficient, adequate, capable*

▹ List 19 3×

ἵππος, -ου, ὁ	horse
κακῶς	badly, harmfully, wickedly
καλλονή, -ῆς, ἡ	beauty, excellence
καπνός, -οῦ, ὁ	smoke
καταλαμβάνω	to take hold of, overtake, capture
καταπίπτω	to fall down, cast down
κενός, -ή, -όν	empty, worthless, pointless
κλῆρος, -ου, ὁ	lot, share, portion
κνώδαλον, -ου, τό	wild animal
κοίτη, -ης, ἡ	bed; sexual intercourse, ejaculation
κτίσμα, -ατος, τό	creation, creature
λανθάνω	to go unnoticed, be ignored
λεπτός, -ή, -όν	small, thin, fragile
λύπη, -ης, ἡ	sorrow, pain
λυτρόω	(*mid*) to redeem, ransom

▹ List 20 3×

μακρός, -ά, -όν	long, far, distant
μάστιξ, -ιγος, ἡ	whip, suffering
μετάνοια, -ας, ἡ	change of mind, repentance
μεταξύ	(+*gen*) among, between
μισθός, -οῦ, ὁ	payment, wages, reward
μνημόσυνον, -ου, τό	memory, memorial, reminder
νεότης, -ητος, ἡ	youth
νοέω	to understand, perceive
ὁδηγέω	to lead, guide
ὁδοιπορία, -ας, ἡ	journey, marching, traveling
ὀδύνη, -ης, ἡ	pain, grief
ὅθεν	from where, consequently
οἰκτίρω	to show mercy (to), have compassion (on)
ὁμοθυμαδόν	with one accord, together
μάρτυς, -υρος, ὁ	*witness*

▷ List 21 — 3×

ὀξύς, -εῖα, -ύ	swift, sharp, severe
ὄρνεον, -ου, τό	bird
πάλαι	long ago, before, previously
παντοδύναμος, -ος, -ον	all powerful, almighty
παράδοξος, -ος, -ον	contrary to expectation, unusual
παραλύω	to weaken, disable, be paralyzed
παρέχω	to bring about, contribute (to)
πάροδος, -ου, ὁ/ἡ	passage, way; traveler, passer-by
παροικία, -ας, ἡ	residence as a foreigner
περιτίθημι	to put on, put around
πληθύνω	to increase, multiply
πλούσιος, -α, -ον	rich, wealthy, abundant
πορεία, -ας, ἡ	journey, course, way
πόσος, -η, -ον	how much?, how many?
παρίστημι	*to place near, present;* (intr) *to stand near, be present to serve*

▷ List 22 — 3×

πρεσβύτης, -ου, ὁ	old man, elder
προγινώσκω	to know beforehand
προσέχω	to pay attention to, be concerned about
πρωτότοκος, -ος, -ον	firstborn
ῥίπτω	to throw (away), defeat, reject
ῥομφαία, -ας, ἡ	sword
σκεπάζω	to cover over, shelter, conceal
σκῆπτρον, -ου, τό	staff, scepter
σκολιός, -ά, -όν	crooked, dishonest, perverse
σπινθήρ, -ῆρος, ὁ	spark, flashing
συμβίωσις, -εως, ἡ	intimate company, close association
συνθήκη, -ης, ἡ	agreement, pact
συνίημι	to understand, notice, ponder
τεῖχος, -ους, τό	(city) wall
τελετή, -ῆς, ἡ	pagan mystic ritual

▷ List 23 3×

τεχνῖτις, -ιδος, ἡ	craftsperson, designer
τοσοῦτος, -αύτη, -οῦτον	so much, so great
ὑπολαμβάνω	to say in response, take up, consider
ὑπόστασις, -εως, ἡ	foundation, possession, substance
ὑψηλός, -ή, -όν	elevated, proud; (*subst*) high place
φθάνω	to come before; to overtake, reach
φθορά, -ᾶς, ἡ	ruin, corruption, decay
φιλάνθρωπος, -ος, -ον	humane, kindly; (*subst*) privilege
φυγάς, -άδος, ὁ	runaway, fugitive
φύσις, -εως, ἡ	nature, natural disposition
φυτόν, -οῦ, τό	plant, bush
χάλαζα, -ης, ἡ	hail
χαλεπός, -ή, -όν	grievous, harsh, difficult
χρυσός, -οῦ, ὁ	gold
ᾠδή, -ῆς, ἡ	song, ode

WISDOM OF BEN SIRA (SIRACH)

▷ **LIST 1**	**47 TO 21×**
ἀνυψόω	to lift up, raise, exalt
ἀφίστημι	to keep away, remove; (*mid*) to depart, withdraw
ἔναντι	(+*gen*) opposite, before, in the presence of
κτίζω	to establish, build, create
μήποτε	lest, in order that . . . not
μιμνῄσκομαι	to remember, recall
μωρός, -ά, -όν	stupid, senseless
παιδεία, -ας, ἡ	training, discipline, instruction
πληθύνω	to increase, multiply
πλησίον	(+*gen*) near, close; (*subst*) neighbor
σοφός, -ή, -όν	wise, skilled, learned
σύνεσις, -εως, ἡ	understanding, intelligence
ὕψιστος, -η, -ον	highest, most high (God)
φίλος, -η, -ον	friendly; (*subst*) friend, associate
χρεία, -ας, ἡ	*necessity, need*

▷ **LIST 2**	**19 TO 16×**
αἰνέω	to praise
ἀνάπαυσις, -εως, ἡ	rest, stopping
ἀσεβής, -ής, -ές	ungodly, wicked, sacrilegious
βουλή, -ῆς, ἡ	plan, advice, council
διανοέομαι	to plan (an action), intend (to do), ponder
δόσις, -εως, ἡ	gift
ἐπιστήμη, -ης, ἡ	skill, competence, understanding
εὐλογία, -ας, ἡ	praise, blessing
εὐφραίνω	to make happy, cheer; (*pas*) to rejoice
καταλείπω	to leave (behind), abandon; (*pas*) to remain
κληρονομία, -ας, ἡ	inheritance, possession(s)
κρίμα, -ατος, τό	decision, judgment, punishment
μνημόσυνον, -ου, τό	memory, memorial, reminder
πλούσιος, -α, -ον	rich, wealthy, abundant
προσέχω	to pay attention to, be concerned about

▷ List 3 — 16 to 14×

ἀλλότριος, -α, -ον	foreign, strange, unfamiliar
ἀμφότεροι, -αι, -α	both
δέομαι	to ask (for), pray (for)
ἐκχέω	to pour out, spill
ἐλασσόω (ττ)	to reduce, lower; (*pas*) to be in want
ἐμπί(μ)πλημι	to fill up, satisfy; [ἐ. τὰς χεῖρας] to consecrate as priest
εὐδοκία, -ας, ἡ	goodwill, approval; satisfaction
εὐσεβής, -ής, -ές	pious, devout, religious
εὐφροσύνη, -ης, ἡ	joy, gladness
λύπη, -ης, ἡ	sorrow, pain
παιδεύω	to instruct, discipline
συνετός, -ή, -όν	sensible, clever, intelligent
συντέλεια, -ας, ἡ	end, conclusion, perfection, annihilation
συντηρέω	to preserve, defend, treasure up
χρῆμα, -ατος, τό	wealth, property

▷ List 4 — 14 to 12×

δυνάστης, -ου, ὁ	ruler, master, official
ἐκδίκησις, -εως, ἡ	vengeance, punishment
ἐκκαίω	to inflame, kindle, burn
ἐλεημοσύνη, -ης, ἡ	kind act, charitable giving, mercy
ἐμπιστεύω	to trust in
ἐξαίρω	to raise up, remove, pack up camp and go
κρύπτω	to hide, conceal
κτάομαι	to get, acquire
μεγιστάν, -ᾶνος, ὁ	noble, magistrate, influential person
μερίς, -ίδος, ἡ	share, part, portion
οἰκέτης, -ου, ὁ	household servant
πονηρία, -ας, ἡ	evil, vice
ταπεινόω	to bring down, humiliate, humble
χάριν	(+*gen*) for the sake of
χρυσίον, -ου, τό	gold

▷ List 5 — 12 to 10×

ᾅδης, -ου, ὁ	Hades, the underworld
ἀδικία, -ας, ἡ	unrighteousness, wrongdoing, injustice
ἄδικος, -ος, -ον	unjust, unrighteous; (*subst*) wrongdoing
αἰσχύνη, -ης, ἡ	shame, disgrace
ἄφρων, -ων, -ον	foolish, senseless; (*subst*) fool
ἐγκαταλείπω	to abandon, leave behind
ἡγέομαι	to go before, guide, act as leader, think, consider
κάλλος, -ους, τό	beauty
κατέναντι	(+*gen*) in front of, opposite, against
πλοῦτος, -ου, ὁ	wealth, riches
πτῶσις, -εως, ἡ	fall, downfall, calamity
στηρίζω	to support, strengthen, establish
ὑπερήφανος, -ος, -ον	arrogant, haughty, lofty
χεῖλος, -ους, τό	lip, language, edge
δικαιόω	*to justify, vindicate, pronounce righteous*

▷ List 6 — 10 to 9×

ἀγρυπνία, -ας, ἡ	sleeplessness, wakefulness
αἰσχύνω	to dishonor; (*pas*) to be ashamed
ἀλλοιόω	to change, alter
ἀνταποδίδωμι	to give back, repay
ἀποκαλύπτω	to uncover, reveal, disclose
ἀπώλεια, -ας, ἡ	destruction, ruin, loss
διηγέομαι	to describe in detail, relate fully
ἐκδιηγέομαι	to describe accurately, tell in detail
ἐκφαίνω	to bring to light, disclose
ἐμπίπτω	to fall into, fall on, attack
νεφέλη, -ης, ἡ	cloud
ὀνειδισμός, -οῦ, ὁ	disgrace, insult
πρίν	before
σοφίζω	to make wise; (*mid*) to be wise
στερεόω	to make strong, establish

▷ List 7 — 9×

ἀπόκρυφος, -ος, -ον	hidden, concealed, obscure
ἀριθμός, -οῦ, ὁ	number, total
βδέλυγμα, -ατος, τό	abomination, detestable object
βρῶμα, -ατος, τό	food, provisions
ἐκλείπω	to abandon, neglect; (*intr*) to fail, run out, cease
ἐκτείνω	to stretch out, reach out, extend
ἐξιλάσκομαι	to propitiate, make atonement
ἐπαγωγή, -ῆς, ἡ	distress
ἐπέχω	to hold in place, bring to a stop, refrain
ἐπιβλέπω	to look at (attentively), observe, anticipate
ἐπιλανθάνω	(*mid*) to forget, overlook, ignore
εὐλαβέομαι	to be concerned, be afraid, show respect
ζυγός/ζυγόν, -οῦ, ὁ/τό	yoke; balance scale
θαυμάσιος, -α, -ον	remarkable, amazing
ἐπιθυμία, -ας, ἡ	*desire, lust*

▷ List 8 — 9×

καταράομαι	to curse
κληρονομέω	to inherit, become heir to, give as inheritance
κοπιάω	to become tired, work hard, strive
μάχη, -ης, ἡ	battle, quarrel, strife
ὅρασις, -εως, ἡ	seeing, appearance, (prophetic) vision
ποταμός, -οῦ, ὁ	river, stream
προσφορά, -ᾶς, ἡ	presentation, offering
στέφανος, -ου, ὁ	crown, (victor's) garland
σφραγίς, -ῖδος, ἡ	seal
ταπεινός, -ή, -όν	humble, abject, oppressed
τελευτή, -ῆς, ἡ	end, death
ὑπερηφανία, -ας, ἡ	arrogance, pride
ὕψος, -ους, τό	height, summit
ὡραῖος, -α, -ον	beautiful, lovely
ὅμοιος, -α, -ον	*like, similar to*

▷ List 9 — 8×

ἀτιμία, -ας, ἡ	shame, dishonor
γλυκαίνω	to sweeten; (*pas*) to taste sweet
διαμένω	to continue, persist, endure
εἰσακούω	to hear, listen to, obey
ἐνδελεχίζω	to continue, persist
ἐξαλείφω	to wipe out, erase, obliterate
ἐπάγω	to bring (up)on
ἐπαίρω	to lift up, raise, magnify
θησαυρός, -οῦ, ὁ	treasure, treasury, storehouse
ἴασις, -εως, ἡ	remedy, healing
κακόω	to do wrong, mistreat
καύχημα, -ατος, τό	object of boasting, pride, glory
κοσμέω	to set in order, adorn, decorate
κριτής, -οῦ, ὁ	judge
καυχάομαι	*to boast (about)*

▷ List 10 — 8 to 7×

ἀπαίδευτος, -ος, -ον	uneducated, untrained, ignorant
ἀτιμάζω	to dishonor
δέησις, -εως, ἡ	supplication, request
διανόημα, -ατος, τό	notion, thought
διήγησις, -εως, ἡ	tale, narrative, discourse
λαλιά, -ᾶς, ἡ	chat, (manner *or* subject of) speech
λέων, -οντος, ὁ	lion
μάστιξ, -ιγος, ἡ	whip, suffering
μεγαλεῖος, -α, -ον	great, magnificent, majestic
νεότης, -ητος, ἡ	youth
παραβαίνω	to deviate, turn away
πληγή, -ῆς, ἡ	blow, wound, misfortune, plague
σαλεύω	to shake, rock, disrupt
συντελέω	to finish, complete, accomplish
φρόνιμος, -ος, -ον	thoughtful, prudent, wise

▷ List 11 7×

ἐκδικέω	to avenge, punish
ἐκζητέω	to search for, seek out, demand
ἐκκλίνω	to bend, turn away; (*intr*) to avoid, deviate
ἐλέγχω	to question, rebuke, reprove
ἐνεδρεύω	to lie in wait for, set an ambush
ἐπισκέπτομαι	to visit, examine, account for
ἐργασία, -ας, ἡ	work, occupation, product
εὖ	well, good
ἰσχύω	to be strong, be capable; (*trans*) to intensify
κάμινος, -ου, ἡ	oven, furnace
καταλαμβάνω	to take hold of, overtake, capture
καταλύω	to lodge, bring down, destroy
καταπαύω	to bring to an end, stop, cease
κατασπεύδω	to hurry up, urge on
κλάδος, -ου, ὁ	branch (of a plant)

▷ List 12 7×

κυκλόθεν	all around, from all sides
μακράν	far away, distant
μισθός, -οῦ, ὁ	payment, wages, reward
μουσικός, -ή, -όν	musical; (*subst*) music, musician
ὀλισθάνω	to fall, cause to slip
ὀνειδίζω	to insult, criticize, taunt
πίμπλημι	to fill, satisfy
πρότερος, -α, -ον	former, earlier, before
προφητεία, -ας, ἡ	prophecy
πτωχεία, -ας, ἡ	poverty
συντρίβω	to break, crush, wreck
τελευτάω	to die
ὕπνος, -ου, ὁ	sleep
ὑποδείκνυμι *or* ὑποδεικνύω	to demonstrate, inform, point out
ψεῦδος, -ους, τό	lie, falsehood

▷ **List 13**	**6×**
ἄβυσσος, -ος, -ον	deep; (*subst*) abyss, depths
ἁγιάζω	to make holy, consecrate, sanctify
ἁγίασμα, -ατος, τό	sanctuary, sacred offering
ἀναστρέφω	to return, change course; (*mid*) to conduct oneself, live
ἄνομος, -ος, -ον	lawless, wicked
ἀντιλαμβάνομαι	to aid, assist
ἀπειθέω	to be disobedient, refuse
ἀσύνετος, -ος, -ον	senseless, witless, unintelligent
γνῶσις, -εως, ἡ	knowledge, understanding
δεσμός, -οῦ, ὁ	chain, restraints
διαβολή, -ῆς, ἡ	slander, false accusation
ἐλάττωσις, -εως, ἡ	defect, (personal) loss
ἐλεγμός, -οῦ, ὁ	refutation, reproof, reprimand
ἐμβλέπω	to look at, evaluate
ἐμμένω	to persist, continue, stand

▷ **List 14**	**6×**
ἐνδύω	to dress, clothe
ἐξιλασμός, -οῦ, ὁ	propitiation, atonement
εὐδοκέω	to consent, accept, be pleased
εὐθύνω	to direct correctly, straighten out
ζηλόω	to be jealous of *or* for, envy, strive for
ἰσχυρός, -ά, -όν	strong, powerful
κακία, -ας, ἡ	evil, harm, misfortune
καταισχύνω	to put to shame, disappoint
κατακληρονομέω	to give as inheritance, become owner, dispossess
κατάρα, -ας, ἡ	curse
κοιλία, -ας, ἡ	belly, stomach, womb
κωλύω	to hinder, prevent, withhold
μακαρίζω	to bless, call happy
μῶμος, -ου, ὁ	defect, blemish
μέλος, -ους, τό	*body part; musical part*

▷ List 15 6×

νέος, -α, -ον	new, young; (*subst*) child
ὁμοιόω	to be similar, make like, compare
οὐθείς, οὐθέν	no one, none, nothing
παγίς, -ίδος, ἡ	trap, snare
πειρασμός, -οῦ, ὁ	test, temptation
πλημμέλεια, -ας, ἡ	(sinful) error, mistake
πλημμελέω	to trespass, err, offend
πόνος, -ου, ὁ	toil, distress, pain
ῥίζα, -ης, ἡ	root
ῥομφαία, -ας, ἡ	sword
σκέπη, -ης, ἡ	covering, shelter, hideout
ταχύς, -εῖα, -ύ	quickly, soon
ὑστερέω	to come up short, fail, lack
ὑψόω	to lift up, raise high, exalt
φωτίζω	to brighten, shine, illuminate

▷ List 16 6 to 5×

ἀγαλλίαμα, -ατος, τό	joy, gladness
ἀδικέω	to do wrong, harm
ἁλίσκομαι	to be captured, be caught
ἀναθάλλω	to flourish, sprout anew, revive
ἀναπαύω	to stop, refresh, rest; to give rest
ἄνευ	(+*gen*) without, far from
ἀνομία, -ας, ἡ	lawlessness, wrongful conduct
ἀνταπόδομα, -ατος, τό	repayment, recompense, reward
ἀπέναντι *or* ἀπεναντίον	(+*gen*) opposite, contrary to, against
ἀποστερέω	to defraud, rob, deprive unjustly
ἀρρώστημα, -ατος, τό	sickness, illness, infirmity
βαρύνω	to make heavy, burden
γῆρας, -ως, τό	old age
δαν(ε)ίζω	to lend; (*mid*) to borrow
χρυσοῦς, -ῆ, -οῦν / χρύσεος, -α, -ον	golden; (*subst*) golden coin

▷ List 17 — 5×

διαλογισμός, -οῦ, ὁ	deliberation, thought, discussion
δοκιμάζω	to prove, put to the test
δυναστεία, -ας, ἡ	power, dominance
ἔδεσμα, -ατος, τό	food, provisions
εἰρηνεύω	to be at peace
ἐκτρίβω	to rub firmly, destroy completely
ἐκφεύγω	to escape, flee
ἐνδελεχῶς	continually, constantly
ἐνύπνιον, -ου, τό	dream
ἐξετάζω	to examine closely, investigate
ἔξοδος, -ου, ἡ	departure, way out
ἐξομολογέω	to acknowledge, admit, confess
ἐξομολόγησις, -εως, ἡ	(confession of) thanksgiving
ἐπιστήμων, -ων, -ον	learned, skilled
ἑταῖρος, -ου, ὁ	friend, companion

▷ List 18 — 5×

εὐοδόω	to lead safely, ensure success, grant; (*pas*) to prosper
εὐωδία, -ας, ἡ	aroma, fragrance
θεμέλιον/ος, -ου, τό	foundation
θλίβω	to press, oppress, afflict
ἰατρός, -οῦ, ὁ	healer, physician
ἴχνος, -ους, τό	footprint, track, sole (of the foot)
καθίστημι	to place, appoint, establish; (*mid*) to stand against
καλύπτω	to cover, conceal
καταβάλλω	to throw down, overthrow, ruin
κατάγω	to bring down, reduce
κατακλυσμός, -οῦ, ὁ	flood, inundation
κατευθύνω	to direct, guide; (*pas*) to prosper
κλίνω	to incline, lean, turn over, bend
κοπάζω	to stop, (cause to) cease, rest
θαυμάζω	*to be astonished, marvel at*

▷ List 19 — 5×

κόπος, -ου, ὁ	difficulty, trouble, toil
κρυπτός, -ή, -όν	hidden, secret
λειτουργέω	to serve (as priest), minister
λυπέω	to vex, displease; (*mid/pas*) to be distressed, grieve
λυτρόω	(*mid*) to redeem, ransom
μανθάνω	to learn, find out
μέλι, -ιτος, τό	honey
μέριμνα, -ης, ἡ	care, anxiety, concern
ὀδούς, -όντος, ὁ	tooth
ὀστοῦν, -οῦ, τό	bone
πανοῦργος, -ος, -ον	shrewd, sly, clever
παρέρχομαι	to go past, pass by, move on
παρίημι	to leave alone, neglect
παροιμία, -ας, ἡ	proverb, maxim, saying
πειρά(ζ)ω	*to tempt, test, try*

▷ List 20 — 5×

πένθος, -ους, τό	grief, mourning
πετεινός, -ή, -όν	winged; (*subst*) bird
πήγνυμι	to put up, pitch (a tent), fasten
πραΰτης/πραότης, -ητος, ἡ	gentleness, meekness
προσδέομαι	to be in need of, beg
πρόσκομμα, -ατος, τό	cause of stumbling, obstacle
σιωπάω	to be quiet, keep silent
σκεπάζω	to cover over, shelter, conceal
σπουδή, -ῆς, ἡ	haste, hurry, exertion
σταθμός, -οῦ, ὁ	lodgings; doorpost; scales
συνοικέω	to live with
τράπεζα, -ης, ἡ	table
ὑπεροράω	to disregard, ignore
ὑπομένω	to remain, endure, wait for
ποῖος, -α, -ον	*what (kind of)?, which?*

▷ List 21 — 5 to 4×

ἀπαντάω	to receive (someone), encounter, befall
ἀπαρχή, -ῆς, ἡ	first portion, firstfruits
ἀφροσύνη, -ης, ἡ	foolishness
βίος, -ου, ὁ	life, existence
βοήθεια, -ας, ἡ	help, support
βουλεύω	to consider, resolve, counsel
βραχίων, -ονος, ὁ	arm, (strength)
δεσπότης, -ου, ὁ	master, absolute ruler
φιλία, -ας, ἡ	friendship, love
φρόνησις, -εως, ἡ	insight, understanding
χίλιοι, -αι, -α	one thousand
χορηγέω	to supply, provide
ψευδής, -ής, -ές	lying, false; (*subst*) liar
ὠφελέω	to profit, benefit, be useful
ἄνεμος, -ου, ὁ	*wind*

▷ List 22 — 4×

εἰσάγω	to bring in, lead in, introduce
ἔκγονος, -ος, -ον	born of; (*subst*) descendant
ἐκλεκτός, -ή, -όν	chosen, select, elite
ἔνδοξος, -ος, -ον	reputable, honored, distinguished
ἐξαιρέω	to take out, remove; (*mid*) to set free
ἐπιβαίνω	to get on, walk over, fall upon
ἐπιθυμέω	to desire, yearn for
ἐπισκοπή, -ῆς, ἡ	inspection, consideration, visitation
ἐρημόω	to make desolate, dry up
ἐφίστημι	to cast over, place on
ζῷον, -ου, τό	living thing, creature
θαυμαστός, -ή, -όν	remarkable, wonderful, astonishing
καίω	to light (a flame), burn
κατασκηνόω	to dwell, settle
καταστρέφω	to turn over, overthrow, ruin

▷ **List 23**	4×
κενός, -ή, -όν	empty, worthless, pointless
κέρας, κέρατος, τό	horn, flank (of an army)
λιμός, -οῦ, ὁ	hunger, famine
λογισμός, -οῦ, ὁ	thought, (line of) reasoning
μεγαλύνω	to enlarge, increase, magnify
μεγαλωσύνη, -ης, ἡ	majesty, greatness
μεθύσκω	to make drunk; (*pas*) to be drunk
μυστήριον, -ου, τό	mystery, secret, rite
ὄνειδος, -ους, τό	disgrace, loss of esteem
ὀρθρίζω	to get up early
ὀσμή, -ῆς, ἡ	fragrance, scent, smell
παύω	to stop, prevent; (*mid*) to cease, come to an end
πένης, -ητος, ὁ	poor person, day laborer
πενθέω	to grieve, mourn
οὐαί	*woe!, ah!*

▷ **List 24**	4×
πικρός, -ά, -όν	bitter
πλήρης, -ης, -ες	full, complete
προσάγω	to bring to, approach
πρόσταγμα, -ατος, τό	ordinance, command
σελήνη, -ης, ἡ	moon
σίδηρος, -ου, ὁ	iron (tool)
στολή, -ῆς, ἡ	robe, cloak
ταπείνωσις, -εως, ἡ	low status, humiliation, humility
τιμάω	to honor; (*mid*) to value (at a price)
τράχηλος, -ου, ὁ	neck, throat
ὑετός, -οῦ, ὁ	rain
φλόξ, φλογός, ἡ	flame
τιμή, -ῆς, ἡ	*honor, value, price*